D1635204

The social geography
of poverty in the UK

Edited by Chris Philo
on behalf of the Social and Cultural
Geography Study Group

CPAG Ltd, 1-5 Bath Street, London EC1V 9PY

CPAG promotes action for the relief, directly or indirectly, of poverty among children and families with children. We work to ensure that those on low incomes get their full entitlements to welfare benefits. In our campaigning and information work we seek to improve benefits and policies for low-income families, in order to eradicate the injustice of poverty. If you are not already supporting us, please consider making a donation, or ask for details of our membership schemes and publications.

Poverty Publication 91

Published by CPAG Ltd, 1–5 Bath Street, London EC1V 9PY

Tel: 0171 253 3406

© CPAG Ltd, 1995

ISBN 0 946744 77 7

The views expressed in this book are the authors' and do not necessarily express those of CPAG.

A CIP record for this book is available from the British Library

Cover and design by Devious Designs, 0114 275 5634
Typeset by Nancy White, 0171 607 4510
Printed by The Alden Press, 01865 249071

CONTENTS

ACKNOWLEDGEMENTS

The idea for this project first surfaced in a letter from Fran Bennett (then of CPAG) to Susan Smith (Department of Geography, University of Edinburgh), as a result of which the Committee of the 'Social and Cultural Geography Study Group' of the Institute of British Geographers took up the idea. Thanks are hence due to Fran and Sue for getting the thing kick-started, and for inadvertently getting me involved as an editor! I must acknowledge the considerable input and assistance provided by various members of CPAG, notably Marie Barenskie and Renée Harris who have helped to smooth the whole process from conception to production. I must also acknowledge the considerable help given by two 'readers', Robin Simpson and Robert Walker, whose critical but constructive comments have certainly aided in improving the chapters. I have received support (as ever) from colleagues at Lampeter, and I would also like to mention Graham Smith (Department of Geography, University of Cambridge) for making printing facilities available to me in the final stages of the editing. The largest thank you obviously goes to the contributors, all of whom have enthusiastically and insightfully entered into the project, meeting whatever deadlines I have set over the past 18 months or so. I would particularly like to thank James McCormick and John Mohan, however, given that they have offered me valuable encouragement and advice at various points when it has most been needed.

Chris Philo
Cambridge, March 1995

ABOUT THE EDITOR

Chris Philo is a Lecturer in the Department of Geography, University of Wales, Lampeter. He is a co-author of *Approaching Human Geography: an introduction to contemporary theoretical debates in human geography* (1991, with P Cloke and D Sadler), the compiler of *New Words, New Worlds: reconceptualising social and cultural geography* (1991), and the co-editor of *Selling Places: the city as cultural capital, past and present* (1993, with G Kearns). His main research interest is the historical geography of 'madness', asylums and mental healthcare provisions.

ABOUT THE CONTRIBUTORS

John Allen is a Senior Lecturer in Economic Geography at The Open University. His publications include *Landlords and Property* (with Linda McDowell 1989), *Housing and Labour Markets* (co-edited 1991) and *Political and Economic Forms of Modernity* (co-edited 1992). He has also written on the geographies of services, with particular reference to the City of London.

Paul Cloke is a Professor in the Department of Geography, University of Bristol. He is founder editor of the *Journal of Rural Studies*, and has longstanding research interests in the geographies of rurality and rural change. He has authored and co-authored some 15 books on these issues, including *The Rural State? Limits to planning in rural society* (with J Little 1990) and *Writing the Rural: five cultural geographies* (with M Doel, D Matless, M Phillips and N Thrift 1994).

Sarah Curtis is a Senior Lecturer in the Department of Geography, Queen Mary and Westfield College, London. Her research focuses on inequalities in health and health/social care from a geographical perspective, with particular emphasis on the European dimension and the particular needs of elderly and deprived inner-city populations. She is the author of *The Geography of Public Welfare Provision* (1989) and co-author of *Changing Perspectives on Health and Societies* (with A Tacket 1995).

Daniel Dorling is a British Academy Fellow in the Department of Geography, University of Newcastle-upon-Tyne. His research interests include the geography of society, politics and housing, data visualisation, cartography and census analysis. He is the author of *A New Social Atlas of Britain* (1995).

Mark Goodwin is a Senior Lecturer in Human Geography at the Institute of Earth Studies, University of Wales, Aberystwyth. He has researched and written widely on urban issues, and his books include *The Local State and Uneven Development* (with S Duncan 1988) and *Reshaping the City: a critical introduction to urban change* (1966).

Ron Martin is the Director of the Graduate School of Geography at the University of Cambridge, and Fellow and Director of Studies in Geography at St Catharine's College there. His research interests include the geography of labour markets, regional economic development, the geography of socio-economic welfare and state intervention, and the geography of money. He has published some 10 books and more than 70 papers on these themes.

Doreen Massey is a Professor of Geography at The Open University. Her publications include *High Tech Fantasies* (with D Wield and P Quintas 1992), *Space, Place and Gender* (1994) and *Spatial Divisions of Labour* (Second Edition 1995). She has also published extensively on industrial geography, regional development, politics and method, gender and space, and aspects of geographical theory.

James McCormick is a Research Fellow at the Institute for Public Policy Research (IPPR) and for the Commission on Social Justice. He co-ordinated the work of the Commission's Services and Communities Panel, and is the author of Citizens' Service (IPPR). He completed a Geography PhD at Glasgow University in 1993, entitled *A Tax too Far? The impact of the poll tax in urban Scotland.*

John McKendrick is a Research Fellow ion the School of Geography, University of Manchester. His research interests cover population and social geography (in particular the geography of the family), along with issues of welfare and social justice. A book, *The Quality of Life of Lone Parents: a deprived population group,* is due out by the end of 1995.

Paul Milbourne is a Research Fellow in the Countryside and Community Research Unit, Cheltenham and Gloucester College of Higher Education. His main research interests are rural housing and homelessness, rural poverty and marginalisation, and cultural change in the British countryside. He is editing two books – *Rural Society: social change in the British countryside* and *Revealing Rural 'Others': diverse voices in the British countryside* – for publication in 1996.

John Mohan is a Lecturer in Geography at Queen Mary and Westfield College, London. He is the author of *A National Health Service? The restructuring of health care in Britain since 1979* (1995), the editor of *The Political Geography of Contemporary Britain* (1989) and the author of numerous articles and book chapters on geographical aspects of health and social policy.

Chris Thomas is a Lecturer in the Division of Geography and Recreation Studies, University of Staffordshire. He is currently completing a PhD thesis dealing with aspects of land, landscape, identity and rurality, and has worked on various projects concerned with rural lifestyles and deprivation.

John Tomaney is a researcher and lecturer in the Centre for Urban and Regional Development Studies, University of Newcastle-upon-Tyne. His main research interest is the impact of European integration on the prospects for Europe's less favoured regions. He is co-editor of *Behind the Myth of European Union* (1995, with A Amin).

Where is poverty? The hidden geography of poverty in the United Kingdom

James McCormick and Chris Philo

[A] study of poverty should mean not simply statistics but an attempt at precise localisation. Since to fix the topographical distribution of poverty is a means of knowing it more exactly, it is doubtless also a means of relieving it and curing it in a less abstract and more efficacious manner.[1]

THE INVISIBILITY OF POVERTY

Recent assertions have claimed that society in the United Kingdom (UK) is presently being 'evened up', made 'classless', and is reaching a situation where it can feel 'at ease with itself'. These are phrases associated with the present Prime Minister, John Major, but similar claims have been made in recent years by other Conservative politicians. John Moore, former Minister for Social Security, announced that the Government had ended poverty once and for all, while Michael Forsyth, former Scottish Office Minister, declined to bid for funding through the European Community's Poverty 2 programme because he considered that poverty no longer exists in Scotland. On different grounds, arguably more defensible, Conservative politicians have objected to the use of the term 'poverty' because it can be stigmatising, and Margaret Thatcher once stated that to call people who depended on income support 'poor' was to defame them. Moreover, observers who might be expected to be suspicious about Thatcher's motives have nonetheless worried that blanket labels such as 'the poor' or 'the underclass'[2] are no more satisfactory in describing lives and aspirations than are other generalisations, and have acknowledged that poor people may not wish to identify themselves as being 'poor' or as part of an 'underclass'.

Alternatively, there is a growing recognition by other politicians and policy analysts that the UK in the late twentieth century has certainly not yet freed itself from the 'curse' of poverty. It is true that poverty appears to undergo periodic phases of rediscovery, but it is probably more accurate to regard any apparent rediscovery of poverty in the mid-1990s UK as more a *revival* of concern about something that had never really gone away. It is not so much poverty that disappears and reappears as its acceptability or relevance to the agendas set by the most influential shapers of public opinion. Furthermore, academic thinking about poverty can easily confuse the issue, not because the arguments being put forward are necessarily wrong, but because it is not uncommon for them to be hijacked and misrepresented. Indeed, this may have happened with debates about 'absolute poverty' and 'relative poverty'.[3] It may be that all claims and counter-claims about the truth of poverty remain fundamentally flawed so long as they are locked into the privileged spaces of Westminster, Whitehall, policy institutes and research centres.

What is needed instead is heightened attention to the real people and places where something called 'poverty', and what the people in these places continue by and large to call 'poverty', can be encountered. Despite the risks inherent in giving priority to the realm of immediate experience there is much to be gained from looking with our own eyes at the physical evidence of such places and from listening to the voices of the people who live in them. And what results from any honest attempt to do just this, as in the examples of the Commission on Social Justice (CSJ) and the recent inquiry of the Joseph Rowntree Foundation (JRF),[4] is surely the acknowledgement that poverty does continue to haunt many people in many parts of the UK.

It is possible to question the prevalence of such poverty in the UK today only because the people and places involved are largely invisible to the individuals and bodies who hold power in our society. They are hidden behind doors or down back alleys away from the brighter thoroughfares of social life, just as Engels writing in the 1840s found the poor of Manchester to be shielded away from the eyes of the middle classes travelling the roads in and out of the city.[5] They are hidden away in whole localities like Meadow Well on North Tyneside (the scene of rioting in September 1991) which comprise a virtual *terra incognita* for many in authority. Yet there is little doubt in Meadow Well itself that poverty still exists – relative, absolute, call it what you will – and that it disfigures people's lifes, excluding them from the basics of what most members of UK society would expect to be able to possess, to access or to take part in. To quote Margaret Nolan, a resident of Meadow Well, 'people should stop pretending that poverty does not exist. It does and it brings despair'.[6]

Margaret Nolan knows that poverty exists, then, and so too does the author of this observation:

> The easiest way to judge the affluence of an area is to visit it, something government statisticians never do ... On a walk around [Meadow Well in Newcastle], you will see burnt-out cars, boarded-up houses, piles of litter and large numbers of young men on the streets in mid-afternoon. The young men are easy to explain. The official unemployment rate is 58 per cent, a 7 per cent rise since the riots – the real rate is much higher when the numbers not registered or on training are taken into account. [7]

As the observation here implies, it is to some extent the failure of government ministers and agents to visit Meadow Well – their failure to look and to listen – which has led to the present situation where a powerful minority is able to deny the existence of poverty in such places, or to claim as 'ideological' those who insist on the existence of these (as we will call them) 'poor places'. It is to some extent precisely because poverty has a geography – because it is present in some places but not in others – that it can remain 'out of sight and out of mind'. It is the task of this book to tease out something of this hidden geography[8] and to reveal the presence of poverty in places which are too readily forgotten about. Demonstrating that poverty exists in many corners of the UK is important if we are to challenge those who speak blandly about an 'evening up' of life-chances for all of the UK's citizens.

THE GEOGRAPHY OF POVERTY

The quotation at the opening of this chapter, taken from the 1920 translation of Brunhes's *La Géographie Humaine*, urges us to appreciate that poverty is a thoroughly geographical phenomenon. For Brunhes, such an appreciation is warranted simply because poverty has to 'take place' somewhere, an apparently banal observation, but one that highlights – as indicated above – the extent to which it is only some people in some places who have to endure this exclusion from a decent 'quality of life'. It also suggests that there is nothing inevitable about poverty, just as there is nothing inevitable about wealth, and that a range of factors which are potentially knowable (and therefore, perhaps, controllable) must be conspiring to generate poverty in 'poor places' and wealth in 'rich places'. Furthermore, this geographical unevenness has important implications, tough personal ones for people living in poorer locations, but also broader ones for the policy-makers who must decide what should be done so these locations do not pose a threat to social order (and see also Chapter 8). Issues such as these are threaded throughout this book, as is the simple message that attempting to research, document and analyse the geography of poverty in the UK today is a more complex task than it might at first appear. Our focus here is to describe that geography and to draw out its implications for the experiences of the people concerned.

DESCRIBING THE GEOGRAPHY OF POVERTY

The geography can be described in terms of nameable places and particular types of settlements, environments and regions, some of which are weighed down with poverty (complete with industrial decline, unemployment, bad housing, deficient services and social problems) and some of which are currently more fortunate. It can also be thought of at differing spatial scales, with a pattern of poverty and wealth at the regional level (eg, the South-East or the North-West) being cross-cut by other patterns which operate along specific axes (town as opposed to country, factory district to farmland, lowlands to uplands) or which are more local in their extent (inner-city contrasted with neighbouring suburb, private estate with adjacent council estate, rural town with sparsely-populated surrounding hills and vales). In addition, at the most local of spatial scales poverty and wealth are sometimes closely intermixed, almost touching, and yet still remain separated by minute distances (think of the plush office block towering above a 'cardboard city') which keep poor and rich strangers to one another.[9]

The book's basic structure, then, covers spatial scales from the most broad-brush regional to the most intimate local. Chapters 2 and 3 examine dimensions to the regional geography of UK poverty, considering first 'the North-South divide' (and demonstrating that this divide persists in the 1990s despite widely-reported claims about its death), and then looking at what McKendrick terms 'the Celtic divide' between the experiences of the Celtic lands (Northern Ireland, Scotland, Wales) and the non-Celtic lands (England). Chapters 4 and 5 start to look beneath the regional picture, at wealth and poverty in urban and rural areas. Goodwin explores poverty in the UK's towns and cities, noting variations between both different urban areas and different localities within the same urban area, while Cloke *et al* explore poverty in the UK's countryside, noting in particular a tension between the common image of the 'rural idyll' and the realities of hard, deprived lives led by many rural-dwellers. Chapters 6 and 7 take another route into the geography of UK poverty, contrasting the fortunes of the UK's old industrial and new industrial districts, hinting in the process at how the 'distribution' of wealth or poverty in different parts of the UK is closely bound up with industrial restructuring (see below). In Chapter 6, Dorling and Tomaney cover the undoubted fall into poverty suffered by regions such as the North-East and the West Midlands, cataloguing the social problems that flow from the shedding of employment opportunities for people born and bred in such regions, while in Chapter 7 Massey and Allen tease out differences in the experiences of different people (from cleaners to scientists) employed in high-technology workplaces, showing the micro-geographies of 'impoverished' and 'enriched' lives which touch in time and space but never properly meet.

These chapters are complemented by Mohan's inquiry (Chapter 8) into the state of the South-East, in many ways the iconic region of New Right dreams. He brings together evidence from various sources to show that the South-East in the 1990s is not immune to poverty – even in the middle-class 'Acacia Avenues' – and that within its boundaries there is undoubtedly an uneven geography of wealth and poverty. Curtis's contribution (Chapter 9) is the only one which does not follow a traditional geographical approach based upon a particular set of places, since here she takes one aspect of social well-being often related to poverty, that of health and healthcare, and investigates spatial inequalities involved in the distributions of sickness and medical provisions across the UK. It would have been possible to include similar chapters on other aspects of social well-being, notably housing, education and childcare, but sections to do with health are arguably less common in the other contributions to the book than are sections on these other aspects, making a separate chapter on 'unwell' geographies highly useful in its own right.[10] As our comments here indicate, though, the book is not as comprehensive as it might have been – it could have included more on welfare geographies, for instance, or maybe a chapter focusing explicitly on poverty in agriculture – and neither is it a comprehensive 'atlas' of UK poverty which maps 1991 Census variables indicative of variations in poverty levels (but see the maps in Chapter 6).[11] Rather, what the book does contain is a selection of cuts into the complex geographies of UK poverty to describe as sensitively as possible the circumstances of poverty in the many 'poor places' which are identified.

EXPLAINING THE GEOGRAPHY OF POVERTY

As well as identifying and describing the 'poor places' where poverty occurs, however, there is the further task of explaining why the places involved have fallen into poverty. It must be reiterated that given the constraints of this book contributors only hint at explanations for the geographies that they describe, but it is nonetheless appropriate here to explain some methods which geographers use when researching poverty and which feature on occasion in the pages that follow.

COMBINATORIAL THINKING

Insofar as contributors shift from description to explanation in the chapters that follow, they generally reject mono-causal explanations in favour of combinatorial ones which specify how particular sets of factors – usually categorised in some way as 'economic', 'political', 'social' and 'cultural' – spin together in specific ways to produce the outcome which is certain forms of poverty for certain people in certain places. The precise mix of causal factors involved, the precise manner in which they combine together, and the precise type, level and experience of poverty produced in the process are all variable, and can only ever be fully appreciated through detailed studies of particular 'poor places' (and hence the suspicion of grand generalisations). What adopting such a approach does not mean, though, is that the poverty of any one place can be explained solely by reference to the properties of that place (a geographical version of blaming the poverty of a poor person on his or her inherent failings). Rather, it is to envisage a variety of different economic, political, social and cultural processes operating on different but overlapping 'surfaces', some of which are national or even international in their extent, and to regard poverty as an outcome arising at given locations thanks in part to the spatial coincidence of 'troughs' in two or more of these interacting surfaces.

A prominent example of this kind of combinatorial thinking is Massey's work on what she terms 'spatial divisions of labour'.[12] Here she explains how capitalism mutates through successive 'rounds of investment' in what she also terms the 'space-economy' – the spatial distribution of all economic activities throughout the country under study (in this case the UK) – and that each such round results in different places (or, rather, the local economies of these places) receiving differing levels of investment. At the same time these places end up with differing mixes of activities, along with differing types of work from the most managerial to the most menial, and in consequence some places end up being successful or 'winners' (more prosperous, more growth, more employment) while other places end up being relatively unsuccessful or 'failures' (little prosperity, limited or no growth, meagre employment). It is possible for the fortunes of different places to change and even to reverse from one period to the next, as has happened to some extent in relation to the UK's North-South divide,[13] but once a place has acquired a tendency towards being unsuccessful it is much less likely to attract favourable investment (and higher status work and jobs) in subsequent years. Many places are hence prone to slipping into a downward spiral of decline which it is then difficult to break (and see below). Massey's ideas are primarily applied to the economy, but she acknowledges how this combinatorial structuring of economic space interacts with the structuring of other spaces (with the political, social and cultural attributes of different places) to create the overall combinations of factors productive of 'rich places', 'poor places' and those places faring somewhere in between.

COMBINED AND UNEVEN DEVELOPMENT

A further set of arguments is sometimes deployed by geographers when explaining why it is that poverty becomes localised in some places and not others, although it must be acknowledged that the arguments here are quite theoretically-driven and speculative. Some years ago Colenutt stated that 'the map of the poorest regions only gives us half the picture, because we can hardly talk about poverty without talking about wealth'.[14] What he meant by this was not simply that we should recognise the co-existence of poverty and wealth across the regions of a nation or city, but that we should attend to 'the flows between regions', to a situation in which affluence in certain regions may well be actively 'causing poverty in rival regions'[15] thanks to complex transfers of capital in various guises (as money, resources, activities and even people) from the latter to the former. The further claim is that such transfers are not confined to the condition of 'zero-sum growth', where there is a limited size of economic 'cake' to be distributed among a given number of places, but is also inevitable in conditions of economic growth (and may indeed be a prerequisite for growth to occur at all). These are controversial claims, not least because they go against the grain of the 'rising ships' or 'trickle-down' arguments of the Right (see also Chapters 2, 4 and 8) which insist that economic growth propelled by the unfettered functioning of the market is the key to ensuring an improvement of all peoples and places.

The view of many economists and geographers is rather that 'poor places' are a structural property of capitalism, arising in all societies with economies organised around the competitive production of commodities for consumption at market. Within capitalist societies[16] the geography of poverty is thereby seen as *necessarily* uneven, in that the innermost workings of capitalism compel it to generate spatial concentrations of capital and resources ('rich places') set apart from areas where capital and resources are more thinly spread or even non-existent ('poor places'). Many theories have emerged in this respect, often linking back to Marx's statement that 'capital grows in one place to a huge mass in a single hand because it has in another place been lost by many'.[17] In the geographical literature, for instance, there is Peet's thesis about capitalism fixing the 'industrial reserve army' or 'underclass' in particular 'poor places' from which extra labour power can be drawn very cheaply whenever production needs to be stepped up.[18] There is also Harvey's thesis about capitalism centralising its activities in certain (probably core urban) locations so as to 'minimise circulation costs as well as turnover times', although he also underlines the need for capitalism constantly to be seeking out fresh (probably peripheral rural) locations where the exploitation of indigenous resources and labour – alongside the opening up of new markets – can promote enhanced capital accumulation.[19] Harvey clearly supposes pivotal locations where capital clumps to be intimately bound to other locations where capital simply 'passes through', the richer centres needing the poorer peripheries and vice versa (once the latter have been sucked into the system), and here we have in crude outline a model which purports to explain the geography of poverty by deducing it from capitalism's need for economic development to be combined but uneven.[20]

POOR PLACES

In this section we offer a rather different framework for the book and in so doing demonstrate the combinatorial approach discussed above. The principal objective here is to spell out a number of the elements which are commonly found today in one guise or another in the 'poor places' of the UK. These elements come together not so much to create poverty at the outset – although some of the elements will play a role in this causal sense – but to entrench the experience of poverty once it has been established. In the process we sharpen the description of what comprises a 'poor place' in the UK, something left understated up to this point, but we also offer the outlines of an explanation for why poverty, once established, tends to become locked into a 'downward spiral' whereby various processes tend to feed off each other in a destructive fashion making it increasingly difficult to redress the balance. Several different elements of 'poor places' are discussed in turn, although our list is certainly not exhaustive.

LACK OF PAID WORK

The single strongest influence on the increasing scale of UK poverty in the 1980s was clearly the growth in unemployment, and particularly in the numbers of people being unemployed for a year or longer. Unemployment figures must be treated with caution, however, not only because the basis on which they are calculated has changed on numerous occasions, but because even accurate statistics can reveal only part of the transition in labour markets presently occurring in many places (including many of the poorer ones). Even so, among people of an age able to undertake paid work, unemployment brings the highest risk of slipping into poverty. Savings are quickly exhausted, leaving fewer resources to fall back on in times of rising prices. Families with dependent children who enter this situation are most in danger of being made poor, however

this poverty is quantified. The longer the duration of unemployment, the lower may be the prospects of finding another job (the
'scarring' effect of long-term unemployment), reflecting both the
attitudes of employers and the diminishing half-life of manual skills.
Relative to 10 or 20 years ago, unemployment is now more likely
to lead to poverty: in 1993 only three in ten of the registered
unemployed were eligible for the contributory unemployment benefit;[21] income support (the means-tested benefit paid at a lower rate)
is now the only form of unemployment support available to the
majority of those who are recorded as jobless. The latter cost £2.6
billion in 1978 and £10.8 billion in 1993, whereas the total cost of
the former remained steady at around £1.7 billion across the same
15-year period.[22] The route out of unemployment is often through
personal contacts with people who are in work and/or who know
about job vacancies as they arise. In areas where high unemployment
(and particularly long-term unemployment) is concentrated, the
chances of being included in a network of people who are in paid
work or who know other employed people are significantly reduced.

Beyond the official unemployment rates, the most telling indicator
of what is going on is that of non-employment, particularly of
men.[23] Over the 15 years to 1992, male employment levels collapsed
by 2 million, resulting in a working age participation rate of only 80
per cent of men (down from 91 per cent in 1978).[24] Yet only half of
this reduction was translated into higher recorded unemployment,
and so evidently something else has been happening. Although the
lower participation rate is affected by more people studying longer
and retiring earlier, the key trend is that many economically active
men – often jobless for more than a year, often as young as 40, and
disproportionately with lower skill levels and fewer qualifications –
have been coming off the unemployment register to claim sickness
and incapacity benefits instead. In a city such as Sheffield, the
combined non-employment rate (of people registered as unemployed,
sick and for incapacity benefit) for 1991 was 31 per cent for men
and 40 per cent for women, and both figures were around 10 per
cent above the average figure for the whole UK.[25] In several wards
the number of men registered as long-term sick exceeds the official
number of unemployed men, and in some of the city's poorest
neighbourhoods, less than one in three people of working age has a
job of any description. The reduction of unemployment benefit
from 12 months to a 6-month 'jobseekers' allowance' (announced
in the 1994 Budget) is more likely to force those still able to claim it

into inactivity and means-tested benefits rather than into jobs, and to strengthen the perverse occurrence of part-time women workers having to give up their jobs when their husbands lose theirs thanks to the off-setting of low wages against means-tested benefits.

Official statistics are unable to capture this revolution in non-employment taking place in many parts of the UK today, or to uncover the emerging, partly hidden spaces of poverty associated with non-employment. Unless the priorities of public policy change, the likeliest future for places such as, for example, Knowsley or Hackney (and see Chapter 4), is written firmly in their non-employment rates. The longer that people in such places are excluded from the contributory basis of the National Insurance system, the greater the likelihood that today's working-age poor will be tomorrow's pensioners in poverty, thus etching poverty ever more deeply into the human environments of these places.

WEAK ECONOMIES

Poverty is not the result only of economic downturn reflected as a shift in demand for specific skills at the local, regional and national labour market scales, it is also the *cause* of decline according to economists like Will Hutton of the *Guardian*.[26] In places where relatively few people are in paid employment, the circulation of money through what are inevitably poor communities is limited. Reducing the purchasing power of low-income households – which are likely to spend money locally rather than saving it, spending it elsewhere or using it on expensive imported goods – damages the economies of 'poor places'. A gradual process of uncoupling hence occurs between local and national economic trends, such that improvements in the latter may no longer feed through into any improvement in the former. Even if new jobs do start to be created, and even if national economic growth does exceed its low level of the previous decade, there are now an increasing number of places with such weak local economies that they are unlikely to experience the benefits which 'trickle down' economics might envisage.

TRAPS

In places where means-tested social assistance benefits are the major source of income, other 'passported' benefits (like school meals, housing benefit and council tax deductions) are often paid as well.

Because of both the rate at which benefits are withdrawn on starting paid work and the low level of the earnings disregard, it makes more sense for many people in these places not to take a job unless a level of income to support a household can definitely be secured. The effective 'tax rate' imposed at this level can reach almost 100 per cent. Research on the poverty trap reveals that when new enterprises are set-up in low-wage areas they experience difficulty in recruiting sufficient women because the *male* unemployment rate is too *high*. Similarly, people in low-paid work are discouraged from increasing their working hours because the tax and national insurance barriers, combined with benefit withdrawal, potentially leave many worse off. In addition to this employment conundrum, the rigid nature of the housing benefit system reduces the work prospects of tenants in the 'social rented' sector still further. Indeed, the steep rate of withdrawal of this benefit (65 pence in the pound), coupled with the loss of council tax benefit (a further 20 pence in the pound) and the rising level of rents in both the council and housing association sectors, compounds the trap of it being economically irrational for many people to work harder for higher wages. Furthermore, it is increasingly the case that only tenants on full housing benefit payments can afford to live in new housing association homes, leading to the fear that housing association estates are becoming new landscapes of poverty.

POOR SERVICES

'Services for poor people tend to be poor services': so various writers have argued.[27] In the UK's 'poor places' there are often fewer or no services available locally or regionally, partly reflecting the declines in both population and economic viability, and partly reflecting the fewer bargaining powers of people in such places when it comes to the political decision-making process. If poverty is most immediately a product of having little or no money, we might say that deprivation is caused by a lack of power in society (see also Chapter 5).[28] School and hospital closures tend to take place first in poor areas considered to be least able to organise politically and to resist the will of the authorities, and Campbell dramatically portrays the results in terms reminiscent of those which geographers have been using for some time when describing the plight of powerless communities in run-down areas:

The estates were a contradiction. ... [A]part from the odd church, shop or hall, they were stripped of urban services and the means of congregation. Estates were space but not place ... The crisis of public space in the estates [was caused by] the extinction of their economy and the erosion of co-operative use of public space.[29]

These places and communities are representative of many others 'at the edge' in functional terms: they are places where poverty in cash terms is made worse by poverty in terms of services and the evidence suggests that the benefits in kind of the 'social wage' also trickle upwards and outwards from 'poor places' (rather than downwards and inwards to them).

Although there is a lack of money circulating locally, there is also a serious shortage of local outlets through which money can be recycled, and those outlets which are used tend to be ones that siphon money out of the places concerned and into national organisations with few local loyalties (and with only limited importance in local job creation). Easterhouse has one of the busiest branches of Ladbrokes bookmakers in Europe, for instance, and also one of the largest Bingo halls in the UK. A further trend is the withdrawal of banking facilities in certain 'poor places', which inevitably prompts difficulties for local people in gaining access to insurance, credit and savings services. When close to one-third of the wards in Birmingham (the UK's second largest city) have either lost their only local bank or are threatened by its closure, and with loan sharks who charge massively inflated interest rates appearing to fill the void in financial services, a process of financial 'red-lining' is in effect occurring for people living in such places.[30] People who can afford to take out a loan from a bank or building society receive credit, but people who cannot get by without a loan receive debt. The floods affecting parts of West Scotland in December 1994 were so devastating in part because of the lack of home contents insurance protection in some neighbourhoods, it being estimated that on one estate only 5 to 10 per cent of households had appropriate insurance cover. In the 'exhausted estates on the edge of British cities a fiscal haemorrhage is ongoing',[31] claims Campbell (see also Chapter 4), and a survey conducted in 1985 (again in Meadow Well) revealed that an average of £10 left each household every week as a repayment on debt at rates of interest between 33 per cent and 100 per cent.[32] In West Belfast one woman explained how people had no choice other than to go to the money-lenders:

In this area I see them every day – the tick men. There must be

bongo drums or something because when they come down the
street, one minute everyone is at their front door, the next minute
everyone is away. There are still places where they take the Family
Allowance books. It still goes on to this day.[33]

People living in 'poor places' are also more likely to lack gardens
and safe play areas for children, and in this respect we find the
environmental deprivation or degradation identified by Townsend
in his *Poverty in the UK*.[34]

HIGH EXPENSES

It is an irony that living in poverty is *not* a cheap option. In relative
terms, and often in absolute terms as well, 'poor places' are expensive
places to live and to shop in. Where only a skeleton local economy
exists, monopoly suppliers of basics – a food shop, a clothes shop, a
bank – will quite commonly be pushing up the cost of living
relative to that endured elsewhere. The chances of having a car and
being able to drive to cheaper supermarkets, or of possessing a
freezer to keep enough food to feed a family for a week, are
considerably lower in such places. The cash-debt economies that
have emerged offer only expensive money options (as compared to
the trend among banks which increasingly discriminate against cash
transactions through steeper handling charges of money compared
with cheque and credit card payments).[35] Moreover, where housing
design is flawed, as in the cases of buildings served by deck-access
'walkways in the sky' common in London, or the four-storey
tenement houses common in Scottish cities, it tends to cost more to
keep them adequately heated. Much of the expenditure in 'poor
places' thus leaks out through poorly insulated walls, windows and
doors, resulting in much higher fuel bills than would be needed
with rehabilitation and improved design.

POOR HEALTH

It is clear that people living in poverty can expect to pay the price
in lives that are on average eight years shorter than those of people
living in the richest neighbourhoods of the same cities. Higher risks
of contracting long-term illnesses are also to be found in the UK's
'poor places', and it is unsurprising to learn that people with
physical and mental disabilities are more likely to be living in such

places as well.[36] One member of Church Action on Poverty from Ancoats in Manchester is not prepared to let these 'facts' have the last word, however:

> We don't accept that those in communities such as ours should be three times more likely to die in infancy, die of heart disease, have children who are killed or injured in accidents or have chronic illness. These people are not simply statistics, they are our friends and neighbours. [Winnie Amir, Ancoats][37]

Places where poverty is rife are places where there are more attempted suicides and cases of bronchial and respiratory disease, and, according to the *British Medical Journal*, the evidence that poverty (and, even more strongly, inequality) is bad for your health and that unemployment can kill 'now verges on the irrefutable'.[38]

There is an intriguing suggestion that places supporting equitable income patterns among the people resident within their boundaries may be generally healthier than places supporting unequal ones. For instance, among the older capitalist countries it seems that those with the most unequal distributions of income have experienced the lower increases in life expectancy over recent years, irrespective of whether they are affluent or relatively poor. Citizens of Spain and Portugal (on average poorer than the UK) as well as citizens of Denmark, Sweden and Germany (on average richer) can therefore expect to live longer than the average British citizen. Wilkinson's research into health and income inequalities indicates that this phenomenon is indeed related to the lower levels of inequality *within* these countries, regardless of the substantial differences *between* them.[39] Evidence which may be relevant here can be drawn from the Scottish experience. Figures reveal that Grampian Region and the Borders had the lowest Standardised Mortality Ratios (SMRs) in Scotland at the 1981 Census.[40] Other figures shows that the former had the highest average earnings in Scotland whereas the latter had among the lowest in the UK.[41] It is at least a possibility that the similar health outcomes in these two places, despite dissimilar earnings profiles, reflects the relatively smaller range of 'deprivation scores' (a composite index of four factors)[42] found in the Borders compared to elsewhere in Scotland (implying less inequality within the region itself as compared to that found in other regions). It may also hint that the effects of low pay and poverty in some rural areas are expressed less obviously in terms of health costs than they are in urban areas (see also Chapter 5).

DANGER AND STIGMA

Goliath, the 1993 study of crime, communities and gender by Campbell, is subtitled *Britain's dangerous places*.[43] The term 'dangerous places' refers here to the neighbourhoods in Newcastle, Oxford and Cardiff (among others) which experienced the summer riots of 1991, but 'poor places' in general are – at least in the popular imagination and probably in actuality too – more dangerous than many other UK localities. If one was to conduct an opinion survey in almost any poor neighbourhhood of the UK, the fear of crime is likely to appear as one of the strongest concerns being voiced by respondents. It is in those areas identified by the Home Office as 'the poorest council housing estates' that the risk of being burgled is highest (four times higher than in the most affluent areas),[44] and it is here that people also have the fewest opportunities to obtain affordable insurance cover for their home and possessions. As illustrated in *Raining Stones*, the 1993 Ken Loach film documenting the lives of poor people in Manchester, the violence of loan sharks is an everyday experience for some households in the UK's poorest and most dangerous places. Economies of corruption controlled by drug barons or paramilitary groups of various kinds fill the space in the local communities previously occupied by mainstream economic activities.

The cumulative result of many of the elements discussed so far is a geography of stigma. Everyone knows the 'no-go areas' in their own towns or cities, and most people have heard about places (sites, localities, regions) which they may never have visited but which they now wish to avoid: and the places concerned are in a very real sense being shaped by such negative perceptions.[45] Having the right address rather than the wrong one can make all the difference between getting a job interview and not getting one for people with similar qualifications. It influences whether the Council will promptly repair street lighting or simply leave it ('because it would only be vandalised anyway'); it affects whether or not taxi-drivers and GPs will go into a locality at night; it affects whether and where residents are 'red-lined' by banks and by other lending agencies. The fate of 'poor places', and thus of their residents who are often unable to move away, is perhaps being sealed for years to come by this process of stigmatisation – notwithstanding the commitment of many individuals and groups to save their places – and here we surely encounter the most disturbing bottom-line of the hidden geography of poverty in the UK under investigation in this volume.

A NEW MAP OF POVERTY?

A recent attempt to 'map injustice' has been made by the Commission for Social Justice (CSJ),[46] which surveyed the extent to which basic human needs remain unfulfilled 50 years after the Beveridge settlement was introduced (and see Chapter 6). The CSJ's mapping exercise represents an important step forward, but we would also argue that this 'mapping' has not yet been geographical enough: it has not been as literal a mapping as is required. Indeed, our view is that the efforts of the CSJ (and of other anti-poverty organisations) need urgently to be supplemented by a drawing of a *new map of poverty*, where the map is one with a strong geographical basis indicating the differing levels, types and experiences of poverty associated with different places throughout the UK.

To some extent it is not so much the actual map itself that is crucial, though, and it should be acknowledged that producing such an atlas of poverty in the UK would be a time-consuming task hedged around with all manner of caveats about the statistics to be employed (including caveats about the strict comparability of statistics from one part of the UK to the next). Rather, it is the principle of always keeping in mind the fact that poverty has a geography which is crucial: it is the constant alertness to the reality of 'poor places' where poverty is concentrated; to the fact that these places are all too often invisible in debates and policy-making; to the details of how poverty becomes entrenched in these places; and to the reasons behind why some places and not others slip into poverty, perhaps because the very wealth of some places may be causally linked to the poverty of others. The aim is to make the features, dynamics and ramifications of this geography more prominent in the debates over poverty, and to spell out the policy implications which lead from a recognition that poverty does not occur 'on the head of a pin' but across a complex landscape full of diverse human environments (see also Chapter 10). It is with these thoughts in mind that the present volume has been put together, not as a definitive last word on the matter, but as a series of snapshots illuminating what the 'geographies' of poverty in the contemporary UK currently entail.

NOTES

1. J Brunhes, *Human Geography: an attempt at a positive classification – principles*

and Examples (George G Harrap, 1920, trans).

2. We could here make a reference to the 'underclass' debate, since the argument that people are poor for different reasons – disability, having children, long-term unemployment, crisis events (divorce, house fire, accidents) – challenges the notion that there is a single coherent under*class* with shared characteristics. See also Chapter 4.

3. Being in 'absolute poverty' is defined as lacking the essential resources to meet the basic needs identified by William Beveridge (architect of the British welfare state) as money, nutrition, shelter, health and education. It is sometimes argued that the assessment of absolute poverty should not only consider peoples' ability to meet these physiological needs, it should also take seriously whether or not they are able to meet psychological needs for care, respect, security and the suchlike. Being in 'relative poverty' is defined as lacking the quality of life which is available to most other people living in the same society (neighbours, fellow citizens), and hence poverty is here measured on a scale which is supposed to shift according to the time and place concerned. An argument about relative poverty is that through time what were once regarded as luxuries become judged as necessities (think of the example of the fridge), and this is the opening which allows right-wing critics to claim that UK anti-poverty activists – who commonly argue in terms of relative poverty – are not dealing with anything more than trivial differences and inequalities.

4. The Commission was established by the late John Smith MP as an independent inquiry into the long-term future of economic and social policy in the UK, and we should acknowledge that James McCormick is a Reasearch Fellow with the Commission. The research undertaken has drawn on a nationwide network of individuals and groups from communities, local government, trade unions, the voluntary sector, education and business, and has conducted a series of outreach visits to each 'nation' and region of the UK. Its final report – CSJ, *Social Justice: strategies for national renewal* (Vintage/Institute of Public Policy Research (IPPR), 1994) – has just been published. The recent Rowntree inquiry is reported in JRF, *Income and Wealth, Vols. I and II* (JRF, 1995): it too has attracted considerable attention and criticism but its findings have appeared too late to be included in this book.

5. Engels's account of working-class life in Manchester is well known. An excellent assessment is S Marcus, 'Reading the illegible', in H J Dyos and M Wolff (eds), *The Victorian City: images and realities, Vol.II – Shapes on the ground/a change of accent* (Routledge and Kegan Paul, 1973), pp257-76.

6. Quoted in Church Action on Poverty, *Making Poverty a Priority* (campaign leaflet).

7. *Observer*, 7 February 1993. The article from which this quotation is taken examined the strange implications of the All Ages Social Index, 'the official

league table of poverty and deprivation' for local authorities, which suggests that places such as Tyneside are actually better-off than places such as Kensington and Chelsea, Richmond, Westminster, Hove and Gloucester. The index is calculated on the basis of several indicators, excluding unemployment, rent arrears and free school meal statistics, but including housing statistics in such a way that the run-down housing stock of a place such as Meadow Well is deemed superior to the housing of Cambridge and Oxford (basically because it boasts adequate plumbing). It does indeed appear that the people responsible for this index, which has an influence on Whitehall grants to local authorities, have never been near many of the 'poor places' which here end up being judged relatively affluent.

8. The same reasoning has been used before to justify exploring the geography of poverty: see B Coates, R J Johnston and P L Knox, *Geography and Inequality* (Oxford University Press, 1977), who claim that inequality is allowed to persist because for 'us' (as for official bodies) there are 'parts of [the local city] which we never visit and with whose residents we have no contact' (p1); R Peet, 'Preface to special issue on the geography of American poverty', *Antipode*, Vol. 2(2) (1970), p. iv, who claims that 'we quite easily ignore the American poor, for they move in a different geographical system [to] the majority' (p. iv).

9. Taylor-Gooby speaks in this respect of 'Comfortable' and 'Miserable' Britain existing side-by-side: on the same street (the theatregoer of 'comfortable' London passes by the homeless people in shop doorways of 'mnMiserable' London): see P Taylor-Gooby, 'Social welfare: the unkindest cuts', in R Jowell *et al* (eds), *British Social Attitudes: the seventh report* (Gower, 1990), pp1-26.

10. The original intention had been to include a chapter on the geographical dimensions of housing and poverty, but this plan had to be adandoned.

11. Particularly useful in this respect, though, is R Forrest and D Gordon, *People and Places: A 1991 Census Atlas of England* (School of Advanced Urban Studies, 1993), and note the use made in Chapter 4 here of the 'deprivation indices' calculated and mapped by Forrest and Gordon. Also very recently published is A E Green, *The Geography of Poverty and Wealth* (Institute of Employment Research, 1994), and we acknowledge that more use could have been made of this source throughout the book.

12. D Massey, *Spatial Divisions of Labour: social structures and the geography of production* (Macmillan, 1984); and see also D Massey, *Space, Place and Gender* (Polity, 1994), especially Part 1.

13. There is a complex story to tell here about the changing economic geography of the UK from the Industrial Revolution to the present, one that to some extent involves a gradual reversal of fortunes for the North (where much of the UK's nineteenth-century heavy industry appeared) and the South (where much of the UK's twentieth-century high technology and service industries are appearing), but one in which London

and the South-East have always fared relatively well in terms of their share of economic activity and employment: see R L Martin, 'The political economy of Britain's North-South divide', *Transactions of the Institute of British Geographers*, Vol. 13 (NS) (1988), pp389-418, reprinted in J Lewis and A Townsend (eds), *The North-South Divide: regional change in Britain in the 1980s* (Paul Chapman, 1989), pp20-60.

14. B Colenutt, 'Poverty and inequality in American cities', *Antipode*, Vol. 2(2) (1970), p56.

15. This is the phraseology of one 'reader' of this paper.

16. In socialist societies (China and the old Soviet Union) considerable effort is clearly made to achieve an equitable distribution of capital and resources, although in practice creating an even map of wealth and poverty has proved impossible. In addition, it is evident that in highly bureaucratised societies dominated by large 'party' apparatuses abuses readily occur which lead to certain cities and places gaining privileges whereas others do not, thus creating peaks and troughs in the geographical patterning of capital and resources: see G E Smith, 'Privilege and place in Soviet society', in Gregory and Walford, work quoted above, pp320-40.

17. Quoted in 'Uneven development', in R J Johnston, D Gregory and D M Smith (eds), *The Dictionary of Human Geography* (Third Edition) (Basil Blackwell, 1994), p649. The whole of Smith's entry on 'uneven development' (pp648-51) is useful in connection with this part of the chapter.

18. R Peet, 'Inequality and poverty: a Marxist-geographic theory', *Annals of the Association of American Geographers*, Vol. 65 (1975), pp564-71.

19. D Harvey, 'The geography of capitalist accumulation: a reconstruction of the Marxian theory', *Antipode*, Vol. 7(2) (1975), pp9-21. Harvey has subsequently refined his attempt to draw out the spatial aspects and implications of Marx's theoretical interrogation of capitalism, most notably in D Harvey, *The Limits to Capital* (Basil Blackwell, 1982).

20. See also N Smith, *Uneven Development: nature, capital and the production of space* (Second Edition) (Basil Blackwell, 1990), which extends these kinds of arguments while talking about 'geographicall uneven development'.

21. E Balls, 'Men not at work', in E Balls and P Gregg, *Work and Welfare: tackling the jobs deficit*, Commission on Social Justice Issue Paper 3, IPPR, 1993.

22. *The Guardian*, 23 September 1993.

23. There is a complex story to tell here about the gendering of both economic restructuring and its social consequences. Indeed, in many 'poor places' like Meadow Well there has been a restructuring of the local job market, leaving many unskilled and semi-skilled men without jobs, as well as bringing more women into full- or part-time employment. There is hence a commendable trend towards increasing employment opportunities for women – on a national basis 70 per cent of working-age women are now in paid employment – but the pay and conditions of

work available to women are often worse than what is available to men (or that has been available in the past). This leaves many of the women concerned scant resources, time and energy to cope with a demanding 'dual role' as wage-earner and home-maker. Conventional household relations have been scrambled as a result, but men have not straightforwardly taken over domestic chores in the absence of their partners, and instead have all too frequently slipped into a demoralised idleness or even a petty criminality. Campbell thus argues that women and men respond in different ways to problems such as unemployment and poverty. More specifically, she sugggests that the twin 'magnets' in the UK's poorest places are currently community development and crime, and she identifies a striking gender difference here: women (particularly mothers) are more likely to be attracted to the first, but men are more likely to be attracted to the second. These claims are made in B Campbell, *Goliath: Britain's dangerous places* (Methuen, 1993), who bases much of her assessment here on the Meadow Well case, and refers to it explicitly as a 'poor place' in her Chapter 3.

24. P Gregg, 'Jobs and justice', in Balls and Gregg (see note 21).
25. Sheffield City Council Directorate of Planning and Economic Development, *Poverty and the Poor in Sheffield, 1993*, (Sheffield City Council, 1993).
26. See, for example, W Hutton, 'The real price of poverty' in *The Guardian*, 24 February 1992.
27. This idea is discussed further in D Donnison, *The Politics of Poverty* (Martin Robertson, 1982).
28. See the claims of J Veit-Wilson, *Dignity not Poverty: a minimum income standard for the UK* (Commission on Social Justice Issue Paper No. 6, IPPR, 1994).
29. Campbell, *Goliath* (see note 23), p320.
30. E Mayo (ed), *Bank Watch* (New Economic Foundation, 1993).
31. Campbell (see note 23), p236.
32. Campbell (see note 23).
33. Northern Ireland Voluntary Trust (NIVT), *A Qualitative Study of Life in the Disadvantaged Areas of Belfast* (NIVT, 1991), p10.
34. P Townsend, *Poverty in the United Kingdom* (Penguin, 1979).
35. A Middleton, 'Don't bank on it', *The Big Issue*, 1-7 February 1994.
36. Rather more could be said in this volume about the apparently growing presence of physically and mentally disabled people, along with members of various other 'vulnerable' populations, in certain urban localities. From the geographical literature comes the useful notion of the 'public city' as the often run-down part of many Western cities where 'welfare-dependent' populations and their support servives (public, voluntary and private) tend to cluster, thereby stirring in a whole new aspect to the problems and poverty faced by these neighbourhoods: see M Dear and J

Wolch, *Landscapes of Despair: From Deinstitutionalisation to Homelessness* (Polity, 1987).

37. Church Action on Poverty (see note 6).
38. Evidence reviewed in R Wilkinson, *The Damage of Deprivation: the effects of widening income differences on the welfare of the young* (Barnados, 1994).
39. Wilkinson (see note 38).
40. V Carstairs and R Morris, *Deprivation and Health in Scotland* (Aberdeen University Press, 1991).
41. See Table 108 in *New Earnings Survey, 1993, Part E: Analyses by region* (Department of Employment, HMSO, 1993). The date is available for full-time manual workers. The UK lacks a comprehensive data set on trends in earning which reflects the significance of low-paid, part-time jobs with low or zero employer contributions.
42. Carstairs and Morris (see note 40) calculated an index of socio-economic deprivation in Scotland using four components: household overcrowding; male unemployment; concentration of social classes 4 and 5; and households without a car.
43. Campbell, *Goliath* (see note 23).
44. Research findings bulletin (Home Office, October 1993).
45. An important theme in recent geographical inquiry concerns the ways in which places of all sizes become 'imagined' and 'mythologised' ('socially constructed'), often with the result that people, communities, institutions and bodies of various sorts treat the places concerned according to the received images rather than on the basis of actual knowledge: see R Shields, *Places on the Margin: alternative georgaphies of modernity* (Routledge, 1991).
46. See chapter entitled 'A new map of injustice' in CSJ, *The Justice Gap* (IPPR, 1993), pp17-48. This chapter 'maps' persistent and more recent injustices experienced by people in the UK, and does so by surveying a range of data sets over time and by making some reference to differences between places on the ground.

2 Income and poverty inequalities across regional Britain: the North-South divide lingers on
Ron Martin

THE NORTH-SOUTH DIVIDE: THE RISE AND DEMISE OF A DEBATE

All governments, of whatever political hue, make grandiloquent claims about their achievements in office. The Thatcher administrations were no exception: indeed, their claims reached unprecedentedly grandiose proportions. By the late-1980s the Conservatives were boasting that they had wrought nothing short of a national 'economic miracle'. The Prime Minister herself announced that 'everyone in the nation has benefited from the increased prosperity – everyone'.[1] In celebrating the growth in wealth the Thatcher governments, like other post-war Conservative administrations before them, displayed little interest in how the nation's wealth is *distributed*.

The underlying Conservative philosophy has consistently been that provided the size of the economic cake is increasing, the shares of the cake will be relatively safe from questioning. In the Thatcherite view, the free market that their policies had unleashed would produce such a vast accretion of income that every section of society would gain. The *theory* was essentially that of 'trickle-down' economics: some portion of the growth in wealth was bound to trickle down to the low income groups (via tax cuts, improved earnings and greater employment opportunities), who would then be released from dependence on the overstretched welfare state, which itself needed to be 'slimmed down'. Uniting the nation through the spread of wealth creation was the Tory credo.

The *reality* of the past decade and a half, however, has failed to bear out this optimistic scenario. On the contrary, as the 1980s wore on, far from becoming more united, the country became more divided. Social inequality increased in numerous ways: between the employed and the unemployed; between those in high-earning managerial and financial professions and those in low-wage, low-skill, unstable and often marginal jobs; between an expanding home-owning majority and a residualised minority of homeless; between those living in deprived inner-city areas and those in the more prosperous suburbs and shires. One aspect of this polarisation that attracted considerable debate was the so-called 'North-South divide'. Numerous observers complained that regional socio-economic disparities had widened dramatically in the 1980s, to reach levels not seen since the inter-war years. Britain, it was argued, had become divided into two geographical nations: into a rapidly growing, low-unemployment, high-wage and Tory-voting 'South' (usually defined as comprising the South-East, East Anglia, South-West and East Midlands), and a slower growing, high-unemployment, lower-wage and Labour-voting 'North' (the rest of the UK).[2] For many critics the divide was not just some unfortunate and unforeseen side effect of the Thatcherite economic project, but an inevitable component of it.[3] It was, moreover, a latent source of contradiction, ultimately constraining and destabilising the growth boom on which that project depended.[4]

Unsurprisingly, Margaret Thatcher herself strenuously dismissed the economic and social divide between North and South as a 'false oversimplification'.[5] Some local areas in the South and in inner London, she argued, had difficulties as great as any to be found in the North. No one, of course, had denied the existence of pockets of economic malaise and high unemployment in the South, or that London contained some of the country's most serious inner-city problems, or that local centres of relative affluence and prosperity could be found in the North. It is also a well-known fact that *intra*-regional disparities are inevitably more pronounced than *inter*-regional differences, since the latter are weighted averages of the former. But the argument was not about intra-regional inequalities. Rather, the charge was that these local disparities mapped out a broader North-South geography of socio-economic inequality,[6] and that this regional divide had become an increasingly prominent feature of British society. To the extent that the divide was acknowledged at all by the Thatcher governments, some ministers (like

Lord Young) sought to defend the more rapid growth of wealth in the South by appealing to the 'justice of history': to the absurd and erroneous notion that, whereas in the nineteenth century the North was the rich part of Britain, now it was the long-overdue 'turn' of the South. Others saw the divide as merely a 'temporary' phenomenon which would soon be eliminated as market forces inevitably diffused the southern-based boom of the mid-1980s outwards and northwards to encompass the country as a whole – a geographical counterpart of the 'trickle-down' thesis.

In recent years, though, the debate over the divide has all but disappeared. As national unemployment fell after 1986 and regional unemployment differentials narrowed, so interest in the North-South divide waned. Then, with the unexpectedly severe impact of the early-1990s recession on the South-East of Britain compared to the rest of the country (see Chapter 8), commentators began to talk not only of the 'end of the divide' but even of its reversal. It is certainly the case that the geography of the recent recession has been rather different from that of previous downturns. In the early-1980s recession, the North lost twice as many jobs as the South (896,000 compared to 368,000). In the recession of the early-1990s, in contrast, the pattern was reversed, and job losses in the South far exceeded that in the North (897,000 compared to 503,000). As a result unemployment increased much more rapidly in the South, and the North-South unemployment gap, rather than widening with recession as has been the typical post-war pattern, continued to close instead.[7] In terms of growth and employment it now seems that the South-East's lead has suddenly evaporated. Yet, announcements of the 'death' of the divide may be somewhat premature.[8] Forecasts of regional output and employment recovery for the rest of the 1990s suggest that the recent setback of the South-East is likely to be only temporary, and that, far from disappearing, the North-South divide will reassert itself as a significant feature of Britain's economic and social experience.[9] In any case, as the remainder of this essay shows, while the divide in employment and unemployment may have temporarily narrowed, the income gap between North and South that also emerged in the 1980s has persisted into the early-1990s, and as yet has shown no signs of following the convergence of regional unemployment rates. The North-South divide is, of course, only one aspect of what is a complex geography of income and poverty, and other chapters in this volume examine the more local dimensions of this geography.

However, the broad regional disparities that I want to discuss here are a real and significant aspect of the economic and social landscape.

RECENT TRENDS IN REGIONAL INCOME INEQUALITIES

The evidence that the income distribution for UK households has widened since 1979 is indisputable.[10] The annual *Family Expenditure Surveys*, which contain information on household incomes and expenditure for a representative sample of around 7,000 households, show that inequality (regardless of the specific dispersion index used) followed a slow overall downward trend through the 1960s and 1970s, reaching its lowest point under the last Labour government in 1977. Income differentials were squeezed between 1972 and 1977 by redistributive taxation and the implementation of incomes policies. However, since 1977 and especially from 1979 onwards, income inequalities have widened sharply, as can be seen from Figure 2.1 where the inequality indices measure the dispersion of gross household incomes (before taxes and living costs) adjusted for housing size (giving 'equivalised' households).[11] Several factors have contributed to this increase in income inequality, including divergent rates of earnings growth between different groups of workers, the emergence of mass unemployment, the shift of employment away from full-time towards part-time work, the expansion in self-employment, the move to a more restricted and discriminatory social security benefit system, and changes to personal and indirect taxation.

My primary interest here is in the regional complexion of this widening of the income distribution. An immediate difficulty in this context is that the Family Expenditure Survey sample sizes for some of the standard regions of the UK are relatively small. Nevertheless, by combining pairs of years it is possible to derive reasonably consistent estimates of recent movements in average household income on a regional basis. These estimates measure average gross weekly household income from all sources, before payment of taxes and before living expenses, such as housing costs (no adjustments are made for variations in household size and consumption across regions). In order to focus on regional differences irrespective of absolute income levels, these data are expressed relative to the national average (that is, UK=100) in what follows.

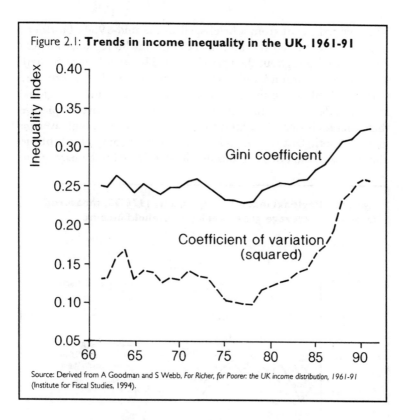

Figure 2.1: **Trends in income inequality in the UK, 1961-91**

Source: Derived from A Goodman and S Webb, *For Richer, for Poorer: the UK income distribution, 1961-91* (Institute for Fiscal Studies, 1994).

The evolution of the regional income structure since the late-1970s shows several clear features (Figure 2.2). The first is that the South-East region (including London) is in a league of its own, and is by far the highest average income area of the country. Moreover, its lead has steadily increased over the past decade and a half. In the late-1970s, average household income in this region was about 10 per cent above the national average; by the early-1990s it had risen to almost 25 per cent above the national level. Second, the three other southern regions, East Anglia, South-West and the East Midlands, have all experienced a net increase in relative average income position over the period, especially in the case of East Anglia and the South-West. Third, by contrast, the remaining regions have all witnessed a steady deterioration in relative average income position since the late-1970s. Relative decline has been particularly marked in the northern region (from 94.9 in 1976-77 to 78.8 in 1990-91), Wales (95.2 to 81.2) and Scotland (96.9 to

87.5). Fourth, apart from a brief spell in the mid-1980s, Northern Ireland has occupied the bottom position in the regional income distribution throughout the period: average household income here has fluctuated around only 80 per cent of the UK mean (see Chapter 3). Although there has been a slight narrowing of regional income differences during the recent recession, the overall picture that emerges is one of an increasing divide between a high average income South-East region and a low average income North of the country, with the other regions usually considered to be part of the

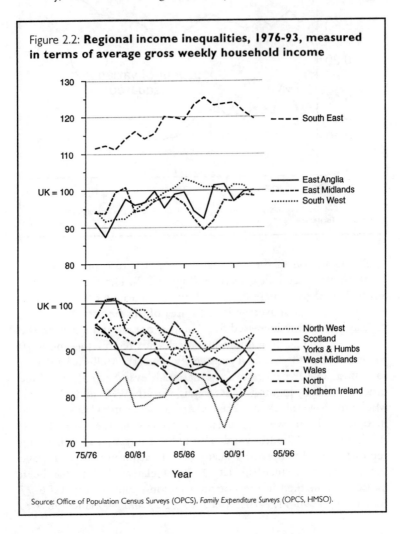

Figure 2.2: **Regional income inequalities, 1976-93, measured in terms of average gross weekly household income**

Source: Office of Population Census Surveys (OPCS), *Family Expenditure Surveys* (OPCS, HMSO).

South (East Anglia, the South-West and to a lesser extent the East Midlands) also – even if more slowly – pulling ahead of the North.

Of course, these regional income inequalities take no account of geographical differences in the cost of living. The single most significant and most regionally variable component of the latter is housing costs. House prices, rentals and costs have traditionally been highest in London and the South-East region. In the first half of the 1970s, for example, house prices in London averaged between 40 and 50 per cent above the UK average, and those in the rest of the South-East about 30 per cent higher. At the other end of the scale, house prices in the North, Wales and Yorkshire-Humberside regions were 20 per cent or more below average national prices. During the second half of the 1970s these differentials narrowed somewhat,[12] but in the 1980s the distribution widened once again with a vengeance. Not only did the national house price spiral of the 1980s emanate from London and the surrounding 'Home Counties', rising house prices and rapid wage inflation fuelled one another to a much greater extent in the South-East than in areas further north. Several observers have argued that this North-South divide in housing costs effectively offsets the regional income divide, so that in *real* terms (that is, after allowing for housing costs) regional average income differences are minimal, or even reversed in the North's favour.

The housing expenditure data included in the *Family Expenditure Surveys* can be used to deflate average gross household income to derive regional estimates of average household income adjusted for housing costs. These adjusted figures should give some test of the claims about the equalisation of regional 'real' incomes. Table 2.1 shows average housing expenditures and 'corrected' regional income relativities for three selected years, 1979-80, 1985-86 and 1991-92. With the exception of the West Midlands, the proportion of average weekly household incomes expended on housing declines northwards away from the South-East, and is some 25 per cent higher in the latter than in Scotland and Northern Ireland. However, as the table shows, while adjustment for these regional housing costs depresses the relative income position of East Anglia and East Midlands, and improves the relative income position of Scotland, these shifts do not alter the basic overall North-South income gap. By the early-1990s, the division between the four southern regions led again by the South-East, on the one hand, and the rest of the UK regions, on the other, is clearly evident. Within the latter group, the West

TABLE 2.1: **Regional income relativities, 1979-80, 1985-86 and 1991-92, adjusted for housing costs**

	Percentage of average weekly income spent on housing			Relative average household income after housing costs		
	1979-80	1985-86	1991-92	1979-80	1985-86	1991-92
South-East	16.8	18.5	19.1	112.7	117.6	117.2
East Anglia	15.8	17.0	16.8	97.3	99.0	102.7
South-West	16.0	17.2	19.1	91.6	102.8	99.8
East Midlands	13.4	15.8	17.3	102.4	97.5	100.6
West Midlands	15.9	16.6	17.4	98.3	92.6	89.0
Yorkshire-Humberside	13.1	15.8	17.0	88.1	86.2	88.9
North-West	14.7	16.5	16.1	95.2	90.4	93.5
North	13.4	15.0	14.0	89.7	84.2	85.3
Wales	12.7	14.0	16.8	94.1	91.8	85.4
Scotland	10.5	12.9	15.1	97.8	96.2	94.0
Northern Ireland	10.4	12.9	11.1	86.1	87.0	85.8
UK	**14.8**	**16.6**	**18.7**	**100.0**	**100.0**	**100.0**

Source: OPCS, *Family Expenditure Surveys* (OPCS, HMSO).

Midlands, the North, Wales and Scotland again display steep falls in their relative real incomes. Thus, notwithstanding the fact that, on average, households in the south of the country have to spend more of their weekly incomes on housing than do their counterparts in northern regions, the evidence suggests that in aggregate terms their residual incomes are still significantly higher. Although substantial, housing cost differentials between the regions are not sufficient to equalise real incomes across the North–South divide.

LOW INCOME AND POVERTY ACROSS THE DIVIDE

While the growing income disparity between these two geographical Britains is disturbing, an equally if not more important issue concerns the regional incidence of poverty. Measuring poverty is notoriously difficult and contentious. There has long been a conceptual debate over the causes, definition and measurement of poverty (see Chapter 1).[13] To compound matters, unlike in some other countries, in Britain there is no official poverty line, no governmentally recognised minimum income threshold which defines the existence of poverty. Different income series have provided different definitions of the poverty line. The *Low Income Families* (LIF) series from 1972-85 defined poverty as the number of people living on or below the old supplementary benefit level (the income level below which state support was deemed necessary). In the new *Households Below Average Income* (HBAI) series, which replaced the LIF series, the poverty line is taken to be 50 per cent of average income, the definition used by the European Commission. Some analysts, however, use the bottom decile (bottom 10 per cent threshold) of the income distribution as the line. Not only do these different series and measures give different estimates of poverty, none is comprehensive, since they all exclude the homeless, the most deprived – and currently the most politically embarrassing – section of contemporary British society.

These statistical problems notwithstanding, the trends are unequivocal. During the 1980s, for the first time in 50 years the proportion of the population living in poverty increased. For example, if we take the former supplementary benefit as the poverty benchmark, then whereas in 1979 some 12 per cent of the population were living on or below this line, by 1987 (the final year of supplementary benefit before it was replaced by income support) that proportion had grown to 19 per cent. Alternatively, if we use the European Commission's definition of the poor as those having an income of less than half of the average of the country in which they live, the numbers living in poverty in the UK have increased from 5 million in 1979 to more than 13 million in 1991.[14] On this estimate, more than a fifth of the population now live in poverty, making the UK one of the poorest countries in the European Union, alongside Portugal, Greece, Spain and Ireland.[15]

The deterioration in the relative position of the poorest section of society, the bottom 10 per cent, has been particularly serious. The latest HBAI results show that, while average real income (after housing costs) rose by 36 per cent between 1979 and 1990-91, the real income (after housing costs) of the poorest 10 per cent actually *declined* by 14 per cent (see Table 2.2).[16] Households receiving income support saw their weekly income rise by only 13 per cent over the period, while those not on benefits – who were on average already 80 per cent better off in 1979 – saw their income rise 39 per cent. As a consequence of these differential movements, the share of total national income received by the poorest 10 per cent of the

TABLE 2.2: **Changes in real income for different income groups: includes self-employed people**

	Per cent change by decile group 1979-1990/91					
	Bottom 10	10-20	20-30	30-40	40-50	Pop mean
Income before housing costs	−1	6	11	17	23	35
Income after housing costs	−14	0	7	16	22	36

Source: OPCS, *Households Below Average Incomes, 1979-1990/91* (OPCS, HMSO, 1993).

population has fallen by half since 1979, from 4 per cent to 2 per cent (see Table 2.3). The poorest 20 per cent have lost more than a third of their share, and the bottom half of the population more than a fifth. By contrast, the top half of society has seen its share of total income rise from just over two-thirds to three-quarters. Over the past 15 years of Tory government, a net upward *redistribution* of income has thus taken place from the poorest to the richest sections of British society (see Chapters 1 and 8).

Predictably, the Conservatives have dismissed the idea that they

TABLE 2.3: **Share of total UK income received by different income groups, 1979, 1988-89 and 1990-91: includes self-employed people**

	Share of income received by individuals below various percentiles of income distribution (after housing costs)			Per cent change in share 1979-1990/91
	1979	1988-89	1990-91	
Bottom 10 per cent	4.0	2.5	2.1	−48
Bottom 20 per cent	9.6	6.9	6.2	−35
Bottom 30 per cent	16	12	11	−31
Bottom 40 per cent	24	19	18	−25
Bottom 50 per cent	32	27	25	−22
Top 50 per cent	68	73	75	+10

Source: OPCS, *Households Below Average Incomes, 1979-1990/91* (OPCS, HMSO, 1993).

have presided over an increase in poverty and social hardship. Indeed, in 1989 the government argued to the contrary, and proclaimed the 'end of the line for poverty'. Drawing a sharp distinction between absolute and relative concepts of poverty, the then Secretary of State for Health and Social Security derided both. 'Relative poverty' or deprivation in his view was a mere euphemism for inequality, a notion used by academics and politicians 'to keep the fires of resentment and envy ... forever stoked'.[17] As for 'absolute poverty', this he claimed had been abolished by the government's 'economic success', and was something that belonged to the era of Dickensian London, not to contemporary Britain. No amount of political rhetoric, however, can disguise the fact that over the past decade and a half both relative and absolute aspects of poverty have increased. Not only have the lowest income groups benefited least from the growth of the 1980s, with the result that their *relative* standard of living has fallen, the very poorest have actually suffered a sharp decline in their *absolute* real standard of living.[18] In addition, the numbers of homeless, who by definition are excluded from the *Family Expenditure Surveys*, have grown dramatically since the end of the 1970s: in England alone, the number of households *officially* accepted as homeless has tripled since 1978, and official figures seriously understate the true extent of the homeless.

The regional geography of poverty bound up in all of this is far from easy to chart (see also Chapter 6). All of the main sources of information on low income are silent on the regional distribution of the poor. Although *Family Expenditure Survey* data on the distribution of household income in the regions are published, the definition of the income bands varies from year to year, and per centile analyses are not produced. In their analysis, Goodman and Webb attempt to throw some light on the issue by amalgamating unpublished *Family Expenditure Survey* data into the following regional groups: southern England (South-East, East Anglia, South-West), the Midlands (East and West), and northern England (Yorkshire-Humberside, North-West and North), together with Wales and Scotland separately.[19] They find that the distribution of the poorest decile of households (the bottom 10 per cent) across these regions has diverged. While in 1961-63 southern England contained 38 per cent of Britain's population but only 35 per cent of the poorest 10 per cent, by 1989-91 southern England's share of national population had increased to 42 per cent yet its share of the poorest group had declined to 33 per cent. More recent data confirm this disproportionate concentration of poorest households in the northern regions of the country (see Table 2.4).

TABLE 2.4: **Regional distribution of poverty**

	Regional shares of households in bottom 10 per cent of income distribution (average 1990-93)	population (1991)	Location quotient (col 1 divided by col 2)
Greater London	11.6	11.8	0.98
Rest of South-East	11.5	18.6	0.62
East Anglia	3.0	3.6	0.83
South-West	6.7	9.0	0.74
West Midlands	8.8	9.1	0.96
Yorks-Humberside	10.1	8.5	1.18
North-West	12.3	11.1	1.69
Northern	9.0	5.3	1.69
Wales	6.4	5.0	1.28
Scotland	11.9	8.8	1.35
Northern Ireland	2.6	2.4	1.08
UK	100.0	100.0	1.00

Source: OPCS, *Family Expenditure Surveys* (OPCS, HMSO).

These findings are reinforced if we look at the proportion of households on low incomes in each region. The lowest gross weekly household income band specified in the 1992 *Family Expenditure Survey* is the less-than-£65 group. This figure corresponds approximately to a gross weekly income of only *one-fifth* of average household income for that year. Using this measure, the incidence of poverty in the northern region, Wales, Scotland and Northern Ireland is almost twice what it is in the South-East, East Anglia, South-West and East Midlands (see Table 2.5). If we follow the European Commission's definition of the poor and consider the proportion of households with gross weekly incomes less than half the national average (£340 in 1992), a similar if less dramatic regional pattern is evident.[20] Nationally, in 1992 a third of households had gross weekly incomes less than half the average income (less than £170), but in all of the four southern regions the proportion was below

TABLE 2.5: **Regional disparities in the incidence of low income and welfare support, 1992**

	Per cent of households with gross normal weekly income		Per cent of household income from social security benefits
	below £65	below £170	
South-East	5.4	26.6	9.7
East Anglia	5.3	26.8	11.5
South-West	6.3	30.9	12.5
East Midlands	6.0	27.9	11.5
West Midlands	6.4	33.2	15.1
Yorkshire-Humberside	8.6	37.1	15.0
North-West	9.1	38.0	15.2
North	10.7	40.9	19.2
Wales	10.1	40.7	18.5
Scotland	10.0	36.8	17.0
Northern Ireland	11.5	40.9	19.1
UK	**7.7**	**33.0**	**13.1**

Source: OPCS, *Family Expenditure Surveys* (OPCS, HMSO); Department of Finance and Personnel, Northern Ireland; Department of Social Security.

this figure, while in all of the northern regions it was above. Only Scotland departs from an otherwise steadily increasing northwards trend in this measure of poverty.

The geography of state benefits tends to mirror these regional differences in poverty, so that expenditure on income support per capita is also concentrated in the low income regions of northern Britain (see Table 2.5). Average expenditure in the South-East is higher than in the other southern regions, reflecting the serious pockets of low income, poverty and welfare need in certain parts of London (see Chapters 4 and 8). Nevertheless, the figure for the region as a whole is still well below the national average, and considerably less than in the North-West, the northern region, Wales, Scotland and Northern Ireland. The very high level of per capita income support in Northern Ireland, more than 50 per cent above the national level, reflects the particularly high proportion of low income households there (see Chapter 3). Were it not for the inter-regional transfers produced by the welfare system, the North-

South disparity in the incidence of low incomes would be even greater.[21] What in fact is striking about the geography of low income is the quite different shape of the income distribution of the South-East compared to those of the northern regions (see Table 2.6). In the South-East the income distribution is skewed towards the top income bands (gross weekly household incomes above £550), whereas in the North, North-West, Wales, Scotland and Northern Ireland, the distribution is skewed instead toward the bottom income groups (less than £95 per week).

TABLE 2.6: **Regional differences in household income distributions, 1994: particularly notice the contrast between the South-East and the northern regions**

Per cent of region's households in each income band (gross weekly income)	South-East	North	North-West	Wales	Scotland	Northern Ireland
Under £65	6.4	10.7	9.1	10.1	9.6	11.5
£65 and under £95	7.4	11.3	10.4	11.0	11.1	12.2
£95 and under £130	7.3	11.1	8.8	8.1	8.7	8.6
£130 and under £170	6.5	7.8	9.7	11.5	7.4	8.6
£170 and under £220	7.0	9.8	8.4	9.5	8.1	11.5
£220 and under £270	7.4	7.5	7.6	6.5	7.1	7.2
£270 and under £320	7.7	9.1	8.8	7.9	9.9	10.1
£320 and under £380	8.0	5.7	6.9	8.1	7.0	6.5
£380 and under £450	8.3	9.1	8.1	7.9	8.1	7.9
£450 and under £550	9.0	7.4	7.2	7.9	8.4	7.2
£550 and under £750	12.6	5.4	7.2	6.7	9.4	5.0
£750 or more	12.4	5.0	7.8	4.8	5.3	3.6

Source: OPCS, *Family Spending: a report on the Family Expenditure Survey* (OPCS, HMSO, 1994).

We know surprisingly little about the causes of these (persistent) regional differences in income and poverty. Problems of low income and poverty are most pronounced among the self-employed, the retired and particularly the unemployed. Although regional unemployment rate disparities are now very much reduced, as we have seen, a marked North-South divide still exists in the relative incidence of *long-term* unemployment, and it is for groups suffering this that poverty, social hardship and economic exclusion are particularly acute. The self-employed group is a highly heterogeneous one, with marked inequalities between the professional categories at one end and the essentially unskilled and casualised categories at the other. Again, we know little about how far and in what ways the opportunities for, and incomes of, different types of self-employment differ across the regions. But not only is there an unemployed poor, a self-employed poor and a retired poor, there is also a sizeable *working poor*. Since the early-1980s, the earnings distribution has widened faster in the UK than in any other OECD country.[22] For both full-time men and full-time women the earnings of the bottom decile of the distribution have fallen progressively behind those of the top decile. But as part of this process the earnings of the bottom 10 per cent have grown faster in the southern regions than in the rest of the country (see Table 2.7), again for both full-time men and full-time women (see Figure 2.3).

Opinions differ as to the reasons for this growth in pay inequality in the UK since the end of the 1970s.[23] Some authors have suggested

TABLE 2.7: **The widening of regional inequalities among the working poor, 1979 compared with 1993: showing bottom deciles of gross weekly earnings**

	Upper point of the bottom decile in the region as per cent of upper point of the bottom decile in Great Britain			
	Full-time men		**Full-time women**	
	1979	1993	1979	1993
Greater London	108.6	119.5	115.0	132.5
Rest of South-East	101.1	104.1	101.5	106.5
South-East	104.2	110.0	106.4	115.1
East Anglia	95.8	99.9	95.3	96.6
South-West	93.9	96.9	96.1	97.8
East Midlands	99.2	96.7	97.5	92.2
West Midlands	102.6	97.1	99.0	95.6
Yorks-Humberside	99.2	95.3	96.3	94.7
North-West	99.0	97.0	99.0	98.0
Northern	100.0	96.5	96.1	92.0
Wales	10.5	90.1	98.8	94.4
Scotland	97.9	97.3	98.8	95.7
Great Britain	100.0	100.0	100.0	100.0

Source: OPCS, New Earnings Survey (OPCS, HMSO, 1993)

Figure 2.3: Regional gross average weekly earnings of full-time male and female workers, 1979–93: bottom decile for each region as percentage of the UK figure

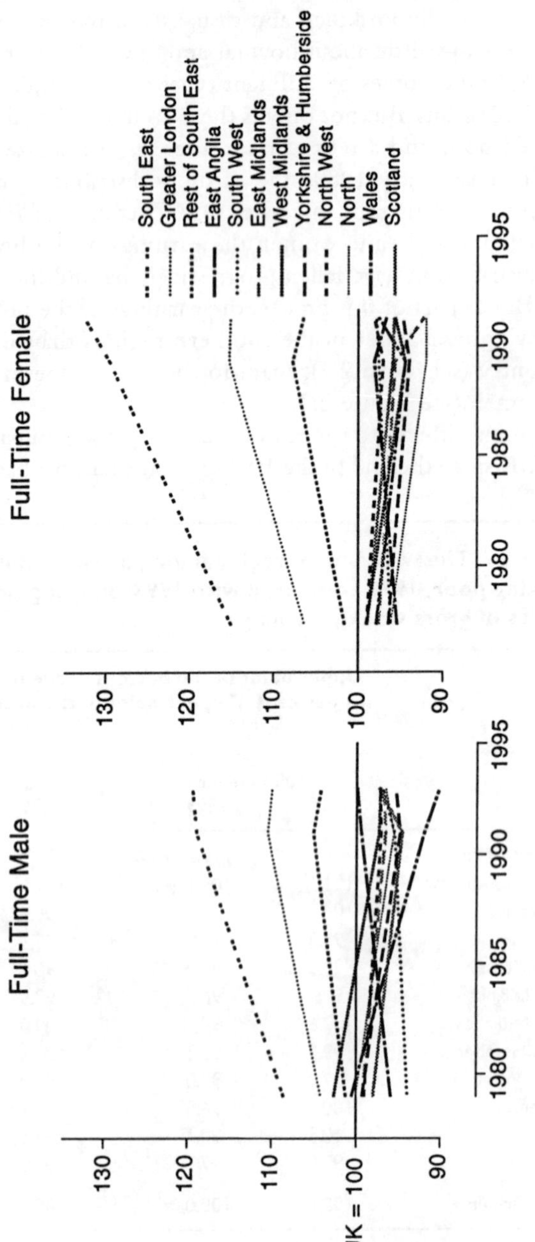

Source: OPCS, *New Earnings Survey* (OPCS, HMSO, 1993).

that it is explained by the relative movements in the demand for and supply of labour.[24] For example, while the demand for the professional and managerial occupations has grown, that for less-educated labour in the manual occupations has fallen. At the same time the supply of qualified labour has not risen quickly enough to match the increased demand, whereas the supply of less-educated labour has not fallen fast enough to match the shrinking demand for unskilled workers. Hence the pay of the former group has increased rapidly while that of the latter group has dropped. Other writers, however, put more stress on the role of institutional factors: in particular, a sharp decline in union bargaining influence, a reduction in the scope of minimum wage protection (with the erosion and then the abolition of the Wages Councils), the decentralisation of pay determination towards the level of the individual firm, and the abandonment of any attempt by the state to control pay trends in the private sector while maintaining more-or-less strict controls on public sector pay.[25] The UK is the only country to have witnessed all four of these institutional trends. Moreover, as Blanchflower and Freeman have recently put it, the UK has 'the worst of two possible worlds',[26] with the widening pay inequality of the decentralised United States labour market running alongside the high aggregate unemployment characteristic of a number of European labour markets. Furthermore, the low-income northern regions have also been the regions with the highest unemployment, contrary to what competitive labour market theory would predict.

All of this is not to suggest that there is little poverty in the South-East (see Chapter 8). As noted above, certain areas of inner London contain some of the most deprived sections of the country's population, and local concentrations of 'poverty amongst riches' – the juxtaposition of extreme wealth and poverty, both of people and places – can be found throughout the South-East region. In recent years local inequalities have increased markedly in every region of the country, including the South-East, and there are many local 'South-South divides' and 'North-North divides'. Yet, the increase in intra-regional inequality has not been sufficient to reduce or to mask inter-regional differences, and overall the proportion of households in the South-East with low incomes is considerably smaller than in the North of Britain.

THE POLITICS OF REGIONAL INCOME DIVERGENCE

A century and a half ago Disraeli, the founder of one-nation Toryism, lamented that Britain consisted of 'two nations between whom there is no intercourse and no sympathy ... the rich and the poor'. For him the elevation of the condition of the people was to be a 'great object of the Tory Party'; but in the Britain of the 1990s the division between rich and poor is very much still with us. Indeed, while successive post-war governments could justifiably claim to have promoted a steady narrowing of the gaps between rich and poor, and between North and South, through the re-distributive tax and welfare system to which all major political parties subscribed, under the past 15 years of Tory government those gaps have widened once again. The politics of 'trickle down' has clearly failed.

This is hardly surprising. 'Trickle-down' economics is an article of faith rather than a natural process. It is, moreover, logically inconsistent with the free market individualism pursued by the Thatcher and Major governments. In the absence of state-imposed safeguards and safety nets, free market economics favours pre-existing advantaged social groups and geographical areas against the disadvantaged: it generates and entrenches social and spatial inequalities. By removing or restricting many of the protections and benefits that shielded the low paid and unemployed from undue poverty, while simultaneously favouring the better off with tax cuts and tax reliefs, the Thatcher and Major governments have been far from innocent bystanders to the increase in income inequality.[27] Instead of market-based 'trickle-down' there has been government-promoted 'trickle-up': from poor to rich, and from lagging North to prosperous South (in much the same way that happened under Ronald Reagan in the United States).[28]

The existence of a much enlarged 'underclass' of poor, as much as a fifth of the population, is an affront to basic notions of democracy, citizenship, and social justice. It makes a mockery of John Major's rhetorical utterances about a 'classless society' and 'a nation at ease with itself' (see also Chapter 1). Yet it is one of the more insidious and pernicious aspects of the new Conservatism that this affront has been ideologically transposed into official indignation *against* the poor and socially deprived. In the government's view the poor, the unemployed and the homeless have only 'themselves to blame' for their predicament. Not only does welfare breed social lassitude and a culture of dependency, it burdens the hard-working and socially-responsible majority with excessive taxes. Welfare benefits should therefore be restricted to the 'deserving poor'. Thus, in order to protect the gains made by the well-off majority, what Galbraith terms the 'culture of contentment',[29] increasingly authoritarian surveillance procedures and benefit allocation controls have been introduced to keep what the government sees as the 'un-deserving' poor, the 'welfare scroungers', 'benefit swindlers' and 'work-shy', in check.[30]

While benefit fraud – like tax fraud – undoubtedly exists, and while standards of individual behaviour are undeniably vital, the majority of the low paid and poor are trapped in their deprived circumstances less by their own shortcomings or laziness than by barriers of social hardship, economic exclusion and geographical inequality. The uneven geography of economic development and employment shapes and conditions the labour market and income opportunities available to local households. In the same way that 'geographically uneven development' fuels local cycles of relative prosperity, so it also fosters local cycles of relative deprivation. The widening of the North-South income divide since the late-1970s is part of this process, and has been the result of divergent but interdependent patterns of regional growth and employment restructuring, patterns promoted in part by government economic policies which have favoured the south-eastern economy over that of the northern half of the country.[31] But, in addition, given this differential economic geography, it was inevitable that the government's restructuring of the tax-benefit system would also impinge unequally on the regions, and thereby serve to reinforce rather than to reduce the income gap between the North and South. According to the present Chancellor of the Exchequer, Kenneth Clarke, the role of the welfare state should be to ameliorate the social uncertainty and dislocation that are inevitable features of a flexible dynamic market economy. One may question how this view can be reconciled with the government's on-going restriction of the welfare system and its unrelenting discrimination against the poor, the unemployed and the homeless. One may also question how this view can be reconciled with the government's signal lack of concern about the growth of income inequalities across the regions of Britain.

ACKNOWLEDGEMENTS

I would like to thank Holly Sutherland (Department of Economics and
Politics, University of Cambridge), Steven Webb (Institute of Fiscal Studies,
London), and M. Kramer (Central Statistical Office, London) for providing
information and advice.

NOTES

1. M Thatcher, speech in the House of Commons, 17 May 1988.
2. See, for example, R J Johnston, C J Pattie and G Allsop, *A Nation Dividing?*
   (Longman, 1988); R L Martin, 'The political economy of Britain's North-
   South divide', *Transactions of the Institute of British Geographers*, Vol 13(NS)
   (1988), pp389-418, reprinted in J Lewis and A Townsend (eds), *The North-
   South Divide: regional change in Britain in the 1980s* (Paul Chapman, 1989),
   pp20-60; D Smith, *North and South: Britain's economic, social and political
   divide* (Penguin, 1988); Lewis and Townsend, *The North-South Divide*.
   Contemporary descriptions of such a North-South 'two nations' divide are
   not new, of course, and were not uncommon in nineteenth-century
   literature and political-economic debate.
3. B Jessop *et al*, *Thatcherism: a tale of two nations* (Polity Press, 1988);
   Martin, 'The political economy of Britain's North-South divide' (see
   note 2).
4. R L Martin, 'Regional imbalance as consequence and constraint', in F
   Green (ed), *The Restructuring of the UK Economy* (Harvester Wheatsheaf,
   1989), pp80-97.
5. M Thatcher, quoted in *The Independent*, 5 January 1988.
6. T Champion and A Green, 'Local economic differentials and the North-
   South divide', in Lewis and Townsend, *The North-South Divide* (see note
   2), pp61-96.
7. R L Martin, 'Remapping British regional policy: the end of the North-
   South divide?', *Regional Studies*, Vol 27 (1993), pp797-806.
8. R L Martin, 'Remapping British regional policy' (see note 7).
9. G Gudgin and A Schofield, 'The emergence of the North-South divide
   and its projected future', in R Harrison and M Hart (eds), *Spatial Policy in
   a Divided Nation* (Jessica Kingsley, 1993), pp19-36.
10. A Goodman and S Webb, *For Richer, for Poorer: the UK income distribution,
    1961-91* (Institute for Fiscal Studies, 1994); S Jenkins, *Winners and Losers:
    a portrait of the UK income distribution during the 1980s* (Department of
    Economics, Swansea University, 1994).
11. Drawing upon Goodman and Webb, *For Richer, for Poorer* (see note 10).
    The 'Gini coefficient' is a statistical measure of the extent to which the
    actual distribution departs from a perfectly equal distribution: it is hence
    a measure of inequality in the income distribution. The coefficient of

variation is the standard deviation of the income distribution divided by the mean income. It measures the 'spread' of the income distribution regardless of the mean level of that distribution.

12. C Hamnett, 'The owner-occupied housing market in Britain: a North-South divide?', in Lewis and Townsend, *The North-South Divide* (see note 2), pp97-113.

13. See, for example, D Donnison, *The Politics of Poverty* (Robertson, 1980); R Holman, *Poverty: explanations of social deprivation* (Robertson, 1978); C Oppenheim, *Poverty: The Facts* (CPAG, 1990); C Oppenheim, *Poverty in London: an overview* (CPAG, 1991); P Townsend *et al*, *Poverty Today* (Centre for Theology and Public Issues, University of Edinburgh, Occasional Paper 7, 1986); T Waxman, *The Stigma of Poverty: a critique of poverty theories and policies* (Random House, 1977).

14. Low Pay Unit, 'Poor excuses: the rise and rise of poverty', *The New Review*, No. 23 (August/September 1993, Low Pay Unit), p7.

15. European Commission, *Final Report on the Second Poverty Programme, 1985-89* (European Commission, 1991).

16. Department of Social Security, *Households Below Average Income, 1979-90/91* (HMSO, 1993).

17. J Moore, 'The end of the line for poverty', speech, 11 May 1989.

18. Jenkins, *Winners and Losers*, see note 10.

19. Goodman and Webb (see note 10).

20. *Households and Families Below Average Income: a regional analysis* (The Social Service Committee, Session 1980-90, 378-I, HMSO).

21. R Walker and M Huby, 'Social security spending in the United Kingdom: bridging the North-South divide', *Government and Policy*, Vol 7 (1989), pp321-40.

22. OECD, *The OECD Jobs Study (Parts 1 and 2)* (OECD, 1994).

23. D Blanchflower and R Freeman, 'Did the Thatcher reforms change British labour market performance?', in R Barrell (ed), *The UK Labour Market* (National Institute of Economic and Social Research, 1994); pp51-92; P Gregg and S Machin, 'Is the UK rise in inequality different?', in Barrell, *The UK Labour Market*, pp93-125.

24. L Katz, G Loveman and D Blanchflower, *A Comparison of the Changes in the Structure of Wages in Four OECD Countries* (Centre for Economic Performance, Discussion Paper No. 144, LSE, 1993).

25. P Robinson, *Is There an Explanation for Rising Pay Inequality in the UK?* (Centre for Economic Performance, Discussion Paper No. 206, LSE, 1994).

26. Blanchflower and Freeman, 'Did the Thatcher reforms change British labour market performance?' (see note 23).

27. D Bull and P Wilding, *Thatcherism and the Poor* (CPAG, 1983); H Glennerster and J Midgeley, *The Radical Right and the Welfare State* (Macmillan, 1991); T Stark, 'The changing distribution of income under

Mrs Thatcher', in F Green (ed), *The Restructuring of the UK Economy* (Harvester Wheatsheaf, 1989), pp177-96.

28. J K Galbraith, *The Culture of Contentment* (Sinclair-Stevenson, 1992); K Phillips, *The Politics of Rich and Poor: wealth and the American electorate and the Reagan aftermath* (Random House, 1990).

29. Galbraith, *The Culture of Contentment*, see note 28.

30. I Gilmour, *Dancing with Dogma: Britain under Thatcherism* (Simon and Schuster, 1992).

31. Martin, 'Regional imbalances as consequence and constraint' (see note 4).

3 Poverty in the UK: the Celtic divide

John McKendrick

BEYOND THE NORTH-SOUTH DIVIDE?

As Ron Martin demonstrated in the previous chapter, the North-South divide is an important faultline in the geography of poverty in the UK. A less obvious, but equally significant, division is that between the Celtic nations of the UK (Scotland, Wales and Northern Ireland) and England. This division can be expressed in terms of poverty statistics, but its real significance is less tangible. The discussion in this paper is organised into five sections. First, given that there is no consensus in defining Celtic UK, a description of and explanation for its usage here must be provided. Following on from this, the concept of poverty in the Celtic core is introduced. It will be argued that two analytical approaches are possible: comparing Celtic to non-Celtic UK using a range of poverty indicators ('poverty in Celtic UK'), and then discussing what may be essentially Celtic about poverty in these areas ('Celtic poverty in the UK'). The second and third sections of the chapter are given over to this analysis, and the results show that Celtic UK fares less favourably than non-Celtic UK. However, there is a twist to the tale. Research has shown that places in the Celtic core are more likely to provide the conditions necessary to support a higher quality of life, and this contradiction is discussed in a fourth section. Finally, conclusions are drawn, which discuss both the key findings and, most importantly, the policy implications that arise from them.

Before turning to these issues, though, it is necessary to explain two concepts which are used throughout the chapter. First, Celtic

UK is used in preference to the more familiar Celtic Britain because Northern Ireland is included in the discussion that follows (Britain encompasses England, Scotland and Wales, whereas the UK comprises Britain and Northern Ireland). Second, the term Celtic core is used in preference to the more familiar term Celtic periphery. This is not to deny the geographical, political and cultural distance that separates Celtic UK from England and, in particular, its south-eastern corner. On the contrary, these realities are central to the analysis that follows. Rather, the term Celtic core is deployed to emphasise that the Celtic is the focus (the 'core' of this paper), and to emphasise that an attempt has been made to avoid the ethnocentric bias that is all too often implicit in accounts of 'the periphery' from 'the core'.

Defining Celtic UK is problematic, but must be addressed for – as the chapter will show – a sense of shared Celtic identity is a crucial framework through which many people in the Celtic lands experience, perceive, conceptualise and act upon poverty. By specifying the limits of Celtic UK, the basis of this shared identity is more readily appreciated. The controversy over defining Celtic UK rests not so much with the criteria to be used, though, as with the interpretation that follows. It is widely accepted that Celtic lands should be defined according to language, and it is commonly claimed that 'with reference to the modern world, the term 'the Celtic nations' can only refer properly to communities whose traditional languages are, or were, Celtic'.[1] Two significant points arise from this. First, there are grounds for distinguishing the Celts as an ethnic as well as a linguistic group, since – as Hiebert has explained – ethnic groups have a common ancestry and culture that distinguish them from other groups.[2] Second, in the modern world Celtic UK need not be restricted to areas where Celtic languages are currently spoken. Rather, Celtic UK is determined on historico-cultural grounds, partly but not exclusively in terms of language. Price seeks to evade what would be an overly restrictive specification of Celtic UK if patterns of current language usage were the only defining criteria, and he thereby acknowledges that 'Celtic consciousness' (Celtic ethnic identity) extends far beyond areas of Celtic speakers. Applying his more inclusive criteria, Price concludes that 'the term 'Celtic nations' in the sense in which it is widely used nowadays refers to Ireland, Scotland, the Isle of Man, Wales, Cornwall and Brittany'.[3]

However, both the definition and the interpretation here remain (geographically) contentious. First, despite avoiding the tendency to underestimate the extent of Celtic UK, their historical grounding ignores the fact that at the present time there are geographical variations in identity *within* Price's Celtic nations. McCrone, in a biographical reflection on his seminal work on the sociology of Scotland, conveys such sentiments: 'born and brought up in Aberdeen, ... I stood outside that region of Scotland – the central belt – where most Scots lived, and shared the sense of separateness, even peripherality, of many folk in the North-East'.[4] A second and related objection is that historically there was more than one community occupying Celtic UK: for Scotland, Kay, writing his vivid account of the social and political history of the Scots language, identifies no less than five groups in tenth-century Scotland, each with its own territorial heartland.[5] Thus, there were the Gaels of the West Highlands, the Picts of the North-East, the Norse of the Northern Islands, the Welsh Celts of central and eastern lowlands and the Inglis (later Scots) of the South-East. Furthermore, Kay describes how the Gaelic language expanded at the expense of the Welsh Celts and how Scots – the dominant language (or dialect, according to your outlook) of lowland Scotland today – is a Germanic language. Clearly, to claim that the whole of Scotland, for example, was an area of Celtic speakers is historically inaccurate. A third and final objection to Price's definition refers specifically to Cornwall. To conceive Cornwall as being part of a 'Celtic nation' seems untenable given that it lacks the national institutions characteristic of Wales, Northern Ireland and Scotland, and the degree of national identity that prevails in these parts of Celtic UK. These 'problems' are compounded by the geographical cleavages examined in subsequent chapters of this volume. In terms of poverty, the experience in Belfast (city) will differ to that in County Fermanagh (rural area); the experience in Grampian (richer region) will differ to that in Monklands (older de-industrialising region); and the experience in the Roath Park, Cardiff (within the city) will differ to that in the St Mellons housing estate (peripheral estate, on the outskirts of Cardiff).

These insights seem to dispute the possibility of a distinctively Celtic dimension in the analysis of UK poverty. What exactly, then, is the Celtic dimension that will be discussed? In this chapter, an aspect of what might be called a 'national' divide in poverty across the UK is the subject of study. This is Celtic inasmuch as the analysis inevitably refers to the non-English nations of the UK which are widely acknowledged to be Celtic nations, despite the inaccuracies and complications referred to above. Historical in-accuracies, however, are here less important than the Celtic identi-ties that undoubtedly do now exist. Of course, as McCrone's reflection demonstrates, identities are fractured at different geographical scales. Focusing, as this chapter does, on the 'national' (Celtic) scale does not deny the importance of localised (for instance, Welsh Valleys, Shankhill Road, Protestant Belfast) or more general (for instance, British versus Northern Irish) terms of reference. These layerings of identity are for others to explore, although the principles underlying this discussion might be usefully applied in the process. Most importantly, the use of the Celtic descriptor signifies that this account of poverty comprises a cultural component. In this way, it should be distinguished from Martin's overview of UK poverty, which deals chiefly with differences across *space*.[6] In this chapter these spaces are given a cultural persona and the discussion is one about poverty in *place*, with the Celtic lying squarely at the core of the analysis. To begin with, though, it is necessary to chart the objective divisions in poverty between Celtic and non-Celtic UK.

POVERTY IN CELTIC UK

> The statistics [proving Scottish poverty] are there. Unfortunately, they're not all that's there. For being poor is never merely statistical. It is specific and individual and sore...[7]

William McIlvanney, award-winning author of many Scottish novels, reminds us in the essay *Being Poor* of what statistics on poverty cannot convey. However, statistics have an important contribution to make in the study of poverty. First, they estimate the probable extent of poverty among the population. Second, and partly because of this first function, indicators of poverty are used to inform those responsible for formulating anti-poverty policies and strategies.[8] In turn, poverty debates and policies reinforce the fact that poverty still exists in the UK, even though the UK is (still) one of the richest nations in the world as we fast approach the twenty-first century. Furthermore, in the context of this particular discussion, a statistical account of poverty is a necessary complement to the cultural interpretation that follows.

The indicators of poverty recorded here have been carefully selected to fulfil three objectives. First, each of the dominant interpretations of poverty are represented.[9] Thus, to represent *subsistence level* poverty (income sufficient to obtain what is necessary for the maintenance of physical efficiency), the proportion of households receiving social security benefits is discussed. To represent poverty as *basic needs* (subsistence level and essential services), the proportion of all patients on hospital waiting lists for more than one year is discussed. To represent poverty as *relative deprivation* (as a social condition whereby those in poverty cannot fulfil the social demands and customs placed upon them by members of that society), ownership of consumer durables is discussed. A second factor underpinning indicator selection was a concern to use contemporary data that provided the means for four-way 'national' comparisons (whereas many poverty statistics are available only for Britain, thus excluding Northern Ireland). Finally, the well-worn indicators of poverty are omitted (such as car ownership, households below average income) in favour of lesser-used alternatives. This is to demonstrate the breadth of poverty, and is in no way a reflection on the utility of standard poverty indicators. On the contrary, the range of indicators that is now discussed has been validated on the grounds that they accurately reflect the key findings arising from the more traditional indicators of poverty.

Table 3.1 facilitates a four-way 'national' comparative analysis of poverty in the UK. For each of the 17 indicators that are discussed, values are given for each nation alongside their rank order. Ranks range from 1 (least poverty) to 4 (most poverty). Clearly, there is what may be termed a 'Celtic divide' in terms of objective poverty. England, the non-Celtic nation, ranks first in 12 of the 17 indicators of poverty, suggesting if not conclusively proving that there is much less poverty in England (in non-Celtic UK) than in Celtic UK. For example, England has the highest proportion of households with an economically active head of household, the highest average weekly household income, and the highest proportion of households owning a video recorder. As the statistics show, though, the division between Celtic and non-Celtic UK is not absolute, and it is found that Wales, Scotland and Northern Ireland each perform favourably on at least one indicator. Yet this observation, while significant, cannot undermine the reality of the Celtic divide in the poverty of the UK.

Furthermore, the Celtic divide is evident for each interpretation of poverty. Thus, defined as *subsistence* and represented by the proportion of households in receipt of social security, it is found that, while 12.6 per cent of households in England are poor according to

TABLE 3.1: 'National' poverty in the UK: comparing poverty in England, Wales, Scotland and Northern Ireland

Indicators of poverty	Estimates				Rank			
	England	Wales	Scotland	NI	E	W	S	I
Economic Indicators								
unemployment (% of working age population, Jan '93)[1]	10.6	10.3	9.9	14.7	3	2	1	4
men long-term (>5 yr) unemployment (of unemployed, Jan '93)[1]	3.3	3.4	5.8	20.7	1	2	3	4
women long-term (>5 yr) unemployment (of unemployed, Jan '93)[1]	2.4	2.4	3.8	10.6	1	1	3	4
economically active head of household (% of households, 1992)[5]	62.5	58.4	58.4	59.0	1	3	3	2
households receiving social security (% of households, 1992)[5]	12.4	18.5	17.0	20.8	1	3	2	4
Household income & expenditure								
weekly disposable income (£Sterling, 1992)[5]	285.74	245.31	257.15	220.70	1	3	2	4
% with weekly gross income under £80 Sterling/week (1992)[2]	11.3	14.6	18.2	17.8	1	2	4	3
weekly expense on holidays/hotels (£Sterling, 1992)[5]	11.64	10.30	10.15	7.80	1	2	3	4
Health & safety								
long term (>1yr) on hospital waiting list (% on list, 1991-2)[4]	8.8	18.3	11.2	22.2	1	3	2	4
still births (per 1,000 births, 1991-2)[4]	4.6	4.6	5.5	4.7	1	1	4	3
fatal & serious road accidents (per 1,000 vehicles, 1992)[3]	189.4	174.7	280.2	246.6	2	1	4	3
Household ownership of selected consumer durables								
telephone (% of households, 1992)[5]	89.3	80.3	85.3	82.7	1	4	2	3
washing machine (% of households, 1992)[5]	87.5	87.4	91.2	92.1	3	4	2	1
fridge freezer/refrigerator (% of households, 1992)[5]	84.4	86.2	76.6	69.8	2	1	3	4
central heating (% of households, 1992)[5]	81.9	78.1	81.9	84.2	2	4	2	1
video recorder (% of households, 1992)[5]	70.2	67.4	64.9	54.7	1	2	3	4
home computer (% of households, 1992)[5]	19.9	18.8	14.6	9.4	1	2	3	4

Sources: 1. *Regional Trends 28* (HMSO, 1993), based on Department of Employment statistics; 2. *Regional Trends 28* (HMSO, 1993), based on Family Expenditure Survey; 3. *Regional Trends 28* (HMSO, 1993), based on Department of Transport statistics; 4. *Regional Trends 28* (HMSO, 1993), based on Department of Health statistics; 5. *Family Spending: a report on the Family Expenditure Survey 1992* (HMSO, 1993); 6. *Monthly Digest of Statistics No. 579* (HMSO, March 1994) this criterion, the incidence of poverty is more prevalent in Celtic UK (17 per cent in Scotland, 18.5 per cent in Wales and 20.8 per cent in Northern Ireland). Similar results are found when poverty is defined in relation to *basic needs* and is represented by the proportion of patients on hospital waiting lists for more than one year (health care being an essential service): once more, England with 8.8 per cent of patients waiting for more than one year has the lowest incidence of poverty, particularly in relation to Wales and Northern Ireland (with 18.3 per cent and 22.2 per cent respectively). Finally, England also fares marginally better when poverty is defined as *relative deprivation*: using ownership of consumer durables that are increasingly acknowledged as 'basic household amenities', England is found to have the highest levels of ownership (the least amount of relative deprivation) on half of the indicators that are discussed, (telephone, video recorder and home computer), although there are higher levels of ownership of washing machines and central heating in Northern Ireland, washing machines in Scotland and fridge freezers in Wales. Thus, while there is a Celtic divide to UK poverty under each interpretation of poverty, it is most acute when stricter definitions of poverty are employed (when the focus is on subsistence or basic needs poverty rather than on relative deprivation poverty).

The existence of a Celtic divide is the key finding to emerge from these results. However, three elements of this divide merit particular attention. First, Northern Ireland fares much less favourably on economic indicators of poverty. Compared to England, the unemployment rate is two-thirds higher (14.7 per cent compared to 10.6 per cent), almost twice the proportion of households receive social security (20.8 per cent compared to 12.4 per cent), and six times the proportion of unemployed have been registered as such for more than five years (20.7 per cent compared to 3.3 per cent). The extent and depth of the economic basis of poverty in Northern Ireland even sets it apart from mainland Celtic Britain (see Table 3.1). Second, the breakdown of data on long-term unemployment by gender is included to demonstrate that the Celtic divide applies to both male and female poverty (the other indicators do not make this explicit). The division is most apparent when comparing England with Scotland and Northern Ireland, given a higher incidence of long-term unemployment for both men and women in the Celtic core. Finally, of the consumer durables that are discussed, it is interesting to note that the greatest Celtic divide is evident for the emerging technologies. This means that Celtic UK, and in particular

Northern Ireland, lags far behind England in terms of ownership of video recorders and home computers. This does not augur well for the future, given that education and businesses of tomorrow are set to utilise these mediums to a much greater extent.

CELTIC POVERTY IN THE UK

What is Celtic about the poverty experienced in the Celtic lands of the UK? Using the example of Scotland, two attempts to outline the Celtic dimension in accounts of prevailing social conditions are considered. First, there are the contentious theories of the 1970s which explained Scotland's social conditions in terms of its colonial status (*vis-à-vis* England) and its peripheral position in the world economy.[10] These are briefly discussed. Second, more recently it has been suggested that social conditions in Scotland are interpreted by the Scots at the 'national' (here meaning Scottish) level, and that this reflects the existence of meaningful frameworks at this spatial scale through which experiences can be judged:[11] that is, the very interpretation of poverty (or any other social condition) as 'Scottish' by the peoples of Scotland is as 'real' as the objective conditions which they experience. While it could be argued that using Scotland here to stand for Celtic UK is problematic, it must be stressed at the outset that the objective of the following analysis is to tease out the significance of the Celtic dimensions of poverty in Scotland. At the very least, it is imperative to get closer to the details of one particular case study in order fully to demonstrate the role of identity in comprehending poverty.

CELTIC UK AS A DEPENDENT COLONY

Underlying the explanations of Scottish social conditions in the late-1970s were two key propositions. First, that Scotland occupied a peripheral position in the capitalist world economy. Second, that historically the development which did occur took the form of 'development by invitation': that is, development was constrained to those sectors of the economy which were complementary to, and not competitive with, English capitalist interests. Scottish poverty, according to these perspectives, is a function of Scotland's 'dependent' position (historically and contemporarily) in the world economy: Scotland was hence *under*developed. As McCrone observes, these structuralist accounts of Scottish development seemed to provide answers to the political concerns of that era (the 1970s).[12]

However, the argument has been criticised on several counts. Carter demonstrated that to characterise Scotland as backward is historically inaccurate;[13] Smout argued that much of Scotland's growth was internally driven, and that dependency on England (to the extent that it existed) was actually beneficial to Scotland;[14] and Nairn questioned whether a nation at the forefront of the transition to industrial capitalism could be legitimately described as under-developed.[15] The foundations of the 'dependency thesis' were duly found to be wanting, and this version of a Celtic explanation for prevailing social conditions does not suffice. Yet, a not dissimilar line of argument is perhaps not insignificant in attempts that many 'ordinary' Scottish people have themselves made to comprehend Scottish social conditions, as will now be demonstrated.

CELTIC TERMS OF REFERENCE IN COMPREHENDING POVERTY

In the course of providing a sociological account of Scotland, McCrone argues convincingly that Scotland is a civil society (a spatially bounded unit within which social interaction is stable and relatively dense), a country (with its own values and image), and a 'nation' (in that it is imagined as bounded and carries with it a sense of community whose people have a right to sovereignty).[16] In the course of validating these claims McCrone offers three propositions which are suggestive of a Scottish (Celtic) dimension to poverty in the UK:

- Scottish national identity mediates local experiences: insofar as these local experiences are made sense of at the national level, poverty in Scotland is hence interpreted as *Scottish* poverty.
- In Scotland meaningful frameworks exist through which social experiences can be judged (as Scottish): many key institutions are hence Scottish (education, law) or are orientated toward the situation in Scotland (media, political parties).
- It is not the measuring of objective conditions that is most significant, but the mobilisation of ideas, beliefs and other conceptual materials which people believe to be true: supposed Scottish injustices at the hands of the English can hence be mobilised to provoke a public outcry, regardless of the actual extent of any particular injustice being protested about.

This is not to suggest that poverty in Scotland is only interpreted at the Scottish scale – at the level of the Scottish nation – since experiences of poverty are undoubtedly interpreted by its sufferers at various scales. Thus, the impoverished partner of an unemployed compulsive gambler may refer to the habit (explanation at household level), to the lack of local employment opportunities (explanation at community level) or to the inadequacy of welfare benefits (explanation at the state level) as contributory factors to a poor existence. However, in Scotland, poverty (as is the case with other social conditions) tends to be analysed at least in part at the Scottish level, as this is one of the scales at which the experience of poverty is most readily rationalised.

The particular significance about these national level explanations in Scotland is that, as just intimated, they are most frequently directed against 'the English'. While the thesis of an underdeveloped Scotland, based on an unequal relationship with England is problematic, it is often mobilised by the Scots as an explanation for (relatively poorer) Scottish social conditions. Opposition to the poverty bound up with the community charge and with the (planned) deregulation of water gets directed against English plans, English Tory plans or Tory plans, and the terms of debate thereby often extend beyond the political and reach toward 'national' opposition. Scottish institutions such as the media provide the frameworks through which lived experiences are judged as distinctively Scottish, and as shaped by the relationship with England. For example, poverty in Scotland reported by the Scottish media is generally set within a British/UK context, reflecting the fact that the most important poverty-alleviating decisions are made (or not made) at Westminster. This framework of reporting tends to suggest that Scottish interests are at best marginalised, or at worst systematically neglected. Perceived thus, Scottish (and more generally Celtic) poverty is a 'reality' understood through a Scottish (Celtic) and often anti-English set of lenses.

This insertion of the Celtic into the analysis of UK poverty is open to criticism. First, the marginalisation of objective poverty is unhelpful. The reality of poverty, as expressed through statistics, must never be ignored in favour of cultural interpretations. Thankfully, these two perspectives need not be mutually exclusive, and the cultural component need not be introduced to the exclusion of the more traditional statistical accounts. Indeed, there is the need to examine the extent to which cultural conceptions are grounded in objective conditions (which is precisely the approach adopted in this chapter). More detailed work is required, but at this general level the results indicate that the search for a Celtic explanation of poverty seems to be based on the reality of greater poverty in Celtic UK. A second challenge is that 'cultural' insights are by no means straightforward to interpret. Thus, while the comprehension of Scottish social conditions *vis-à-vis* England implies inequality and leads to a focus on the severity of Scottish poverty, consider this reflection of McIlvanney:

> I believe one of the highly developed national skills the Scots have is the ability to deny the reality of their own circumstances ... Scots pride, that formidable quality, has always tended to rebound upon itself. For generations, the poor of this country have equated poverty with shame and have consequently hallucinated adequacy in a desert of deprivation.[17]

Thus, on one hand there is the tendency to draw attention to poverty, while on the other there is a tendency to ignore it. These contradictory tensions may coexist as part of a complex Scottish psyche, or they may be generational (with the younger generation more willing to recognise their state of poverty), or they may vary by context (with a poor person prepared to voice their state of poverty to those outside their community, yet denying its presence to those within the local community). As yet, these tensions are not fully understood, but such criticisms are not raised to deny the relevance of applying McCrone's thinking to an analysis of Scottish poverty. Rather, they merely identify particular challenges to be faced in developing the cultural dimension in the analysis of poverty. These challenges must be faced beyond this essay. In the current context, the objectives have been met: that is, it is now apparent that poverty requires a cultural appreciation, and that the poverty divide between Celtic and non-Celtic lands (between the Celtic 'nations' and the English 'nation') is an important cleavage in the *cultural* geography of poverty in the UK.

ALL DOOM AND GLOOM IN THE CELTIC CORE?

So far, a negative caricature of Celtic UK has been drawn of there being considerable poverty in Celtic UK, and of this poverty being widely attributed (at least in part) to an unequal relationship with non-Celtic UK. Yet there is a sense in which Celtic UK fares more favourably to non-Celtic UK. A consistent finding of geographers from Glasgow, based on a series of studies of the quality of life in Britain,[18] is that the districts and cities of Celtic Britain are the places in which the average British citizen is most likely to find what he or she deems important from their local area.

The Strathclyde Quality of Life Group approach involved five stages:[19]

1. Identifying similar geographical units for meaningful comparison.
2. Specifying the components that contribute toward quality of life, such as health, housing and crime.
3. Calculating an 'unweighted' measure of quality of life for each geographical unit using appropriate indicators for each component specified in (2), and then aggregating the results to give a single quality of life index for each geographical unit.
4. Conducting a British public opinion survey to establish the relative importance of the different components specified in (2) as evaluated by 'lay people'.
5. Refining the estimation of quality of life by weighting the indicators from (3) according to the evaluations uncovered in (4), and aggregating the results to give an overall scale of quality of life values for comparison with the summary indices calculated for each of the geographical units.

In effect, the research asked people what was important to them in terms of providing a decent quality of life, and then found out which places (geographical units) in Britain could best provide this. Three analyses were conducted: for large cities (Figure 3.1), for smaller urban settlements (Figure 3.2), and for large, non-metropolitan district councils (Figure 3.3).

In each analysis the results have shown that places in the Celtic core apparently offer the highest quality of life, often higher than that offered outside of this core. This is particularly true for Britain's largest cities (see Figure 3.1), where four of the five best performing cities are to be found in Celtic Britain (Edinburgh, Aberdeen, Cardiff and Motherwell). Similarly, Dundee and Swansea are among the best performing intermediate-sized cities (see Figure 3.2). For non-metropolitan district councils, five of the best performing places are from the Celtic core, including the two highest ranked districts of Perth & Kinross and Kyle & Carrick (see Figure 3.3). While there are some poorer performing areas in Celtic Britain (for

Figure 3.1: **Where in mainland Britain the 'average person' can get what they want: the 'quality of life' in Britain's largest cities**

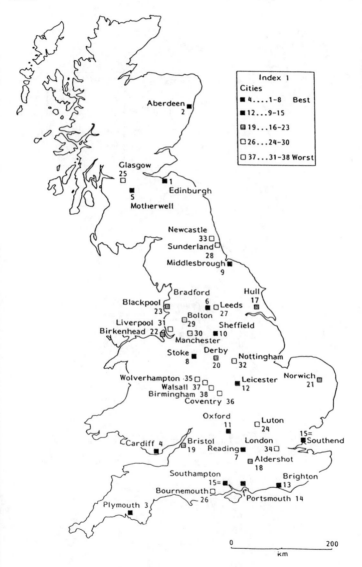

Source: A Findlay, R J Rogerson and A S Morris, 'Quality of life in British cities in 1988', *Cities*, Vol 10 (1988), pp268-76.

Figure 3.2: **Where in mainland Britain the 'average person' can get what they want: the 'quality of life' in Britain's intermediate-sized cities**

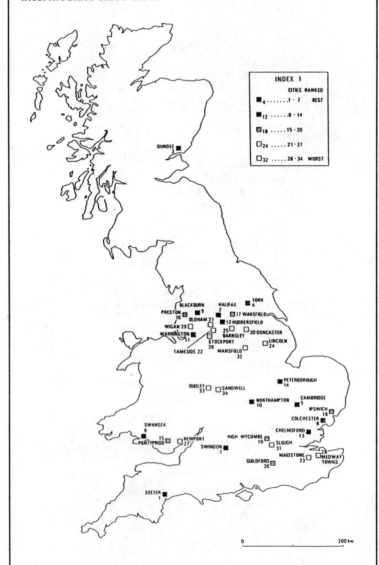

Source: R J Rogerson et al, Quality of Life in Britain's Intermediate Cities (Quality of Life Group, University of Strathclyde, 1989).

Figure 3.3: **Where in mainland Britain the 'average person' can get what they want: the 'quality of life' in Britain's largest non-metropolitan district councils**

Source: R J Rogerson et al, Quality of Life in Britain's District Councils (Quality of Life Group, University of Strathclyde, 1992).

example, Monklands is one of the poorer performing districts, as shown in Figure 3.3), the clearest and most consistent geographical division in Britain's quality of life is the Celtic divide separating Celtic lands from England.

Thus, while Celtic UK experiences more poverty, the places of Celtic Britain appear to offer more of what the average British citizen wants. What is the explanation for this seemingly contradictory situation? First, it may be argued that because poverty and quality of life 'describe' different aspects of living in the contemporary UK, the findings may not be so contradictory. Quality of life differs from poverty in two important respects, in that it takes into account the relative importance of different life concerns (poverty measures tend not to include such a weighting dimension)[20] as well as involving a more comprehensive assessment of conditions of life (poverty being mainly concerned with economic well-being). These differences raise the possibility that Scotland (and Celtic UK more generally) can have more poverty, and yet still offer a higher quality of life than non-Celtic UK. Scotland hence performs better on the noneconomic life concerns, which themselves are valued more highly by people in Scotland than are the basically economic ones, and the (greater) poverty experienced in Scotland *vis-à-vis* non-Celtic UK therefore ends up being relatively less significant than the (greater) quality of life as bound up with non-economic life concerns. Implausible as this explanation may seem, such a conclusion can be deduced from further research undertaken by the Quality of Life Group, which demonstrates the different outlook between Scots and people from the South-East of England in terms of what constitutes a high quality of life.[21]

It is unlikely, however, that this alone is an adequate explanation for the apparent paradox between quality of life and poverty. A second explanation, also related to the differences between the two 'concepts', is that individuals can themselves be poor but benefit from a good quality of life as enjoyed by a whole community. In conceptual terms poverty deals with individuals/households whereas quality of life deals with wider environmental conditions. In this way, higher quality of life performs – or has the potential to perform – a compensatory role in alleviating the severity of poverty experienced in Celtic UK (see also Chapter 5 for similar claims about the alleviation or obscuring of deprivation in many rural areas). It may be some consolation for Celtic UK that there is greater potential for this compensation occurring in Celtic lands, where quality of life is high, than in non-Celtic UK.

Finally, the paradox may reflect the possibility that there is a greater polarisation of quality of life within Celtic UK. That is, as inquiry has focused on the 'best' places (and has found that the Celtic lands provide a disproportionately large share of these), it has inadvertently ignored the location of the 'worst' places (with Celtic UK arguably also providing a disproportionately large share of these). In some respects this looks a valid explanation: in Figure 3.1 Glasgow ranks as one of the worst-performing of Britain's largest cities, and in Figure 3.3 Monklands ranks as one of the worst-performing of Britain's non-metropolitan district councils. Indeed, it can be claimed that more of the population of large cities in Scotland (see Figure 3.1) live in localities where the quality of life is below average (more people live in Glasgow than in Aberdeen, Edinburgh and Motherwell combined). Even so, the weight of evidence suggests that polarisation is only of limited value as an explanation, given that a tendency towards there being a higher quality of life in the Celtic lands emerges across all scales of analysis.

CONCLUSION: FROM PARADOX TO POLICY

Teasing out the implications of the paradox – that there is more poverty in those places (of the Celtic core) offering more of what the average British citizen apparently wants from life – takes the final part of the discussion here into the realms of policy. Indeed, should tackling the greater poverty experienced in Celtic UK or redressing the quality of life disadvantage experienced in non-Celtic UK be the priority for policy? Given that quality of life involves the comprehensive appraisal of various conditions of living, it could be argued that quality of life is the key issue. A critical dilemma with this conclusion, however, is that it is extremely difficult to mobilise quality of life insights into practical policy interventions. In fact, it has recently been observed that policy interventions are incompatible with quality of life research.[22] In any case poverty imbalances surely should not be ignored: steps must be taken to overcome poverty, and the Celtic divide is probably one cleavage along which interventions should be formulated.

In terms of policy interventions, quality of life and poverty are not mutually exclusive, and nor are they necessarily in competition with one another (as implied above). On the contrary, the quality of life results should be mobilised in the fight against poverty in the contemporary UK. Thus, it is incumbent upon those promoting the Celtic core (inward investment agencies, local authorities, entre- preneurs) to utilise to a greater extent than they do at present the knowledge that many places in the Celtic core offer a higher quality of life than places in non-Celtic UK. Technological changes and financial incentives ensure that both the relocation of existing economic enterprise and the 'peripheral' siting of new economic enterprises are feasible and attractive propositions. More effective marketing of places, and the economic-led assault on poverty that is associated with it, is hence a positive strategy which should be implemented from (and for) the Celtic core of the UK.

It is not enough, however, to conceive of the crusade against poverty in Celtic UK as a task of (say) redirecting investment and jobs from non-Celtic UK (England). If, as was suggested earlier, a polarisation of poverty *does* exist within Celtic UK, then anti- poverty strategies must be applied to redress these internal inequali- ties. An excellent example of such a strategy is Strathclyde Regional Council's *Social Strategy for the Nineties*, which has as its prime concern a commitment to reduce disadvantage and to build better communities.[23] This is the third decade of such anti-poverty plan- ning in Strathclyde, which has achieved considerable successes since its introduction in the late-1970s.

Thus far, the concluding discussion has neglected the cultural dimension to Celtic poverty in the UK. It is likely that greater Celtic control over poverty-alleviating strategies would not make a substantial reduction in the actual level of poverty experienced in Celtic UK. That is, the poorer social conditions of the Celtic nations – as the case of Scotland shows – cannot be straightforwardly attributed to an injustice relative to non-Celtic UK. More effective poverty-alleviating strategies need to be formulated, to be sure, but in objective terms these may not need to be implemented at the 'national' scale (formulated specifically for, say, Scotland as opposed to England). Objectively, the spatial basis for implementation may therefore be relatively unimportant, but it may remain vital that Celtic solutions (specific to the different Celtic nations) are *perceived* to be used in the assault upon *perceived* Celtic poverty. As was demonstrated, Scottish citizens interpret their social condition at the Scottish scale. To ignore these frameworks through which experiences are judged is to erect unnecessary barriers for initiatives seeking to alleviate poverty. While the example of Scotland was discussed, these principles also apply to Wales and Northern Ireland. Therefore, the most important lesson, based on Scottish evidence and drawing upon a cultural interpretation of poverty, is that poverty-alleviating policies for Celtic UK must be sensitive, *and be seen to be sensitive*, to the Celtic context.

Yet it is on this very point where much criticism can be directed at the British state, centred in England but claiming legitimacy to govern in a very direct fashion throughout non-Celtic UK. Not only has devolution of power not been encouraged, the ruling political party has actively sought to centralise power and to minimise the power of local government. Until the British state decentralises and is seen to decentralise; until the British state understands Celtic concerns and is seen to understand Celtic concerns; and until the British state enables rather than provides and is seen to enable rather than to provide, then the *Celtic* dimension will continue to be writ large as a cleavage within the geography of UK poverty.

NOTES

1. G Price, 'The Celtic languages', in G Price (ed), *The Celtic Connection* (Smythe, 1992), p2.
2. D Hiebert, 'Ethnicity', in R J Johnston, D Gregory and D M Smith (eds), *The Dictionary of Human Geography (Third Edition)* (Blackwell, 1994), pp172-4.
3. Price, 'The Celtic languages' (see note 1), p1.
4. D McCrone, *Understanding Scotland: the sociology of a stateless nation* (Routledge, 1992).
5. B Kay, *Scots: The Mither Tongue* (Grafton, 1988), Chapter 2.
6. R Martin, Chapter 2 of this volume.
7. W McIlvaney, 'Being poor', in G Brown and R Cook (eds), *Scotland – The Real Divide: poverty and deprivation in Scotland* (Mainstream, 1983), pp23-6.
8. See, for example, the Department of Environment commissioned work on the 1991 Census, conducted by members of the School of Geography at the University of Manchester in 1993. See M G Bradford, B T Robson and R Tye, *Constructing the 1991 Urban Deprivation Index* (School of Geography, University of Manchester, School of Public Administration Working Paper No. 24, 1993).
9. P Townsend, *The International Analysis of Poverty* (Harvester Wheatsheaf, 1993), Chapter 2.
10. M Hechter, *Internal Colonialism: the Celtic fringe in British national development* (Routledge & Kegan Paul, 1975); I Wallerstein, 'One man's meat: the Scottish Great Leap Forward', *Review*, Vol 3 (1980), pp.631-40.

11. McCrone, *Understanding Scotland* (see note 4), p26.
12. McCrone, *Understanding Scotland* (see note 4), p55.
13. I Carter, 'The Highlands of Scotland as an underdeveloped region', in E DeKadt and G Williams (eds), *Sociology and Underdevelopment* (Tavistock, 1974), pp279-311.
14. T Smout, 'Scotland and England: is dependency a symptom or a cause of underdevelopment?', *Review*, Vol 3 (1980), pp601-30.
15. T Nairn, *The Break-Up of Britain* (Verso, 1977).
16. McCrone, *Understanding Scotland* (see note 4), Chapter 2.
17. McIlvaney, in *Scotland – The Real Divide* (see note 7).
18. A M Findlay, R J Rogerson and A S Morris, 'Quality of life in British cities in 1988', *Cities*, Vol 10 (1988), pp268-76; R J Rogerson *et al*, *Quality of Life in Britain's Intermediate Cities* (Quality of Life Group, University of Strathclyde, 1989); R J Rogerson *et al*, *Quality of Life in Britain's District Councils* (Quality of Life Group, University of Strathclyde, 1992).
19. R J Rogerson *et al*, 'Indicators of quality of life: some methodological issues', *Environment and Planning A*, Vol 21 (1989), pp1,655-66.
20. J H McKendrick, *The Quality of Life of a Deprived Population Group: lone parents in Britain* (unpublished PhD thesis, Department of Geography, University of Glasgow, 1995).
21. A S Morris, A M Findlay and R J Rogerson, 'In search of the quality of life: some Scottish dimensions', *Scottish Geographical Magazine*, Vol 104 (1988), pp130-7.
22. McKendrick, *The Quality of Life* (see note 20).
23. Strathclyde Regional Council, *Social Strategy for the Nineties* (Strathclyde Regional Council, 1993).

4 Poverty in the city: 'you can raise your voice, but who is listening?' [1]

Mark Goodwin

INTRODUCTION

> After one hundred years of debate on how to plan the city ... the city itself is again seen as a place of decay, poverty, social malaise, civil unrest and possibly even insurrection ... [and] certain trends seem to reassert themselves; perhaps because, in truth, they never went away.[2]

Cities have long been synonymous with poverty, and concern about the urban poor has been evident ever since the 'industrial revolution' first ushered in an urbanised society. Indeed, some of the very earliest social research in this country, carried out over a century ago, concentrated on documenting levels of urban poverty. The work of Booth, Mayhew, Mearns and Rowntree, and their followers and associates, powerfully influenced a range of policy proposals. From the initial half-hearted fumblings of nineteenth-century reform through to the emergence of the post-war welfare state, the introduction of new measures in the fields of housing, planning, sanitation, health, education, social security and pensions was partly driven by a desire to alleviate the worst problems of the urban poor. Whether such a desire was underpinned more by moral zeal and by a fear of social unrest than by a true compassion for the poor remains contentious, but the point stands that urban poverty has long been at the forefront of social concern.

The fact that it remains so today, after a century of urban reform, is both depressing and disturbing. Depressing because the affluent society initially promised by the post-war boom, in which people had supposedly 'never had it so good', has transparently failed to materialise for so many urban residents. Disturbing because, despite some 25 years of specific urban and inner city policy, notionally designed for and targeted at the urban poor, poverty in Britain's cities is deepening rather than declining. This chapter examines the contours of this worsening urban poverty. It looks at the geography of such poverty, the experience of those who live with it on a daily basis, and at the social construction of such poverty as an 'inner-city' problem with supposedly familiar and common characteristics. It does not set out to explain how such poverty arises, although throughout what follows there are indications of the types of economic, political and social processes involved.

In developing these themes, the chapter will move beyond the charting of a simple dichotomy in terms of poverty between the city and the countryside. The geography of poverty is much more complex, with differences evident both between urban areas as well as within them. Hence poverty varies greatly across the many different towns and cities of the UK, and some of these variations – between Celtic and non-Celtic urban areas, between those in the North and the South, between those which were heavily industrial and those which were not, and between different urban places within the richer regions – are pointed to elsewhere in this collection. But, in addition to considering differences among urban areas, the chapter will also look at variations within urban areas. For no single urban area can be regarded as a uniform space with respect to poverty, and each one will possess an internal geography – of housing estates, of suburbs, of industrial and commercial areas, of open spaces, of ethnic and social groups – which helps to produce distinctive patterns of poverty and deprivation.

THE GEOGRAPHIES OF URBAN POVERTY

PROBLEMS OF DEFINITION AND MEASUREMENT

In order to look in detail at the picture of contemporary urban poverty, we need to clarify some issues of definition and measurement. Whether using relative or absolute definitions of poverty,[3] most researchers use some measurement of income as a means of drawing a poverty line. However, an immediate problem faced by those attempting to assess the extent and the shape of urban poverty is the difficulty of obtaining reliable data on income, especially at those spatial scales which allow comparisons to be made within, as well as between, urban areas. For this reason, researchers usually base their work on measurements of urban 'deprivation' rather than on the identification of urban poverty by itself. In this procedure, the existence of deprivation is taken as a surrogate for the existence of poverty. It is thus important at the outset that we clarify the difference between the two concepts. People are said to be 'deprived' if they lack the material standards (such as diet, housing and clothing) and the services and amenities (recreational, educational, environmental, social) which would allow them to participate in commonly accepted roles and relationships within society. They are said to be in 'poverty' if they lack or are denied resources to obtain access to these conditions, and for this reason are unable to fulfil membership of society. Deprivation is therefore linked to the level of conditions or activities experienced, while poverty is tied to the level of incomes and resources available.[4] Because the former are more easily measured, and because we lack any systematic small-scale data on household income, wealth or living standards, researchers tend to use indices of deprivation as indicators of urban poverty.

This leads to a further difficulty, in that different pictures of poverty are produced by different sets and combinations of deprivation indicators. The Department of Environment's (DoE's) 'official' definition of urban deprivation, for example, uses a combination of eight indicators – consisting of measures of unemployment, overcrowding, lack of exclusive household amenities, single parents, pensioners living alone, population change, mortality and ethnic origin.[5] Using such a list skews the identification of deprivation towards particular types of places. Thus inner London boroughs score heavily on indicators of overcrowding, household amenities, single parents and ethnic origin, while northern cities are ranked as more heavily deprived on the indicators of unemployment and mortality. Although inner London scores reasonably heavily on unemployment and lone pensioners, the northern cities, and also outer urban estates, score very low on ethnic minorities, lone pensioners and lack of exclusive amenities. Overall, the result is arguably to exaggerate the extent of deprivation in some cities (notably London), and to underestimate deprivation in other areas – a serious concern when such calculations are used to inform the distribution of government grants.

Other more complex and sophisticated measures of deprivation are not immune from similar difficulties. Begg and Eversley used 160 indicators to rank places on a combined list of favourable and unfavourable indices, but their study tends to underestimate deprivation in London because all of the London boroughs scored well on the more favourable indicators.[6] Thus Hackney, often cited as the most deprived borough in Britain using the DoE indicators, is only listed as the twenty-fifth most deprived using Begg and Eversley's indicators. However, Begg and Eversley use functional areas rather than local authority districts as their unit of classification, and therefore combine Hackney with Islington, a neighbouring borough which is less deprived. This brings us on to yet another problem, that of spatial scale. Some studies use local authority boundaries, and will thus discuss whole cities such as Manchester, Glasgow and Liverpool as single entities. Others use functional classifications, dividing the larger cities into cores and peripheries. Others use parliamentary constituencies, thus dividing the larger cities into five or six units, while some use ward and even enumeration district data, allowing a more fine-grained analysis to be undertaken. As with the choice of indicators, the point is that different spatial scales of analysis will result in different delineations of urban poverty.

This factor is obviously crucial when we interrogate the geography of poverty. As Townsend put it:

> However we care to define economically or socially deprived areas, unless we include nearly half the areas in the country, there will be more poor persons or poor children living outside them than in them. There is a second conclusion. Within all or nearly all defined priority areas, there will be more persons who are not deprived than there are deprived.[7]

This means that the spatial concentration of poverty is relatively low, and that we should reject any conclusions which casually draw a link between certain types of urban locality – say, the inner city – and high concentrations of poverty. We will return to the policy implications of this later in the chapter, but for now we can note that the evidence points to a social, rather than a spatial, concentration of deprivation.[8] In short, we find urban poverty wherever we find the urban poor. Sometimes this will be in the redeveloped high-rise estates of the inner city, but equally we may find the vulnerable and disadvantaged in the outer estates, or, if they are denied access to social housing, in the run-down rented terraces fringing the inner city. As Harrison graphically states, 'the poor, wherever they live, carry their own inner city round with them, like snails their shells...'[9] The geography of urban poverty is therefore complex, and the sifting and sorting of the unemployed, the sick, the elderly, the unskilled, and the disadvantaged, through the operation of intricate labour and housing markets, is far from straightforward. There are, however, some broad trends which we can pick out, and it is to these that we now turn, and in so doing we will use (as elsewhere in the chapter) ranking lists of deprivation. In the interests of both brevity and clarity we will illustrate our arguments by reference to the most depressed urban places, but this should not imply that poverty is absent elsewhere or that poor people living in less deprived places are themselves in any less poverty than are their counterparts from the most deprived places.

THE SCOPE AND EXTENT OF URBAN POVERTY

A good place to begin in order to gain an overall picture of contemporary urban deprivation is with an analysis of the 1991 Census, undertaken at the local authority level by Forrest and Gordon.[10] Their work is especially useful because it distinguishes between material and social deprivation, so avoiding some of the compositional problems of a single index. The 20 most deprived places in the country according to each index are listed in Table 4.1. Several points can be drawn from these listings. Most obviously, they confirm that England's urban areas are the most deprived in the country. (Conversely, the least deprived areas in the index, socially and materially, are those local authority districts dominated by small and medium sized towns.) The only non-urban area to climb into the top 20 of either index is the Scilly Isles, ranked highly because it has so many households with no car, one of the indicators used to calculate the material deprivation index. They also confirm the predominance of inner London as a site of material deprivation, with 13 of the area's 14 boroughs coming in the top 20 (the exception being the City of London). In addition, Brent and Waltham Forest, two outer London boroughs, also rate highly in terms of material deprivation. This means that 15 of the 20 most deprived districts in the country, in material terms, are in London. Apart from the Scilly Isles, the other four areas present confirm the urban bias of material deprivation – Liverpool, Knowsley, Birmingham and Kingston-upon-Hull. However, the presence of Kingston-upon-Hull confirms that there is no simple linear relation

TABLE 4.1: **Ranking of the 20 most deprived local authority areas in England on two different scales: one measuring 'material deprivation', the other measuring 'social deprivation'**

Material deprivation	Social deprivation
1. Newham	1. Knowsley
2. Hackney	2. Manchester
3. Scilly Isles	3. Liverpool
4. Westminster	4. Hackney
5. Kensington & Chelsea	5. Tower Hamlets
6. Hammersmith	6. Easington
7. Haringey	7. Southwark
8. Tower Hamlets	8. Middlesbrough
9. Camden	9. Salford
10. Lambeth	10. Newham
11. Liverpool	11. South Tyneside
12. Waltham Forest	12. Islington
13. Islington	13. Newcastle-upon-Tyne
14. Brent	14. Sunderland
15. Wandsworth	15. Nottingham
16. Knowsley	16. Hartlepool
17. Birmingham	17. Lambeth
18. Lewisham	18. Kingston-upon-Hull
19. Southwark	19. Gateshead
20. Kingston-upon-Hull	20. Greenwich

Source: R Forrest and D Gordon, *People and Places: a 1991 Census atlas of England*, School of Advanced Urban Studies (SAUS), 1993.

between size of city and level of deprivation. We cannot therefore automatically state that the larger the conurbation, the greater the concentration of poverty, but the appearance of so many London boroughs in the material index, along with Liverpool and Birmingham, does indicate that the degree of deprivation is likely to be more severe in the conurbations.

The index of social deprivation produces a different picture. Although it confirms the urban dimension of disadvantage, the majority of the top twenty are northern cities rather than London boroughs. Moreover, many of them are outside of the large conurbations, and the presence of smaller urban areas such as Easington and Hartlepool indicates even more strongly that urban size is not a straightforward indicator of deprivation. Perhaps the most indicative aspect of the index, however, is the appearance of Knowsley as the most socially deprived local authority in the country. Knowsley is on the edge of Merseyside, and although the 'inner city' of Liverpool appears at number three in the index, the position of the 'outer city' at number one confounds our preconceptions about the inner and outer city. We might expect the inner city to be more deprived, but in this case the reverse is true.

This study, using 1991 Census data, confirms many of the broad trends pointed to in a range of work on urban deprivation undertaken throughout the 1980s.[11] The body of this research consistently shows that it is inner urban areas, along with specific outer estates, which are the most deprived places in the UK. Which particular cities are ranked higher than others depends on the exact indicators used, but there does seem to be what we might term a gradient of deprivation, running downwards and outwards from the cores of Britain's large metropolitan areas. Thus, the inner areas of London, Birmingham, Glasgow, Liverpool and Manchester regularly appear at the top of most tables of urban deprivation and poverty. But not all of the areas scoring badly are inner cities and not all inner city areas score badly, hence adding to the complexity of any analysis.

This point can be illustrated by looking at the experience of the 'outer estates'. This generic name is given to those large estates on the edge of many urban areas, built in the 1950s and 1960s to house overspill population. Some are the size of small towns, with populations of up to 50,000, and nationally they house over two million people.[12] Detailed research carried out in the mid-1980s found that average income levels on these estates were lower, and unemployment and overcrowding higher, than in those inner city areas designated for special help by the government. The report on Easterhouse in Glasgow concluded that 'Easterhouse has among the worst combinations of housing problems, poor health, unemployment, lack of services and low income of any area of similar size in Britain'.[13] It notes overcrowding at over seven times the national rate, levels of car ownership at half the national rate, and infant mortality at almost five times the national rate with almost one in 20 infants dying in their first year of life. The origin of these estates means that they are often socially homogenous, and their relative lack of white–collar and skilled populations has made them disproportionately vulnerable to economic decline and rising unemployment. The grim and monotonous system-built environment of the estates themselves adds to the pervading sense of despair, as does their relative isolation and distance from city centre services and facilities.

These estates are not geographically located anywhere near the inner city, yet they carry levels of housing defects, vandalism, unemployment, physical and mental illness, drugs and crime which match, and even outweigh, those found elsewhere in our cities. The Archbishop of Canterbury's Commission on Urban Priority Areas reported that 'many outer estates [are] in greater need of special measures to combat multiple deprivation than the traditional inner-city neighbourhoods'.[14] Such conclusions show that urban poverty cannot be thought of as solely an inner-city phenomenon. Urban poverty is found wherever the conditions of economic decline, physical decay and social disintegration combine in such a way as to prevent residents 'from entering fully into the mainstream of the normal life of the nation'.[15] Such a combination can, and indeed does, manifest itself in a variety of locations within our towns and cities.

We can piece together a broad picture of the resulting levels of suffering from a variety of sources. Many areas of urban poverty and deprivation have official unemployment rates of over twice the national average;[16] they have levels of claimants receiving income support/supplementary benefit running at almost three times the national average;[17] they suffer from levels of overcrowding which are up to four times the national rate;[18] and their population has significantly higher levels of ill-health and mortality.[19] Moreover, the picture is getting worse rather than better. A recent study which looked at a number of deprived urban areas concluded that in terms of the proportion of the population on income support/supplementary benefit, the gap between these areas and the rest of the country had widened since the mid-1980s.[20] Townsend, drawing on studies of London and Manchester in the 1980s, also points to the widening of social and geographical inequality, when he concludes that in the richest and poorest boroughs in each city 'there has been a tendency to depart further from average conditions and circumstances'.[21] This is confirmed by some initial ward level work on the 1991 Census results for Greater London.[22] This research replicates that undertaken by Townsend on the 1981 Census, and uses the same four variables to calculate an index of multiple deprivation for each ward.[23] The results show that Spitalfields, in Tower Hamlets, is still the most deprived ward in London, as in 1981, but that its level of deprivation is now much further from the average.

This deepening of urban poverty has been accompanied by an increasing social polarisation.[24] Labour markets are increasingly divided between the highly paid professional sector on the one hand, and the casual and de-skilled sector on the other, resulting in a 'growth in social inequality on almost every measure'.[25] In addition, some urban areas have been the recipients of literally millions of pounds of public sector subsidies which they have used to stimulate regeneration and development through a variety of urban policies. However, helping deprived places is not necessarily the same as helping deprived people, and the open nature of most urban labour markets means that those jobs which have been created in deprived places have rarely gone to the urban poor who live there. Indeed, property-led urban regeneration may only serve to increase social and spatial inequality by promoting new housing, commercial and retail developments which only benefit a minority of privileged property owners, speculators, 'incomers' and commuters.[26] This in turn may increase social tension and unrest if the end result of regeneration is a range of speculative 'prestige' developments which do little to address the housing and employment needs of local residents.[27] As one study of London's Docklands concluded, with regard to the influx of new residents into the locality's 'up-market' housing developments, '[w]hile in strictly statistical terms each borough [now] has a more 'balanced' population profile, in reality it is an increasingly divided population'.[28]

Table 4.2 illustrates these increasing divides, and is drawn from research being carried out on the 1991 Census results in the Geography Department at the University of Wales, Aberystwyth.[29] It compares the most deprived with the least deprived wards in London, ranking them on an index of material deprivation combining the four separate measures listed. It shows that the differences between the least and most deprived parts of the city are extreme, with the percentage of people suffering from unemployment in the poorer wards being up to eight times greater than in the richer wards. The differences exposed by the other indicators are even more substantial: 30 per cent of all households in the poorest ward were suffering from overcrowding, compared to only 0.3 per cent in the least deprived; up to 96 per cent of households in the most deprived wards did not own their own home, compared to only 3 per cent in the least deprived wards; and up to 74 per cent of households in the poorest wards did not own a car compared with only 5 per cent in the least deprived wards of the city. These are

TABLE 4.2: **Ranking of Greater London wards on measures of multiple deprivation: highest ranked ten wards and lowest ranked ten wards**

Ranked ward	Borough	Z-score index	Unemployed	Over-crowded	Percentage Not owning home	Percentage Not owning car
1. Spitalfields	Tower Hamlets	16.8	32.5	29.8	81.9	73.6
2. Liddle	Southwark	10.9	30.8	12.1	96.4	74.4
3. St Dunstan's	Tower Hamlets	10.8	27.4	16.2	83.8	68.6
4. St Mary's	Tower Hamlets	9.1	22.0	14.7	79.5	68.8
5. Weavers	Tower Hamlets	8.9	25.1	12.7	82.2	66.8
6. Shadwell	Tower Hamlets	8.9	22.6	15.8	78.4	58.1
7. Haggerston	Hackney	8.7	26.4	10.0	88.5	69.6
8. Holy Trinity	Tower Hamlets	8.5	25.2	12.0	80.7	65.0
9. Golbourne	Kensington & Chelsea	8.2	23.8	9.9	88.2	70.2
10. Kings Park	Hackney	8.1	27.6	8.2	89.2	67.5
755. Woodecote & Coulsdon West	Croydon	−5.6	4.7	1.3	10.1	12.2
756. Upminster	Havering	−5.8	4.1	0.6	6.9	17.6
757. West Wickham North	Bromley	−5.8	4.8	0.3	6.7	17.1
758. Crofton	Bromley	−5.9	4.2	0.5	5.5	17.1
759. Emerson Park	Havering	−5.9	5.1	0.8	5.3	12.6
760. Cranham West	Havering	−6.2	5.0	0.4	3.3	13.2
761. Biggin Hill	Bromley	−6.2	4.6	0.9	7.9	7.9
762. Cheam South	Sutton	−6.2	4.1	0.4	7.4	11.0
763. Selsdon	Croydon	−6.3	3.9	0.7	4.6	11.5
764. Woodcote	Sutton	−6.5	5.8	0.3	4.8	5.4

Source: OPCS, *1991 Census of Population* (OPCS, HMSO): data analysis conducted as part of ongoing research at the Department of Geography, University of Aberyswyth.

differences of a huge magnitude, and we can expect them to be replicated in other cities across the country.

The divisions between the overall scores of deprivation are stark, as illustrated by the z-score index, which shows how many standard deviations above or below the London mean each ward is. The accompanying map (see Figure 4.1) shows the varying distribution of material deprivation across London. It provides a ranking of all wards into five classes, using the same multiple index of deprivation. The patterns here are quite clear, and in the main they follow the gradient of deprivation referred to above, with the inner areas suffering the most deprivation. However, we can also see substantial clusters of the most deprived wards to the north and west of inner London, and a scattering of less deprived wards close to the centre. Each city, as with London, will have its own particular distribution of poverty, shaped by the specific geographies of those processes – such as unemployment, poor housing, social polarisation, declining public services – which combine to produce deprivation. We thus need to consider differences within, as well as between, cities when we come to trace the contours of urban poverty.

THE EXPERIENCE OF URBAN POVERTY

This juxtaposition of social polarisation with a deepening spiral of poverty helps to highlight urban deprivation, and perhaps defines it more starkly for those who suffer from it. It is often remarked that for those on their own, nowhere is as lonely as a crowded city. In the same vein, poverty, and the experience of it, is perhaps more keenly felt in the midst of affluence. In their study of Urban Priority Areas, the Archbishop of Canterbury's Commission stated that:

> Poverty is not only about shortage of money. It is about rights and relationships; about how people are treated and how they regard themselves; about powerlessness, exclusion, and loss of dignity.[30]

Although lack of income may be at the heart of urban poverty, the poor also suffer from a lack of self-esteem, and in the city they face constant reminders of those who are wealthier and more fortunate. The material and subjective aspects of deprivation are fused in an urban environment which highlights the multifaceted nature of poverty: part lack of income, part material deprivation, part social deprivation and part subjective experience.

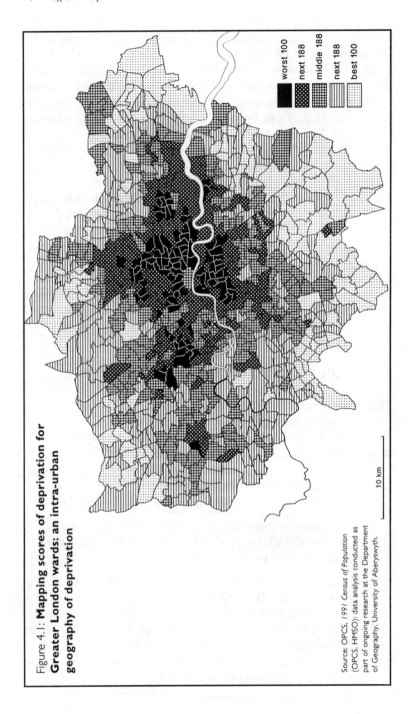

Figure 4.1: **Mapping scores of deprivation for Greater London wards: an intra-urban geography of deprivation**

worst 100
next 188
middle 188
next 188
best 100

10 km

Source: OPCS, *1991 Census of Population* (OPCS, HMSO); data analysis conducted as part of ongoing research at the Department of Geography, University of Aberyswyth.

Studies which have explored the links between these different aspects of poverty show how they reinforce one another, and how they are shaped by a specifically urban experience. In his study of deprivation in London, Townsend found that different forms of material, social and subjective deprivation were more closely correlated than might be supposed.[31] Through interviewing almost 3,000 residents, the study revealed that those in the most deprived parts of the city suffered disproportionately, not only from poor housing, lack of household facilities and possessions and inadequate clothing, but also from risk of road accidents, litter problems and lack of garden and play facilities. They also moved house more often and had more health problems than those residents in less deprived areas. In terms of subjective feelings, a very high proportion of the population of the most deprived wards felt anxieties about the health of both family members and themselves, as well as generally worrying about having enough money to make ends meet. In the words of one inner London resident:

> We're getting low now. We've got food for today, but there's none for tomorrow. Last week we ran out of money for the electric meter … I just have one meal a day, sometimes I don't eat at all … I've had to get the little ones out of nappies – I couldn't afford them any more … We're going steadily downhill.[32]

Many feared eviction, were concerned about isolation and experienced racial harassment, and almost one-fifth had encountered street or estate violence in the previous 12 months. Just over a fifth felt that they suffered from poor public transport, while just under a fifth considered that they owed money. Indeed, debt and the consequences flowing from it often turns out to be a key moment in the slide towards long-term poverty. The following tale illustrates the hardships which can follow unpaid bills:

> They cut my electric off … just after my husband left … My baby (one of five children) was four weeks old. It wasn't warm weather. I had to give her four-hourly feeds with no cooker, no light, no nothing. We were without electric for two years. We cooked our meals in a friend's house … We had candles, and then I got one of those miner's lamps. We had no TV, we just sat around like zombies getting on each other's nerves. At night when it was cold my babies slept in my friend's house … I sold all my home to keep going, I was taking the mirrors off the wall to get £4 … Then I exchanged my

gold wedding ring for a second-hand sofa and a sideboard. The ring was nothing to me, but it takes all your pride away. I ain't got none left.[33]

By taking into account the subjective dimensions of deprivation we can construct a broader picture of urban poverty. The implications of such poverty for the quality of people's day-to-day lives in the city are manifold. Poor people are not only materially deprived of acceptable standards of diet, clothing and accommodation, but also feel excluded, fearful, worried and constantly concerned – about their health, about their safety, about their housing, about their employment prospects and about their ability simply to make ends meet. Their mobility is limited, their social opportunities curtailed, and their immediate surroundings are dominated by squalor and dilapidation.

People experience these deprivations differently, and we should perhaps speak of their varying *experiences* of poverty. Different groups are affected in different ways, although some sections of society are more prone to poverty than are others. In this regard the elderly, those with a disability, those from ethnic minorities, those with long-term illnesses, those reliant on benefits, lone parents and women are all over-represented. We should be wary of homogenising the different experiences of these different sufferers, and including a subjective element in our analysis reinforces this point. Whatever is argued in this respect, though, Townsend's survey of poverty in London unearthed conclusive evidence showing the combined effects of material and subjective elements to be 'more pervasive than many suppose',[34] presenting a picture which was at once depressing and unrelieved. The cumulative effects are captured by Sarah:

> You can only take so much. I'm a human person. I'm not an animal. When you're left on your own your two shoulders don't seem to balance any more. Who do you go to for help? ... I can't see no light at the end of the tunnel. What's the good of my living, every day and every night? It's not a life, it's not a life ... When I get up I think, Christ, I've got to get through till 8 o'clock tonight. If I had tablets here, I'd have taken the lot. But then I look at the two babies.[35]

THE SOCIAL CONSTRUCTION OF URBAN POVERTY

To be a participant in this 'unrelieved' picture of poverty is to be caught up in the spiral of economic decline, physical decay and social disintegration so graphically identified by the Archbishop's Commission on Urban Priority Areas.[36] It is important to remember that this spiral is created and sustained by broader sets of economic, social and political processes, whose origins lay outside of the immediate urban sphere, and that 'above all the inner city and the peripheral estate are creatures of the whole society, not simply of their inhabitants'.[37] It is easy to forget this point, especially in the face of continuing political concern with an 'inner-city problem', which implies that such poverty is spatially bounded and restricted to isolated pockets of deprivation.[38]

The assumptions which lay behind such a concern have fostered a whole series of 'area-based' policy responses, from the urban programme of the 1960s, through urban partnerships in the 1970s, to enterprise zones and urban development corporations in the 1980s and 1990s. Although introduced by different governments, these policies have in common the fact that they are spatially constrained and targeted at specific parts of particular cities, and in so doing they reflect the dominant social constructions of urban poverty. They view poverty as the property of 'deviant' individuals and households, who are supposedly concentrated in a few places of particular need (conveniently labelled the 'inner city'). The appropriate policy response then becomes a fairly limited one of dealing with problem people in problem areas.[39] By constructing poverty and deprivation in this way, as rooted in the characteristics of specific people and places and as only found in a few 'deviant' communities, mainstream society is assumed to be functioning properly. In this manner, urban poverty is seen as a problem *of* people rather than as a problem *for* them, and as a problem *of* the inner city rather than as a problem *in* the inner city.[40] In each instance blame is centred on the victims of poverty, rather than on the conditions of a wider society. Governments of both political persuasions have consistently used this construction since urban poverty reappeared as a politically sensitive issue in the mid-1960s, and they currently show little evidence of reformulating it.[41] Indeed, the emergence of the notion of an urban 'underclass' has helped to reinforce the idea that feckless individuals are solely to blame for their own plight. Instead of addressing the structural factors within the wider economy and society that combine to produce urban decline, politicians can use the idea of the underclass to focus debate on the habits of supposedly apathetic and 'deviant' individuals.

Such a construction is open to argument, however, since when used in this way the very concept 'inner-city' becomes an ideological category heavily loaded with political and moral symbolism. As Ward puts it:

> When the inner city, as such, is discussed as a social problem, the description is not used as a geographical expression at all. The phrase does not describe derelict or run-down buildings. It is used as a euphemism for the urban poor. The 'inner city' is an idea rather than a place.[42]

Like all ideas, it then becomes open to discussion and debate. This is crucial because, somewhat paradoxically perhaps, the idea and the rhetoric of a specifically urban poverty needs to be challenged if the true roots of urban deprivation are to be uncovered and understood. For it is only by situating such poverty and deprivation in their wider economic and social contexts that we can begin both to tackle and to remedy their causes. Until we do this the numerous anti-poverty initiatives now being developed locally within urban communities, such as credit unions, although offering a valuable form of support to the urban poor, will remain nothing more than sticking plasters on an ever-deepening wound (see also Chapter 10). Tackling the results of urban poverty in this way undoubtedly helps those suffering at the moment, but it does little to modify the underlying causes of their poverty. Unfortunately, the task of tackling causes rather than results remains as urgent today as it was over one hundred years ago when urban reform was in its infancy. Along with Tony, the unemployed resident of Hackney, we can still legitimately ask 'who is listening' to the plight of the urban poor?

NOTES

1. 'Tony', unemployed resident of Hackney, inner London, quoted in P Harrison, *Inside the Inner City* (Pelican, 1985), p164.
2. P Hall, *Cities of Tomorrow* (Blackwell, 1988), pp11-12.
3. C Oppenheim, *Poverty: The Facts* (CPAG, 1993), pp6-10.
4. P Townsend, *Poverty and Labour in London* (Low Pay Unit, 1987), pp85-101.

5. Department of the Environment, *Urban Deprivation* (Inner Cities Directorate, Information Note No. 2, 1983).

6. I Begg and D Eversley, 'Deprivation in the inner city: social indicators from the 1981 Census', in V Hausner (ed), *Critical Issues in Urban Economic Development*, Vol 1 (Clarendon Press, 1986), pp11-49.

7. P Townsend, *Poverty in the United Kingdom* (Penguin, 1979), p56.

8. A Sills, G Taylor and P Golding, *The Politics of the Urban Crisis* (Hutchinson, 1988), p59.

9. Harrison, *Inside the Inner City* (see note 1), p24.

10. R Forrest and D Gordon, *People and Places: a 1991 Census atlas of England* (School of Advanced Urban Studies Publications, 1993).

11. See, for example, Archbishop of Canterbury's Commission, *Faith in the City* (Church of England Commissioners, 1985); A Champion and A Green, *Local Prosperity and the North-South Divide: winners and losers in 1980s Britain* (Institute for Employment Research, University of Warwick, 1988); Hausner (ed), *Critical Issues in Urban Economic Development* (see note 6); P Redfern, 'Profile of our cities', *Population Trends*, Vol 30 (1982), pp21-32; B Robson, *Those Inner Cities* (Clarendon Press, 1988); D Sim, 'Urban deprivation: not just the inner city', *Area*, Vol 16 (1984), pp299-306; Townsend, *Poverty and Labour* (see note 4). For a North American perspective, see P Knox, 'The vulnerable, the disadvantaged and the victimised: who they are and where they live', in D Herbert and D Smith (eds), *Social Problems and the City: new perspectives* (Oxford University Press, 1989), pp32-47. Other essays in this latter volume usefully consider individual aspects of urban deprivation which cannot be covered here, such as healthcare, education, housing, crime, unemployment, drugs, alchoholism, welfare services and economic decline.

12. CES Ltd, 'Deprived areas beyond the pale', *Town and Country Planning*, February (1985), pp54-5. See also Centre for Environmental Studies, *Outer estates in Britain* (CES Working Paper 23), and also the Centre's Working Papers 24-27 dealing with individual outer estates.

13. Centre for Environmental Studies, *Easterhouse* (CES Working Paper 24), p1.

14. Archbishop of Canterbury's Commission, *Faith in the City* (see note 11), p177.

15. Archbishop of Canterbury's Commission, *Faith in the City* (see note 11), p9.

16. J Bailey, '1991 Census results for local authority districts in Britain', *Population Trends*, No. 73, pp8-17.

17. Oppenheim, *Poverty: The Facts*, see note 3, pp146-7.

18. Archbishop of Canterbury's Commission, *Faith in the City* (see note 11), p18.

19. P Townsend, 'Living standards and health in the inner cities', in S MacGregor and B Pimlott (eds), *Tackling the Inner Cities: the 1980s*

revisited, prospects for the 1990s (Clarendon Press, 1991), pp93-126.

20. Oppenheim, Poverty: The Facts (see note 3).

21. Townsend, 'Living standards' (see note 19), p119.

22. Analysing Small Area Statistics drawn from the 1991 Census using Small Area Statistics Package (SASPAC), via University of Manchester Computer Centre: The 1991 Census, Crown Copyright, Economic and Social Research Council (ESRC) Purchase. I am very grateful to Tony Moyes, a colleague at Aberystwyth, for allowing me to use his initial findings here.

23. Townsend, Poverty and Labour (see note 4).

24. S Fainstein, I Gordon and M Harloe (eds), Divided Cities (Blackwell, 1990).

25. D Massey, 'Local economic strategies', in MacGregor and Pimlott, Tackling the Inner Cities (see note 19), pp251-70.

26. S Brownhill, Developing London's Docklands: another great planning disaster (Paul Chapman, 1990); M Goodwin, 'The city as commodity: the contested spaces of urban development', in G Kearns and C Philo (eds), Selling Places: the city as cultural capital, past and present (Pergamon Press), pp145-62; Robson, Those Inner Cities (see note 11).

27. C Forman, Spitalfields: a battle for land (Hilary Shipman, 1989); J Short, 'Yuppies, yuffies and the new urban order', Transactions of the Institute of British Geographers, Vol 14(NS) (1989), pp173-88; R Woodward, 'One place, two stories: two interpretations of Spitalfields in debate over its redevelopment', in Kearns and Philo, Selling Places (see note 26), pp253-66.

28. A Coupland, 'Docklands: dream or disaster?', in A Thornley (ed), The Crisis of London (Routledge, 1992), p160.

29. See note 22.

30. Archbishop of Canterbury's Commission, Faith in the City (see note 11), p195.

31. Townsend, 'Living standards', in Tackling the Inner Cities (see note 19).

32. 'Terry', quoted in Harrison, Inside the Inner City (see note 1), p153.

33. 'Sarah', quoted in Harrison, Inside the Inner City (see note 1), pp248-9.

34. Townsend, Poverty and Labour (see note 4), p104.

35. 'Sarah', quoted in Harrison, Inside the Inner City (see note 1), p252.

36. Archbishop of Canterbury's Commission, Faith in the City (see note 11).

37. Archbishop of Canterbury's Commission, Faith in the City (see note 11), p24.

38. S MacGregor, 'The inner-city battlefield: politics, ideology, and social relations', in MacGregor and Pimlott, Tackling the Inner Cities (see note 19), pp64-92; Robson, Those Inner Cities (see note 11).

39. MacGregor, Tackling the Inner Cities (see note 19), p79.

40. Sills, Taylor and Golding, The Politics of the Urban Crisis (see note 8), p59.

41. John Major's self-declared 'war on beggars' is the most recent case in point: see The Guardian, 30 June 1994.

42. C Ward, Welcome Thinner City (Bedford, 1989), p12.

5 Poverty in the countryside: out of sight and out of mind

Paul Cloke, Paul Milbourne and Chris Thomas

INTRODUCTION

One of the most draining and debilitating aspects of poverty in the UK or USA is that the poor person lives in a rich society where people are valued according to what they own. In a situation of absolute poverty it may be easier to retain dignity even in the midst of awful suffering. Where a whole people suffer, poverty does not point the finger of failure at the individual as poignantly and mercilessly as where poverty comes in the midst of affluence.[1]

The overwhelming vision of Britain during the 1980s and 1990s is one of increasing affluence and prosperity. A trip into the countryside will usually yield 'evidence' of a rich tapestry of landscapes and villages, stitched together by the consumer possessions of wealthy people who by dint of family tradition or adventitious in-migration have inherited or bought their place in the very heartland of British heritage, community and environment. Significant trends of population movements from city to countryside reinforce this image, as do surveys such as that publicised recently by the research organisation Mintel which indicated that some 4.5 million people had plans to move to the country over the next five years, and that a further 8.5 million would like to move into the countryside were they to have the opportunities and resources so to do. In addition to the long-standing imagery of rural areas as being 'idyllic' places to live, work and visit,[2] it would appear that the countryside of the 1990s has become not only passively imagined as such but actively striven after as a precious (and prestigious) social and cultural commodity. Moreover, recent political rhetoric has allowed these rural areas to become representative of the 'success' of Conservative governments, and in effect to offer a legitimation of their policies and practices.

Many rural people, however, experience lives characterised by poverty rather than prosperity. Much has already been written about some of the underlying structural causes of rural poverty: the restructuring both of traditional rural industries (notably agriculture) and of those industries (particularly in the manufacturing sector) which have replaced them; the persistence of low pay and poor working conditions; the paucity and cost of 'affordable' housing to rent or to buy in numerous rural areas; the withdrawal of available services and the collapse of public transport systems, the latter obliging poorer rural families to deplete their disposable incomes by buying and running a car; and so on. To explain these processes in detail would require considerably more space than is available here, and so in line with the overall logic of the volume (see Chapter 1) our objective in this chapter is to describe something of the contours and experiences of poverty in rural areas, rather than attempting to lay out an explanatory framework for thinking about how rural poverty arises.

In addition, though, we want to suggest that rural areas have been implicated in an important discursive reshaping of the previous codes, symbols and concepts of welfare and poverty which has marked the Thatcher era in Britain. In a series of contested developments, the relationship between individual, state and society in the provision and receipt of welfare has been redefined, and in these transformations rural areas have been constructed as 'model' environments often suggesting codes and symbols of self-help apparently negating the need for state intervention in welfare. Thus, historical ideas of the 'rural idyll' have been used discursively as a counterpoint to the problematic nature of many urban areas (see Chapter 4), and in so doing rural people have been represented as living happy, healthy and problem-free lifestyles. In such circumstances, ideas of poverty in rural areas are anathema both politically and culturally, thus reinforcing the tendency for evidence of social hardship to remain 'out of sight and out of mind' in the rural context.

Yet recent surveys carried out for the *Lifestyles in Rural England* research programme[3] have confirmed previous suggestions that significant numbers of households and individuals in rural areas are positioned in or on the margins of poverty. Moreover, these research findings also suggest that a number of different social groups – the elderly, single parent households, the young unemployed or underemployed, along with those of other ages who are unemployed, the disabled or otherwise dependent on state benefits – are likely to be experiencing poverty in rural areas. These experiences will often be evaluated by the people concerned against the cultural expectations of 'idyll-ised' rural lifestyles, as well as perhaps being exacerbated through living cheek-by-jowl with the affluent and the adventitious in rural communities.

POVERTY OF WORDS? A DISCURSIVE TRANSFORMATION OF WELFARE

In a series of by now very familiar analyses, the background to the changing welfare state in the UK from the 1970s onwards has been painted partly in terms of ideological change in government,[4] and partly in terms of the wider changes in material conditions that have characterised the post-Fordist (ie, new industrial) era with its collapse of previous social compacts.[5] The shifting nature of power within the Conservative party led to a rejection of ideas of 'one nation' Conservatism with its broad acceptance of the need for interventionist welfare policies, and as a consequence the scope and scale of direct welfare provision became increasingly restricted. Greater incentives for the rich took the form of tax cuts: greater incentives for the poor took the form of benefit cuts, and the 1980s became a time when governments sought to reassert order, discipline and morality, with each of these codes being implanted in the changing habits, practices and forms associated with welfare provision. These ideological strands were accompanied by discourses of welfare in which particular social and cultural constructs of poverty were highlighted, others were appropriated politically, and yet others were denied any existence in the dialogues of government. Thus a series of symbolic statements emerged about the codes of behaviour which were branded 'appropriate' or 'dysfunctional', and attempts were made to shift the dominant cultural norms about poverty.

Meanwhile, non-governmental reports on the changing distribution of income over the years of the Thatcher government reached the clear conclusion that, in direct contrast to the claims made by ministers, the least affluent groups in the population suffered a decrease in real disposable income during the 1980s.[6] Townsend's analysis of changing income levels in that decade concluded that:

> each of the poorest two fifths of the population are recorded as losing between 10 per cent and 20 per cent of their relative share of disposable income, whereas the richest fifth are recorded as gaining by about 15 per cent in their share up to 1987. This is a very rapid shift in aggregate income from poor to rich.[7]

Having suggested that cultural codes, symbols and concepts of poverty have been transformed by a new political discourse into very different approaches to welfare, and that such a transformation took place in a context of a state-led redistribution of income from poor to rich, it is further possible to suggest that the imagined sites or 'repositories' of that discourse are spatially variegated. In speaking of specific socio-cultural construct(ion)s of rural areas, it is important to stress that great care is necessary before ascribing any particular characteristics to rural areas in general, for 'rural' is not a homogeneous category and regional and intra-regional variations within what are recognised as 'rural' areas will often be significant. Equally, it should be stressed that people are not passive to the changes which are happening around them, and that their struggles over production and consumption will affect the particular characteristics of different rural places, and will also shape the form and context of any 'regulatory' strategies employed in giving coherence to the socio-economic characteristics of these places.[8] However, there do appear to be significant differences in the discourses employed for discussion of welfare and poverty in 'rural' as opposed to 'urban' contexts. In broad terms, urban areas are seen to be those where 'disadvantaged' or 'underprivileged' people are concentrated, whereas rural areas *by their very nature* represent places where happy, healthy lifestyles are lived and therefore are symbolised as relatively problem-free.

It is certainly the case that in Britain, where the very notion of poverty has been contested in the alternative political discourse of dependency, aspects of rural poverty – or even rural problems more generally – have been kept out of sight and out of mind. Indeed, it has been extremely difficult for pressure groups, charities and researchers to get any symbolism of poverty, deprivation and disadvantage to stick to the Teflon-like surface of rural life.[9] It may be that poverty and rural life combine in an interlocking discursive device which ensures that rural poverty *cannot* be an issue. Rural areas have been regarded idealistically as a form of 'model' area where 1980s values about welfare are supposedly already being realised, notably in the provision of care by friends and relatives (as seen through an historical lens celebrating the importance of self-help as a response to social problems) and in the broadly self-supporting nature of the local community. If rural areas are to represent politically a form of idealised lifestyle in which welfare is self-delivered, then it would be contradictory to accept that they are also repositories for the social locations, status and identity associated with the (undeserving and dependent) poor. It therefore seems likely that rural areas can indeed be portrayed as the 'natural' heartlands of the Thatcherite values of welfare. This may be due to the actual occurrence of self-helping and self-supporting communities, or to a history of public service decline which renders them devoid of access to more formal state-provided social services, or simply because these characteristics fit into dominant social constructs of what rural areas are (or should be) like. In this way, ideas about rural life may well be linked to the symbolic marginalisation of the undeserving and dependent poor into the real and/or imagined spaces of urban deprivation.

Furthermore, and in more specific policy terms, it appears that for rural areas indigenous and grassroots socio-economic initiatives are viewed as the 'natural' (and best) answer to social problems, with the consequence that such areas are not seen as the proper realm for interventions (by central or even local state bodies, or by other supra-local agencies) which might bring 'something new' (in the way of external assistance, investment, skills training) to the localities concerned. In the 'exclusive' preview of the *Lifestyles in Rural England* report carried by *Country Life Magazine*, for instance, the suggestion in the report that multiple job-holding occurred in rural areas – as in, say, a post office worker also being a part-time decorator and gardener – was interpreted thus:

> The news that rural people throughout the country have been combining jobs as a way of beating the recession is welcome, and *should be encouraged through national policy-making* [emphasis added].[10]

While multiple job-holding may be understood as a pragmatic response to personal and local circumstances, or even as 'traditional' in many rural areas, surely it does not suggest itself as the basis for a government policy to break the recession. Once again, then, what we see here entails an ideological position calling in effect for state 'intervention' to reduce the responsibilities of the state (the state is thus manifested as a passive 'facilitator' of local, time-honoured and self-help solutions). The rural arena appears to suffer in particular from this curious mixture of ideology and (non-)practice, presumably as a result of the socio-cultural constructs mentioned above.

Any overarching image of the rural idyll, which might suggest what rural life should be like, is also important in terms of how poverty might be viewed within rural areas themselves. Certainly the idea that rural lifestyles can be problematic will be undermined if particular 'idyll-ised' representations of what rural life is like and should be like are dominant in the minds of relevant politicians, professionals and rural dwellers. Constructs of rurality dominated by idyll will lead to rural areas being symbolised using happy, healthy and problem-free images of a rural life safely nestling within both a close social community and an adjacent attractive natural environment. As has been suggested elsewhere:

> Should such an idyll in any sense define the cultural domain of a place or an area, the ideas of poverty, deprivation and disadvantage can become a contradiction in terms both for those who do experience hardship (but will perhaps see this as an acceptable trade-off for the benefits of rural living) and for those who don't (and perhaps are anxious to reproduce the culture of an idyll by playing down any hardship that comes to their attention).[11]

Ideas about the rural idyll have gained common currency over recent years, and the pervasive manner in which these myths of idyll have permeated many different arenas of debate over rural policy suggests to us that they should be repeatedly questioned in our interpretations of rural life and lifestyle. Yet our knowledge about rural idylls is at best speculative at this stage, and more needs to be learned: about the ethnocentricity of idyll; about the varying nature of idyll; about the relative significance of pro-rural or pro-nature factors (as opposed to anti-urban factors) in the envisaging of idyll; the interconnections between idyll and gender, class, race and other axes of identity. Indeed, a search for *the* idyll will inevitably reveal multiple different representations in lay, academic and policy discourse, with each having particular forms of social relations naturalised within them. Nevertheless, it does appear that the spatial implications of the discursive transformations of poverty and welfare in Britain over the last two decades have led to a presentation of rural poverty as a contradiction in terms, and that symbols of rural idyll have been used powerfully and persuasively as an antidote to any suggestions of rural poverty.

EVIDENCE OF POVERTY IN THE COUNTRYSIDE

Unlike in the USA, where an official (if much disputed) definition of poverty permits statistical analyses of the spatial distribution of poverty that cannot be gainsaid by government, the refusal by governments in Britain to define a specific 'poverty line' not only makes the analysis of poverty more difficult but also permits them to reject the findings of any such analyses on the grounds that illegitimate indicators have been used. However, it is not only the selection of poverty indicators that have hampered any official recognition of research into rural poverty. Much of the data available, for example on levels of income and wealth, tends to be aggregated into administrative areas (districts, counties, regions) which can only very crudely be related to areas which can be thought of as rural.[12] As a consequence, there have been very few studies which have presented findings at a disaggregated level and which can be equated with a 'rural' phenomenon of poverty.

One such study which has attracted significant attention is that by McLaughlin, whose research on the incidence of deprivation in rural Britain for the Department of the Environment and the Rural Development Commission involved intensive surveys of house-holds in five study areas in rural England in 1980.[13] One particular indicator from McLaughlin's research hit the headlines. He generated an index based on the annual gross disposable income of a household expressed as a percentage of supplementary benefit scale rates, plus actual housing costs, and fixed a threshold on this index to indicate the margins of poverty:

> using this calculation, households with incomes of up to 139 per cent of their supplementary benefit entitlement are identified as living in or near the margins of poverty.[14]

The following percentages of households were found to be at or below the 139 per cent threshold in each study area: Essex 24.9 per cent, Northumberland 27.3 per cent, Shropshire 24.9 per cent, Suffolk 21.4 per cent, Yorkshire 25.8 per cent. These findings soon became established in several different discourses on rural life as reflecting a 25 per cent poverty rate, not only in these case study areas, but throughout rural England as a whole. For example, the report of the Archbishop's Commission on Rural Areas, *Faith in the Countryside*, suggested that:

we are convinced by the arguments in the report to the Department of the Environment by McLaughlin (1985), which indicated that approximately 25 per cent of households in rural areas were living in or on the margins of poverty ... [W]e would suggest that since that survey was undertaken, the degree of relative deprivation in rural areas may well have increased.[15]

McLaughlin's work has been the principal source of information on rural poverty through the 1980s, and has therefore been adopted well beyond its own terms of reference as persuasive evidence that poverty exists in rural areas. There have been major criticisms (as might be expected) of this research, however, both in terms of it having been 'over reverentially received'[16] and in terms of the research technique which was based on only 150 interviews in each of the five study areas.

In 1990 a significant new research programme – the *Lifestyles in Rural England* study[17] – was carried out with the task of painting a picture of what rural life was like in 1990, and of then placing that picture in the context of changing policies and changing opportunities in rural areas. The study involved detailed interviews with a sample of 250 households in each of 12 study areas in rural England (see Figure 5.1) which were selected to reflect different levels of geographical peripherality and different labour market characteristics. Part of the survey focused on details of income, benefits and housing costs. In addressing the question of whether poverty occurred in the study areas, the initial analysis of findings produced three standard indicators which have been widely used in other studies of poverty (see Table 5.1). The indicators using less than 80 per cent of mean and median income are derived from the work of Bradley *et al*,[18] and they serve as indications of relative poverty, while the indicator using less than 140 per cent of income supplement entitlement derives from Townsend's work on measures of poverty in relation to state benefits (the approach also used by McLaughlin).[19] This level of benefit is generally regarded by specialist agencies as a reasonably strong indicator of low income, and Townsend suggests that it is still in general use as a critical indicator of poverty in the 1990s.[20]

Inevitably these three indicators offer rather different pictures of the number of households in each area experiencing low income and poverty. The first column of Table 5.1 shows the proportions of households whose incomes are less than 80 per cent of the mean

Figure 5.1: **The 12 study areas used in the *Lifestyles in Rural England* programme**

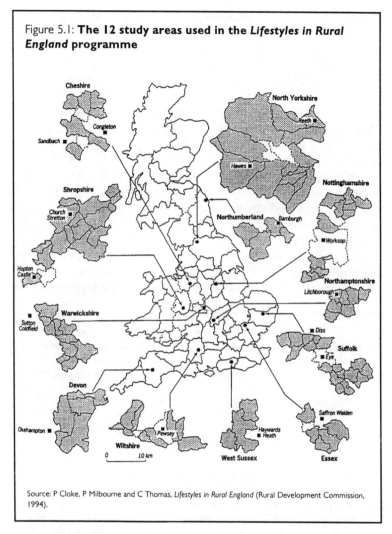

Source: P Cloke, P Milbourne and C Thomas, *Lifestyles in Rural England* (Rural Development Commission, 1994).

household income for that study area. By this indicator, the degree of 'poverty' ranges from 61.9 per cent in the North Yorkshire area to 43.6 per cent in the Northamptonshire area. Even accounting for the likelihood that a few very high incomes in particular areas can push the mean figures upwards – mean income ranges from £10,247 in the Nottinghamshire area to £17,962 in the West Sussex area – the fact that in six of the case study areas more than half of the households surveyed had incomes of less than 80 per cent of that mean, with the remaining areas close behind, suggests that the issue of low household income has not disappeared from rural areas such as these during the 1980s.

The second column of Table 5.1 substitutes a median income figure for the mean. The proportions of households with less than 80 per cent of the median income for their area were (as would be expected) lower than the values relating to the 'mean' indicator. These proportions ranged from 47.1 per cent in the Devon area to 34.5 per cent in the Northamptonshire area, and they reflected the spread of median incomes in the areas from £6,474 in the Nottinghamshire area to £15,885 in the West Sussex area. This indicator results in some changes in the rank ordering of study areas compared with the 'mean' findings, and some of the more pressured localities such as West Sussex, Cheshire and Suffolk – ones which are close to metropolitan areas and therefore subject to various urban pressures – figure more prominently here. Even so, the proportions of households defined on this indicator as experiencing low income or 'poverty' remain significantly high, confirming the suggestion that

TABLE 5.1: **Percentage of households in or on the margins of poverty: study areas ranked for each of the three indicators**

Mean*		Median**		Income support***	
North Yorkshire	61.9	Devon	47.1	Nottinghamshire	39.2
Northumberland	61.1	West Sussex	45.8	Devon	34.4
Nottinghamshire	58.8	Essex	44.4	Essex	29.5
Essex	53.3	Cheshire	43.6	Northumberland	26.4
Shropshire	51.4	Suffolk	42.6	Suffolk	25.5
Devon	50.0	Nottinghamshire	41.2	Wiltshire	25.4
Wiltshire	49.3	North Yorkshire	40.5	Warwickshire	22.6
Warwickshire	48.4	Warwickshire	38.7	North Yorkshire	22.0
Cheshire	46.2	Northumberland	37.5	Shropshire	21.6
West Sussex	45.8	Wiltshire	36.6	Northamptonshire	14.8
Suffolk	44.7	Shropshire	35.1	Cheshire	12.8
Northamptonshire	43.6	Northamptonshire	34.5	West Sussex	6.4
Across 12 areas	51.2		40.6		23.4

NB: * in or on the margins of poverty: <80% mean
      ** in or on the margins of poverty: <80% median
      *** in or on the marrgins of poverty: <140% income support entitlement

Source: P Cloke, P Milbourne and C Thomas, *Lifestyles in Rural England* (Rural Development Commission, 1994).

between one-third and nearly one-half of households in the study areas might be associated with poverty.

It is feasible that indicators of poverty solely on income levels will be distorted by other localised factors, such as different scales of housing costs (see Chapter 2), numbers of households of pensionable age, degrees of savings and investments, and so on. It is therefore the third column of Table 5.1 which provides the most rigorous indicator of the position of a household in or on the margins of poverty. Use of the Townsend indicator serves again to reduce the proportions of households represented as being within the margins of poverty, and it has the helpful effect of identifying more clearly those study areas where poverty is most evident. By this analysis, the 39.2 per cent of households in the Nottinghamshire study area, the 34.4 per cent in Devon and the 29.5 per cent in Essex suggests that particular circumstances prevail in these areas which warrant further specific investigation. Equally, the 6.4 per cent level in West Sussex, the 12.8 per cent in Cheshire and the 14.8 per cent in Northamptonshire suggest that income-related poverty was not so severe in these study areas.

The authors of the *Lifestyles in Rural England* report identified three significant conclusions from these analyses:

(i) the fact that 9 out of 12 study areas contained 20 per cent or more households in or close to poverty itself suggests a severe problem of rural lifestyle in most areas of the country. Neither should we in any way discount the severity of problems experienced by the 14.8 per cent of households in Northamptonshire, the 12.8 per cent in Cheshire and the 6.4 per cent in West Sussex who suffered the additional burden of being a smaller minority with income problems in areas of greater affluence.

(ii) there appears to be a mix of rural geographies at work here. Although the more urbanised study areas tended towards having a lower proportion of households categorised by this index, and the more remote areas tended to have a higher proportion, the cases of Essex, Suffolk, Wiltshire, Warwickshire, North Yorkshire and Shropshire indicate that such tendencies were subject to alteration by local circumstances. We need to look beyond all-encompassing structural factors and broad concepts such as 'remoteness' or 'under urban pressure' in the understanding of the spatiality of these phenomena.

(iii) it has been argued that the issue of poverty and deprivation is an out-dated phenomenon, becoming anachronistic in the 'prosperity' of the 1980s. Our findings suggest that the issue is not only very important in our 1990 surveys, but is also being reproduced by patterns of in-migration.[21]

This last finding relating to in-migration is an important one. There is a traditional wisdom in rural planning circles that in those areas where planning controls are tight, house prices are high, and affordable rented housing is shrinking, the opportunities for impoverished households to move into the areas are inexorably diminishing. Consequently, the 'problem' of rural poverty will also diminish as the real poor either 'move out, or die off'. Table 5.2 demonstrates the connection between households moving into different study areas during the period 1985-90 and low levels of household income (indicated here by incomes below £8,000 per annum). It is apparent from these findings that those case study areas where aggregate incomes were lowest, and poverty indicators were most significant, were also ones which can be identified as the major reception areas for low-income in-migrant households. However, it is also the case that a number of other study areas were also experiencing the in-migration of lower-income households. Only Cheshire, Worcestershire and Wiltshire, which possessed the most protected and gentrified housing markets of all of the study areas, had less than 15 per cent of in-migrants with incomes of less than

---

TABLE 5.2: **Percentage of households moving into the areas over the last five years with annual incomes of under £8,000**

Northumberland	38.8
Nottinghamshire	35.6
North Yorkshire	35.4
Devon	22.5
Suffolk	20.0
Essex	17.0
Northamptonshire	16.2
West Sussex	16.1
Shropshire	15.7
Cheshire	9.8
Warwickshire	8.5
Wiltshire	7.9

Source: P Cloke, P Milbourne and C Thomas, *Lifestyles in Rural England* (Rural Development Commission, 1994).

£8,000. This evidence does suggest that the problems associated with low income and poverty are being reproduced more generally, as well as in the expected 'low–income' areas.[22]

EXPERIENCING RURAL POVERTY

The *Lifestyles in Rural England* study also investigated the composition of those households who were categorised as being in or on the margins of poverty using the Townsend index. These households were often dominated by elderly people: single elderly householders were a major group experiencing poverty in areas such as Cheshire, Devon, Essex, Northumberland, North Yorkshire, Shropshire and Wiltshire, and households with two elderly people were also characteristic of those in poverty in Cheshire, Essex, Northamptonshire, Northumberland, Suffolk and West Sussex. Clearly, some elderly people in rural areas are prone to the problems of poverty caused by low income, with many still having to rely on state pensions for their lifestyle needs. Yet some of the study areas were marked by different poverty characteristics, with the Nottinghamshire and Warwickshire areas in particular having much younger households in poverty, and elsewhere householders in their 50s could be categorised as on the margins of poverty. In some case study areas (Devon, Essex, Northumberland, North Yorkshire, Shropshire, West Sussex and Wiltshire) poverty was found to occur among those households which had been resident for a considerable time in the area. Elsewhere (Cheshire, Northamptonshire, Nottinghamshire, Suffolk and Warwickshire) poverty occurred among recent in-migrants. The surveys also found that there were significant local differences in the relationship between poverty and housing characteristics, economic activity and mobility, and so it seems likely that individuals and householders on low incomes will experience their rural lifestyles differently according to local housing, service, job and access 'markets'.

Thus far, the findings of the *Lifestyles in Rural England* study have been used to present empirical evidence of the occurrence of poverty amongst various types of households in different rural areas. Earlier in the chapter, though, we suggested that socio-cultural constructs of rurality and rural life will serve to obscure possible 'real' instances of such poverty, either because those experiencing hardship will adopt coping strategies whereby aspects of poverty become almost acceptable trade-offs for the benefit of living in a rural area, or because those who do not experience hardship will tend to deny the difficulties of those who do in an attempt to reproduce a learned culture of rural life which filters out the possibilities of poverty and disadvantage in the rural arena. It is, therefore, very important to understand the different *experiences* of poverty and associated rural problems, as well as charting some interpretations of these problems.

As part of the *Lifestyles in Rural England* research, respondents were offered the opportunity to respond freely to open questions about disadvantage and deprivation in their communities. Although these answers were about deprivation and disadvantage only, they do offer some interesting reflections on how issues such as poverty are reflected upon by some rural residents. To place these answers in context, it is worth noting that when asked whether disadvantage or deprivation occurred in rural areas only 33.8 per cent on average thought that such problems did occur. These answers ranged from 46.2 per cent in North Yorkshire to 21.0 per cent in Nottingham-shire (see Table 5.3), and it can therefore be suggested that the majority of the respondents to our survey *did* deny the existence of the rural poverty which is so strongly suggested by the empirical indicators. Those respondents who did perceive deprivation and disadvantage in rural areas pointed it out in terms of such

TABLE 5.3: **Percentage of respondents in the areas who thought that disadvantage or deprivation did occur in the countryside**

North Yorkshire	46.2
Devon	43.9
Shropshire	39.8
Northumberland	36.3
Wiltshire	35.7
Suffolk	34.7
West Sussex	33.3
Cheshire	32.1
Essex	29.3
Warwickshire	28.6
Northamptonshire	25.1
Nottinghamshire	21.0
Mean for 12 areas	33.8

Source: P Cloke, P Milbourne and C Thomas, *Lifestyles in Rural England* (Rural Development Commission, 1994).

conventional issues as the lack of opportunities and the problems experienced by particular groups of people:

> Low wages, lack of education, social and economic deprivation – a result of lack of education. (2432 Devon)[23]

> Old people living on their own who are not catered for as well as they should be. (4505 Cheshire)

> Unmarried women with babies, living in caravans. Lots of farm workers live in cottages and mobile homes in poor conditions. (0314 Shropshire)

Alternatively, our qualitative information from respondents also pointed to some stigma amongst the rural poor:

> Some older people would go without rather than ask for what they are entitled to. They are often too proud. (1351 Suffolk)

And the notion that rural problems are hidden away from sight was also a motif of these responses:

> I don't see any deprivation but I am sure there are deprived people in all areas. (3273 Northumberland)

> Deprivation? I don't know what you mean. We all help each other. (0118 Warwickshire)

In other responses, it became clear that deprivation was being filtered out of accounts of rural lifestyles because of differing levels of expectations regarding town and country life:

> There is no deprivation – if you're used to living in the town you think differently to people living in the country, and *vice versa*. (2111 Wiltshire)

> If there is any deprivation I suppose that those people that live in the country have more simple ideals and don't feel deprived. (3272 Northumberland)

> If you live in a village, you live in a village. If you want the facilities, you must move to a built-up area. (3056 Wiltshire)

> It seems that people have lower expectations in rural areas, so they put up with it. (7673 Shropshire)

These brief glimpses of different recorded responses to the idea of deprivation and disadvantage open up a number of issues. The principal focus of this chapter has been on poverty, and therefore the experiences of the rural poor are assumed to be important in terms of marginalisation through lack of income, as indeed they are. However, in rural areas individuals and households in poverty are not merely marginalised economically, they also appear to be marginalised socially and culturally. Their experience is reflected on by others as being an acceptance of lower expectations, simple ideals, different ways of thinking. In other words, their poverty does not fit the socio-cultural constructions of rural life which are continually being reproduced as the backdrop to the rural stage. In rural areas you have to accept lower levels of services, less employment opportunities, inaccessibility and housing difficulties, because culturally that is just the way things are (especially if you have sufficient affluence to overcome these difficulties). Socio-cultural marginalisation could be painted solely in terms of these power-relations if it were not for the fact that many of the disadvantaged people that we encountered in our survey accepted their difficulties as a 'natural' part of rural life. They eschew the labels of 'poverty', 'disadvantage' or 'deprivation', perhaps because of the stigma attached to these labels, but also because at least some of these people have 'bought into' (despite their seeming poverty) the cultural expectations of rural life as suggested by notions of rural idyll. Problems associated with rural lifestyles are therefore restricted to discrete issues, for example associated with housing, work, transport and services, as the following observations indicate:

> Those coming in are wealthier. It's hard on young people. Our daughter will not be able to live locally unless new starter homes are built. (0059 Cheshire)

> There is not other work except for farm work in the village, so you have to travel and there are no buses, so you have to have your own transport. (3056 Wiltshire)

> You have to be well under 40 years to get employment in our experience. (4270 Nottinghamshire)

> The young people are forced out as there is no work. (Parish Clerk, Northumberland)

> The disadvantage of this area is being isolated. People can't take advantage of all opportunities offered in larger towns because of lack of transport networks. (2836 Devon)

But while many such specific experiences of difficulty do seem to be acceptable in lay discourses of rural life, overall experiences of poverty, disadvantage and deprivation are often denied as being inappropriate (and hence in actuality not present) in these socio-cultural contexts.

Experiences of poverty in rural areas hence differ enormously, and will depend to some extent on whether the individuals and households concerned have any choice about where they live. For those with no choice, it seems likely that the potential isolation, inaccessibility and lack of opportunity could make for some very problematic experiences of hard living conditions, particularly when the relative nature of these conditions is highlighted so starkly by the trappings of affluence that surround them. For those with choice, these difficulties may be offset to varying degrees by beneficial experiences of living in the countryside, where community and landscape may be perceived in a sufficiently positive light to be worth suffering some hardship for. Either way, poverty is likely to be filtered out of the reflexivity of the non-poor, whose referential representations of 'idyll-ised' rural life do not seem to allow for the existence of, or the experience of, poverty in rural areas.

CONCLUSIONS

The *Lifestyles in Rural England* research has added considerable weight to the suggestion that low income and poverty are of continuing significance in rural areas. Findings using the Townsend indicator which point to 39.2 per cent of households in the Nottinghamshire study area, 34.4 per cent in the Devon study area and 29.5 per cent in the Essex study area, all being in or on the margins of poverty, appear to us to be of considerable importance. In these areas (and in others to a lesser extent) these is a strong case for suggesting that a significant minority of households in rural areas have income levels which will create difficulties for them in the purchase of housing, mobility, leisure activities and many other kinds of opportunity. Although any threshold on such an indicator of poverty is likely to be arguable politically, it also seems significant to us that 9 out of our 12 study areas contained 20 per cent or more households classified by this indicator as being in, or on the margins of, poverty. Such levels were, for example, at least *twice* as high as unemployment levels, which are often used as a 'litmus test' of an area's prosperity (and which often elicit specific policy responses). Our study shows that there is, at an aggregate level, a very important problem of low incomes and poverty in many, if not most, rural areas in England.[24]

However, there was clearly some geographical variation in income levels. Some of our case-study areas – notably West Sussex, Cheshire and Northamptonshire – exhibited relatively low levels of poor incomes. These were areas where those moving into the area tended not to include low-income households, presumably because the high prices of housing markets (which had been restricted over a long period by tight planning policies) were prohibitive to these kinds of households. Nevertheless, it is also notable that outside of these 'elite' areas, not only was there a significant presence of low-income households, but the presence of 'have nots' in these places is *not* gradually reducing in the face of restrictive housing market characteristics. A number of our study areas had recently received significant proportions of lower income in-migrants, and therefore it may also be suggested that the problems associated with low income and poverty were being reproduced more generally across rural England, and *not* just in the well-defined 'low income' areas. The juxtaposition of wealth and poverty merely heightens the relative impact of low income lifestyles in these supposedly better-off areas.

Finally, it should be acknowledged that our respondents were on the whole reluctant to admit the existence of poverty and deprivation in their rural localities. Although an average of 33.8 per cent did perceive that disadvantage and deprivation existed in their home areas, the qualitative comments from our survey suggested that the notion of deprivation was stigmatic for some of our respondents, and often 'out of sight, out of mind' for others. It would seem that the perceived benefits of living in the countryside were felt to offer some compensation for those people who might otherwise find a low income lifestyle a severe problem. Equally, though, the supposed compensations of the rural idyll were not shared by all, and living in a rural environment can generate a particular spatiality in the experience of poverty for a not inconsiderable number of people.

NOTES

1. R McCloughry, *The Eye of the Needle* (Inter Varsity Press, 1990).
2. See B Short (ed), *The English Rural Community: image and analysis* (Cambridge University Press, 1992); J Trollope (ed), *The Country Habit* (Bantam

Press, 1993); R Williams, *The Country and the City* (Chatto and Windus, 1973).

3. P Cloke, P Milbourne and C Thomas, *Lifestyles in Rural England* (Rural Development Commission, 1994). See also P Cloke, 'Rural geography and political economy', in R Peet and N Thrift (eds), *New Models in Geography*, Vol I (Unwin Hyman), pp164-97; P Cloke, 'On "problems and solutions": the reproduction of problems for rural communities in Britain during the 1980s', *Journal of Rural Studies*, Vol 9 (1993), pp113-21.

4. M Loney (ed), *The State or the Market* (Sage, 1991).

5. R Martin, 'Industrial capitalism in transition: the contemporary reorganisation of the British space economy', in D Massey and J Allen (eds), *Uneven Redevelopment* (Sage, 1988), pp202-31.

6. See, for example, T Stark, *Income and Wealth in the 1980s* (Fabian Society, 1992); P Townsend, *Poverty in the United Kingdom* (Allen Lane, 1979); P Townsend, *The International Analysis of Poverty* (Harvester Wheatsheaf, 1993).

7. Townsend, *International Analysis* (see note 6), p25

8. P Cloke and M Goodwin, 'Conceptualising countryside change: from post-Fordism to rural structured coherence', *Transactions of the Institute of British Geographers*, Vol 17 (1992), pp321-36.

9. P Lowe, T Bradley and S Wright (eds), *Deprivation and Welfare in Rural Areas* (Geobooks, 1986); B McLaughlin, 'The rhetoric and the reality of rural deprivation', *Journal of Rural Studies*, Vol 2 (1986), pp291-307; H Newby, *Country Life: A Social History of Rural England* (Weidenfeld and Nicholson, 1987); J Short, *Imagined Country: society, culture and environment* (Routledge, 1991).

10. N Farndale, 'The future of our countryside', *Country Life*, 24 March 1994, p59.

11. P Cloke, 'Poverty and the welfare state: a discursive transformation in Britain and the USA', forthcoming in *Environment and Planning A*, Vol 27 (1995).

12. See, for example, C Thomas and S Winyard, 'Rural incomes', in J M Shaw (ed), *Rural Deprivation and Planning* (Geobooks, 1979).

13. B McLaughlin, *Deprivation in Rural Areas* (Research Report to the Department of the Environment, 1986); McLaughlin, 'Rhetoric and reality' (see note 9).

14. McLaughlin, 'Rhetoric and reality' (see note 9), p294.

15. Archbishop's Commission on Rural Areas, *Faith In The Countryside* (Churchman, 1990).

16. D Scott, N Shenton and B Healey, *Hidden Deprivation in the Countryside* (a report commissioned by the Peak Park Trust, 1991).

17. As written up in Cloke, Milbourne and Thomas, *Lifestyles in Rural England* (see note 3). The *Lifestyles in Rural England* project was carried out by a team of researchers, including Shaun Fielding, Katherine Hurd

and Rachel Woodward, as well as the authors of this chapter.

18. T Bradley, P Lowe and S Wright, 'Rural development and the welfare tradition', in Lowe, Bradley and Wright, *Deprivation and Welfare in Rural Areas* (see note 9), pp1-39.

19. P Townsend, *Sociology and Social Policy* (Penguin, 1975); Townsend, *Poverty* (see note 6).

20. Townsend, *International Analysis* (see note 6).

21. Cloke, Milbourne and Thomas, *Lifestyles in Rural England* (see note 3), p95.

22. This reproduction is likely to be a complex phenomenon. The number of households only recently taking up residence at a given address certainly indicates in-movement: but this movement may be highly localised (occurring within the same village or immediate locality), it may indicate a level of retiree in-movement (and retired people, although notable for having lower incomes, may nonetheless also be reliant on assets), and it may indicate the operation of housing policies which are tending to limit access to 'social rented housing' to families on housing benefit. None of these complexities, however, alters the significant continued *presence* of lower income households in rural areas. Rather, the suggestion here is that this issue is one which must receive further research, particularly regarding the spatial mobility of households of differing income levels.

23. Quotations from surveys are anonymised, and then indexed by a survey response number along with the case study area concerned.

24. It is acknowledged that more should have been said here about the experience of rural areas in what McKendrick is calling 'Celtic UK' (in Northern Ireland, Scotland and Wales), and that distinctive aspects of 'Celtic' rural poverty would probably have emerged in the process. For details see P Cloke and L Davis, 'Deprivation and lifestyles in rural Wales: I, towards a cultural dimension', *Journal of Rural Studies*, Vol 8 (1992), pp349-59; P Cloke and P Milbourne, 'Deprivation and lifestyles in rural Wales: II, rurality and the cultural dimension', *Journal of Rural Studies*, Vol 8 (1992), pp360-74. These papers grow out of an extension to the Lifestyles programme which dealt with the experience of poverty and deprivation in rural Wales, as fully reported in P Cloke, M Goodwin and P Milbourne, *Lifestyles in Rural Wales: a final report to the Development Board for Rural Wales, Welsh Development Agency and Welsh Office* (Research Report to the Welsh Office, 1994).

6

Poverty in the old industrial regions: a comparative view

Dan Dorling and John Tomaney

INTRODUCTION

The United Kingdom, in common with countries such as the United States, is said to be an increasingly divided society. Contemporary society, some argue, is characterised by the existence of a 'culture of contentment' which allows a prosperous social group to live alongside a severely disadvantaged group.[1] Some contend that we witnessed a worsening of inequality during the 1980s and 1990s:

> For those at the top these are the best of times. For those at the bottom, horizons are even narrower than they were a decade ago and the gap between the rich and poor is greater than at any time since the 1930s. For most people – those in the middle – insecurity and anxiety are rife.[2]

It is certainly difficult to quantify changes in the overall pattern of inequality, but what is certain is that contemporary British society is marked by profound inequalities, and that the image of a society in which one third of people are increasingly disadvantaged is widely held:

> The famous one-third/two-thirds society – where one third is dependent upon a diminished welfare state with only partial access to secure jobs, housing and reasonable incomes – is the product of economic and social fragmentation. Moreover, the erosion of institutions such as universal welfare benefits or high-quality state

education which attempt to embody a notion of obligations as well as rights has further deepened the divide.[3]

As writers such as Hutton point out, the emerging recognition of a 'dispossessed third' is crucially linked to wider social and economic transformations. Chief among these transformations has been the process of deindustrialisation, which appears to have affected the UK to a greater degree than it has most other industrialised countries.

The aim of this chapter is to present a map of contemporary inequality in England and Wales, paying particular attention to the effects of deindustrialisation. We aim to show that poverty is clearly concentrated in some parts of the country, whereas people living in other parts of the country largely escape it. In particular we aim to show how poverty is heavily concentrated in what have become known as the 'old industrial regions', those regions most badly affected by the deindustrialisation of the UK over recent years.

As part of its regional policy, the European Union has designated a number of old industrial regions in various member states. Such regions are defined in relation to the objectives of the European Structural Funds, and in European Union jargon are known as 'Objective 2 regions'. Objective 2 of the Structural Funds is 'to promote the conversion of areas affected by industrial decline'.[4] In the period 1989-93, seven such Objective 2 regions were designated

---

TABLE 6.1: **Objective 2 regions in England and Wales, 1989-93**

1. North East	South East Northumberland, Tyne and Wear, Durham, Cleveland
2. Eastern England	Humberside, South Yorkshire, West Yorkshire, Derbyshire, North Lincolnshire, Nottinghamshire
3. West Midlands	West Midlands County
4. North West	Greater Manchester, Merseyside and adjacent areas of Lancashire and Cheshire
5. West Cumbria	Workington and Whitehaven
6. North Wales	Clwyd
7. South Wales	Mid Glamorgan, West Glamorgan, Gwent (excluding Monmouth), part of Cardiff and South Glamorgan, adjacent areas of Powys and Dyfed

(The designation here provides only a summary of the localities included within the boundaries of each Objective 2 region, and for a more detailed designation see European Commission, *Community Support Frameworks, 1989-1991: United Kingdom* (European Commission, 1991). Merseyside has been redesignated as an Objective 1 region for the period 1993-97.)

Source: European Commission documentation.

in England and Wales (see Table 6.1).[5] Previously the centres of the industrial revolution, the old industrial regions – located mainly in the north of England – have seen their relative positions decline over a long period, but perhaps more intensively over the last 20 years. Such regions incorporate relatively large and highly concentrated population centres. But these old industrial regions, as defined by the European Union, often do not fit neatly into the 'standard region' format which the government uses for the purposes of statistical reporting. For this reason we have prepared a dataset which allows us to paint a more disaggregated picture of poverty and inequality, and which allows us to gain a better insight into the position of the old industrial regions in relation to the one-third/ two-thirds society.[6]

We seek to develop this map of current patterns of poverty in Wales and the English regions based on contemporary indicators of the 'five great evils' of want, ignorance, idleness, squalor and disease, the defeat of which William Beveridge saw in the 1940s as the task of the welfare state.[7] It has only recently become possible to construct indicators of the extent of these 'evils' at a very local level, using quantitative data supplied by official bodies. We have developed a technique in this chapter which uses official information to show how poverty is distributed across and within the regions of England and Wales. In order to illustrate the huge spatial variation in levels of poverty, we conduct our analysis at the level of local government wards. These are the smallest areas for which our indicators of the evils can be estimated with confidence. The geographical complexity of poverty is illustrated through the use of ward level population cartograms (in essence maps of England and Wales which have been transformed in line with how population is distributed between wards: see Figure 6.1).[8] In order to highlight the situation at the more usually used standard region level, the information contained within these cartograms is summarised for this level in a number of tables.[9]

Five separate sources of data were used to generate contemporary indicators for the 'five great evils' at ward level. 'Want' was estimated using data on children living in households without earners provided by the 1991 Census (statistics used by Department of Environment, provided by Office of Population Census Surveys, OPCS). 'Ignorance' was estimated using the results of all GCSE examinations held in schools in 1993 (provided by Department for Education). 'Idleness' was gauged through the proportion of the

Figure 6.1: **Key cartogram: showing scale, identifying counties and providing 'key' for the following poverty cartograms (Figures 6.2–6.6)**

Scale
☐ = 250,000 people

Showing wards where the
■ most
and
▨ least
of poverty is found

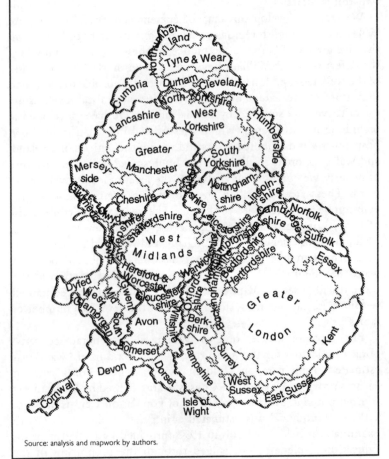

Source: analysis and mapwork by authors.

workforce claiming benefit for over a year in 1991 (data from Department of Employment via National On-Line Manpower Information System – NOMIS). 'Squalor' was the most difficult evil to measure, and we have replaced it with a measure of 'housing wealth' using building society data. 'Disease' was represented through the traditional measure of mortality rates (with information from the Department of Health, via OPCS).

This approach is not without its weaknesses. The choice of a particular statistic to represent a 'great evil' is somewhat arbitrary and our choices were governed by the available information. The official and industry data sources on which we have drawn have their own limits. Nevertheless, they provide a basis for illustrating the spatial dimensions of poverty and inequality and allow us to pick out the position of the old industrial regions in this picture. Our data contain a bias toward measures of poverty that affect children and their social and economic prospects or 'life-chances'.[10] Partly this reflects the paucity of information on poverty among the elderly. More importantly, however, we are concerned with the prospective trends that will affect the development of old industrial regions and their role in the wider national economy and society. We are concerned to identify the possibilities and constraints which individuals face in 'making' their lives, and a focus on the life-chances of children and of young people is suggestive of the kind of society which has emerged – and which may be emerging – in the old industrial regions and in Britain as a whole.

Using the data sources described above, we estimate the extent of the five forms of poverty in each one of over 9,000 wards in England and Wales. For the purposes of analysing this complex and detailed information in an understandable manner, we have taken literally the metaphor of the one-third/two-thirds society. Thus, taking each indicator in turn, we have divided the 'society' of England and Wales into three equal parts, and have mapped these three parts spatially by 'allocating' all of the country's wards to one of the thirds involved. On Figures 6.2-6.6 every black and grey dot corresponds to an individual ward, the size of each dot being proportional to ward population: the black dots identify the 'poorest' third of wards, the grey dots identify the 'richest' third of wards, and the remaining white spaces coincide with the 'middle' third of wards. We can then tabulate the proportions of the affluent third of society and the poorest third of society present in each standard region according to each indicator. The tables (Tables 6.2-6.6) provide a summary of the spatial dimensions to the one-third/two-third society, but the cartograms – showing the ward level data – serve to highlight the complexity of the pattern in practice and to illustrate how local patterns overlie regional ones.

WANT: THE UNEQUAL GEOGRAPHY OF FINANCIAL INDEPENDENCE

The notion of 'want' has changed since Beveridge first proposed it as an evil. We are concerned with developing a picture of how unequal access to financial resources affects children's life chances. Ideally, a measure of the level of want to which children are exposed would include information on the numbers of children living in families eligible for income support benefit, but such information is not available in the systematically disaggregated ways which would allow us to draw up this detailed picture of spatial inequalities in financial means. Thus, in seeking to establish the level of want, we have used as a proxy the number of children living in households in which nobody is (officially) earning. This measure of benefit dependence can be derived from the last census which showed that in 1991 over one million children (or 9 per cent of children) in England and Wales were living in households in which nobody was earning.

We are concerned with the location of these disadvantaged households. We can divide the six million households with dependant children into three types of ward. In the poorest third, between 10 and 42 per cent of children live in households without an earner. In the most prosperous third, less than 5 per cent of children live in households without earners. In one third of the country 'want', as measured by lack of financial independence, is therefore common-place, while in another third it is confined to a minority. Figure 6.2 illustrates where these families are located, the darkly shaded areas representing the poorest third, the lightly shaded areas representing the prosperous third. The areas left blank illustrate the location of the 'middle' third of families who live in wards where between 5 per cent and 10 per cent of children live in households without earners. Referring to the map key (Figure 6.2) and to the list of officially designated Objective 2 or 'declining industrial regions' (Table 6.1) it is clear that in each case these regions are included within the poorest third.

Figure 6.2: **The geography of 'want' in the UK**
(for explanation see text and Table 6.2)

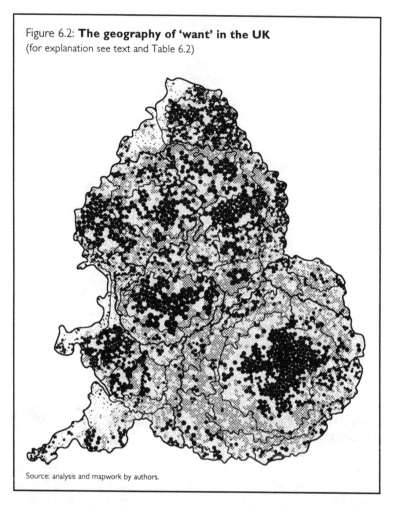

Source: analysis and mapwork by authors.

Table 6.2 summarises the data at the level of standard regions and illustrates the proportion of the population (in this case families with children) of each region which belonged to each third in 1991. The table shows that almost half (49 per cent) of families in the North and in Wales belonged to the poorest third, while less than a quarter (24 per cent) of families in the North and less than one Welsh family in seven (14 per cent) lived in the most affluent third of wards. By contrast, Table 6.2 shows that almost half of all families in East Anglia live in the most affluent third of society according to this measure of poverty.

TABLE 6.2: **Proportion of families living in each third of society in each region**

Society divided according to the likelihood of children living in each ward being in households where an adult was earning in 1991

Region	Poor %	Middle %	Affluent %	%
England & Wales	33	33	33	100
North	49	27	24	100
Yorks & Humberside	43	27	29	100
East Midlands	27	34	40	100
East Anglia	16	36	48	100
South-East	27	36	37	100
South-West	19	44	38	100
West Midlands	40	28	32	100
North-West	43	31	26	100
Wales	49	37	14	100

Society is divided into three groups of wards, each containing as equal a number of families as possible. The 'poorest' third comprises all wards in which less than 89.6 per cent of children are in households with earners; the 'affluent' third comprises all wards in which over 95.1 per cent of children are in such households; the 'middle' group is the remainder. Only dependent children are included (aged 0-15, or also 16-19 if in full-time education living at home, not married and financially dependent). Families in this analysis only include ones with dependent children.

Source: OPCS, *1991 Census of Population* (OPCS, HMSO).

IGNORANCE: THE UNEQUAL GEOGRAPHY OF EDUCATIONAL ATTAINMENT

Educational achievement is an increasingly important factor in determining the life-chances of children. Typically, passing five or more GCSE exams at grade C or above is taken as a measure of whether a child has succeeded or failed at school, mainly because this level of educational attainment is stipulated as a minimum level of qualification for many jobs. Only 41 per cent of children in England and Wales achieved this goal in 1993.[11]

Figure 6.3 again shows a ternary division of the country, this time on the basis of where less than 34 per cent of school leavers pass five or more GCSE exams at grade C or above (the darkly shaded areas) and where more than 48 per cent achieve at least this level of qualification (the lightly shaded areas). The unshaded areas represent the middle third of school leavers, 35 per cent to 48 per

Figure 6.3: **The geography of 'ignorance' in the UK**
(for explanation see text and Table 6.3)

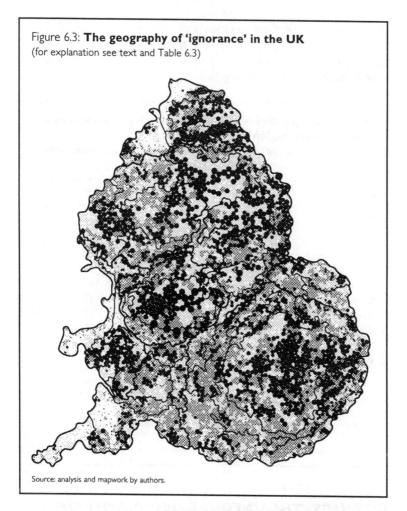

Source: analysis and mapwork by authors.

cent of whom passed at this level in 1993. A very similar pattern emerges to that which we saw for lack of financial independence, with particularly strong concentrations of wards with high levels of educational achievement in southern England, especially to the south and east of London. Again, areas in the old industrial regions are clearly marked now by low levels of educational achievement. And again we have summarised the data in the cartograms at the level of the standard regions. The North clearly has the largest relative proportion of school-leavers in the bottom third, with Yorkshire and Humberside and the West Midlands also performing poorly. In each of these regions well over 40 per cent of school leavers are in the worst performing third. By contrast, East Anglia, the South-West and the South-East have over 40 per cent of school leavers in the best performing third.

TABLE 6.3: **Proportion of school leavers living in each third of society in each region**
Society divided according to the likelihood of pupils living in each ward passing five or more GCSE exams at age 15 in 1993

Region	Lowest %	Middle %	Highest %	%
England & Wales	33	33	33	100
North	47	30	23	100
Yorks & Humberside	43	40	17	100
East Midlands	33	38	29	100
East Anglia	18	41	41	100
South-East	31	26	43	100
South-West	21	36	44	100
West Midlands	44	28	28	100
North-West	29	34	37	100
Wales	35	47	18	100

Society is divided into three groups of wards, each containing as equal a number of school leavers as possible. The bottom group comprises all wards in which less than 34 per cent of school pupils passed five or more GCSE exams at grades A to C in 1993; the top group comprises all wards in which over 48 per cent of school pupils passed at this level in 1993; the middle group is the remainder. Only children aged 15 not in special schools are included. Children are allocated from wards containing their school to the nearest wards in which unallocated 13-year-old children were living in 1991.

Source: Department of Education and the Welsh Offices, exam results by schools.

IDLENESS: THE UNEQUAL GEOGRAPHY OF AVAILABLE EMPLOYMENT

Employment levels are perhaps the chief indicator of the economic well-being of an area (see also Chapter 1). We noted earlier that the old industrial regions are generally regarded to have been most afflicted by the deindustrialisation of the UK economy over recent years, and that these areas are marked by high rates of unemployment. Yet the recession of the 1990s has meant that many other areas of the country, ones which had previously experienced low levels of unemployment, have now seen rates increase rapidly. In order to gauge the structural rather than cyclical nature of the problems facing certain regions and localities, however, we have chosen to use the existence of long-term unemployment as our measure of 'idleness'. Long-term unemployment has a particularly corrosive effect on the moral and material fabric of communities, and the available data illustrates that there is a wide spatial variation in this indicator. The locations of people claiming benefit are available for research from the Department of Employment (through NOMIS), which means that we can map this estimate of poverty relatively easily. We have divided the working age population of the country

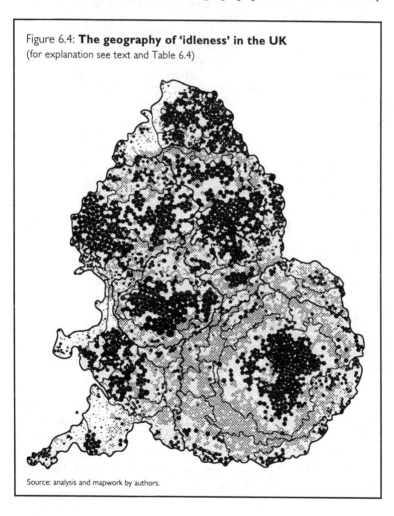

Figure 6.4: **The geography of 'idleness' in the UK**
(for explanation see text and Table 6.4)

Source: analysis and mapwork by authors.

into three groups on the basis of the likelihood of each worker in each ward being out of work for 12 months or more in the period before April 1991. This exercise reveals that the most affluent third of the population had a nil to 0.6 per cent chance of having claimed benefit for the previous 12 months or more. By contrast, in the poorest third of the country between 1.6 per cent and 18.2 per cent of all working-age people available to work in those wards had been claiming benefit for over 12 months.

TABLE 6.4: **Proportion of working-age adults living in each third of society in each region**

Society divided according to the likelihood of workers in each ward having claimed unemployment benefit for over 12 months by April 1991.

Region	Lowest %	Middle %	Highest %	%
England & Wales	33	33	33	100
North	57	29	14	100
Yorks & Humberside	48	32	20	100
East Midlands	30	35	35	100
East Anglia	15	38	47	100
South-East	23	31	46	100
South-West	19	43	38	100
West Midlands	41	31	29	100
North-West	47	34	19	100
Wales	46	39	15	100

Society is divided into three groups of wards, each containing as equal a number of all adults of working age (18-59/64) as possible. The bottom group comprises all wards in which more than 1.6 per cent of the workforce had been claiming unemployment benefit for 12 months or more by April 1991; the top group comprises all wards in which less than 0.6 per cent of the workforce had been claiming benefit for this length of time; the middle group is the remainder. Only people eligible to claim unemployment benefit are included. This number is divided by the number of economically active adults aged 18 to pensionable age in each ward in 1991 (termed the 'workforce' and taken from the Census) to produce long-term unemployment rates.

Source: NOMIS and Department of Employment statistics.

This measure reveals a stark divide between different communities in Britain, and Figure 6.4 shows the location of these two groups. Wards with a strong likelihood of high levels of long-term unemployment (represented by darkly shaded areas) are clearly concentrated in the old industrial regions as defined in Table 6.1, with Greater London also being strongly represented. Table 6.4 provides a summary of the data for the standard region level. It shows that most people of working age (57 per cent) in the North live in wards classified by this measure to be in the bottom third of society. Almost half of the population of Yorkshire and Humberside and of the North-West can expect to live these wards. Conversely, almost half the working-age populations of East Anglia and the South-East live in the most affluent third of wards.

SQUALOR: THE UNEQUAL GEOGRAPHY OF HOUSING WEALTH

'Squalor' is the most difficult of Beveridge's evils to estimate today. The term 'squalor' referred to poor housing conditions, but it is extremely difficult to generate relevant sub-regional level data on housing conditions. Moreover, the kinds of 'squalor' with which Beveridge was concerned have largely been eliminated through state intervention. However, poor housing conditions still exist. The 1991 English House Condition Survey estimated that 1.5 million dwellings in England were unfit to live in, but figures could only be produced at a standard region level. In order to map poor housing conditions we are forced to use a surrogate indicator. As the English House Condition Survey found, the key factor producing poor housing conditions is low levels of housing repair. The most important factor determining levels of housing repair is levels of housing wealth, given that the more a property is worth, the easier it typically is to raise the finance necessary to keep it in good condition and the more likely the owners are to be able to afford to keep it good repair. Housing wealth exists in the form of positive equity, which we can measure using building society records.[12] More generally, in an age when large amounts of personal wealth are tied up in housing equity – half of all personal wealth in the UK is held in bricks and mortar – inequalities in the level of positive equity provide another indicator of the spatial distribution of poverty. Finally, through the legal mechanism of inheritance this wealth is transferred between generations.[13]

We have divided the mortgage holding households ('borrowers') of England and Wales into three equal-sized groups on the basis of their estimated average levels of positive equity. The wealthiest third live in wards where the average positive equity is at least £28,450 per borrower (the lightly shaded areas). The poorest third live in wards where borrowers have £17,950 positive equity or less each on average (the darkly shaded areas). Figure 6.5 provides a map of housing-based wealth. Although such an indicator has obvious limitations, this figure shows that these wards are generally located in the same areas where other forms of poverty occur. Particularly noteworthy is the swathe of prosperity which characterises the outer South-East and adjacent areas of other regions. Table 6.5 summarises the data at the standard region level in the same format as used previously. Once again, according to this measure, the North emerges as being particularly disadvantaged. Below average levels of positive equity are characteristic of all regions except the South-East, but the North stands out as being particularly disadvantaged in this regard.[14]

TABLE 6.5: **Proportion of home buyers living in each third of society in each region**
Ternary division of wards on the basis of average positive equity in 1993 held in dwellings bought there between 1988 and 1991.

Region	Poor %	Middle %	Affluent %	%
England & Wales	33	33	33	100
North	58	26	16	100
Yorks & Humberside	41	35	24	100
East Midlands	45	35	20	100
East Anglia	42	33	24	100
South-East	19	33	48	100
South-West	37	35	28	100
West Midlands	38	36	25	100
North-West	35	34	31	100
Wales	46	30	24	100

Society is divided into three groups of wards, each containing as equal a number of all borrowers as possible. The 'poorest' group comprises all wards in which less than an average of £17,950 is held as housing equity; the 'affluent' group comprises all wards in which more than an average of £28,428 is held in housing equity by borrowers who bought there between 1988 and 1991 and have positive equity; the middle group is the remainder. Only a sample of mortgage holders who bought their homes between 1988 and 1991 and have property with positive equity is included. The sample is assumed to be representative of all recent mortgage-holding households ('borrowers'), using the 1991 Census to provide estimates for borrowers.

Source: Building Society individual mortgage records for property transactions between 1980 and 1991, personal communication to the authors.

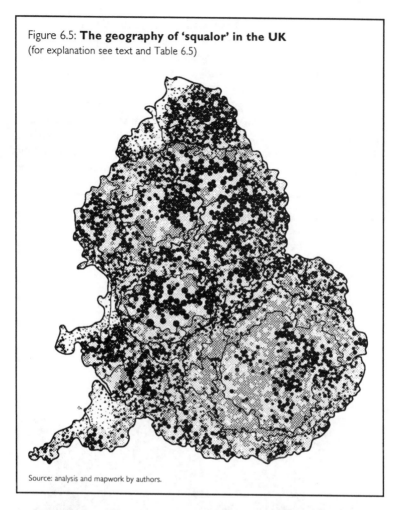

Figure 6.5: **The geography of 'squalor' in the UK**
(for explanation see text and Table 6.5)

Source: analysis and mapwork by authors.

DISEASE: THE UNEQUAL GEOGRAPHY OF ILL-HEALTH

One of the oldest indicators of poverty is the incidence of ill-health or 'disease' (see also Chapter 9). An indicator of health inequality can be estimated by examining the likelihood of people dying from diseases in an area before they reach a certain age. Here we have used mortality records provided by the Department of Health for the period 1981-89 (via the OPCS medical section) to look at the relative likelihood of residents in a ward dying from disease before

their 65th birthday.[15] We have undertaken this exercise for each
ward in England and Wales for all deaths excluding accidents,
suicides and homicides for the period 1981 to 1989, using at the
same time both the 1981 and 1991 censuses to estimate the
population profile of wards.

Figure 6.6 shows the geography of early deaths by disease in
England and Wales, when society is divided into three equal-sized
groups of all residents according to standardised mortality ratios.
The lightly shaded areas represent wards where a person is relatively
unlikely to die of disease before the age of 65 (15 per cent or more

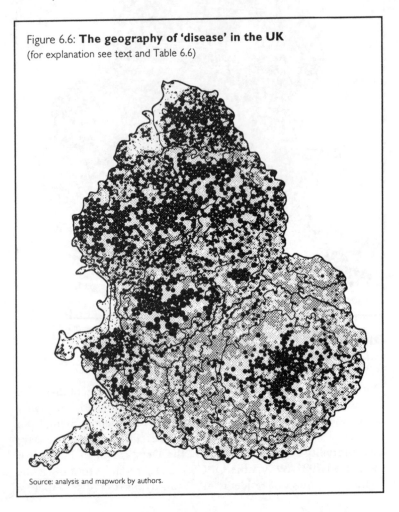

Figure 6.6: **The geography of 'disease' in the UK**
(for explanation see text and Table 6.6)

Source: analysis and mapwork by authors.

less likely than the average). The darkly shaded areas represent wards where a person has a greater than average likelihood of dying before the age of 65 (between 9 per cent and 342 per cent more likely). The data reveals that there can be up to a six-fold difference between the richest and poorest wards in the likelihood of dying young from disease. The results are all the more significant because they do not include homicides or suicides, the inclusion of which would probably further widen the division between localities. Table 6.6 summarises the distribution at the standard region level. The inequalities between regions are marked, with the southern regions having low shares of wards in the bottom third, while the northern regions generally have high shares in the bottom third and vice versa. Once again, the North emerges as particularly disadvantaged according to this measure.

TABLE 6.6: **Proportion of residents living in each third of society in each region**

Society divided into three groups of wards classified by the likelihood of dying there before 65 due to a disease, 1981-89.

Region	High %	Middle %	Low %	%
England & Wales	34	34	32	100
North	62	27	12	100
Yorks & Humberside	49	36	15	100
East Midlands	29	41	30	100
East Anglia	9	29	62	100
South-East	20	36	44	100
South-West	14	37	49	100
West Midlands	44	31	25	100
North-West	59	27	14	100
Wales	45	35	20	100

Society is divided into three groups of wards, each containing as equal a number of all residents as possible. The highest or 'sickliest' group comprises all wards in which SMRs are above 108 (the highest SMR calculated was 442); the lowest or 'healthiest' group comprises all wards in which SMRs are below 86; the 'middling' group is the remainder. All deaths between 1981 and 1989 of people aged below 65 (resident in England and Wales) attributed to disease (ICD 1 to 799) are included. Standardised Mortality Rates (SMRs: see also Chapter 9) are calculated for each ward by dividing the number of deaths from disease among those aged under 65 in the period 1981-89 by the numbers of deaths expected, given the age and sex profile of the ward's population, and assuming that its residents are typical of the nation's population.

Source: OPCS individual mortality records for England and Wales, 1981 to 1989, for all causes of death excluding accidents, suicides and homicides, together with 1981 and 1991 Census population estimates.

HOME TRUTHS: DEINDUSTRIALISATION AND THE POLITICAL ECONOMY OF POVERTY

In this chapter we have shown that an examination of various measures of poverty reveals a marked but consistent geography of poverty and inequality. The cartograms reveal complex patterns, it is true, but there are still some fairly evident trends which can be extracted for further consideration. The cartograms illustrate that all of the standard regions contain some prosperous wards, but they also reveal that – along with inner London (see also Chapters 4 and 8) – the old industrial regions contain a grossly disproportionate share of the most impoverished third of society. At the standard region level a marked 'North-South divide' emerges (see also Chapter 2), but one region, the North, stands out as particularly disadvantaged. The most prosperous third of society, by contrast, is heavily concentrated in large parts of the southern regions of England, excluding inner London.

The impact of the recent recession on southern England has focused attention on rising levels of social and economic stress there (see also Chapter 8). Our analysis has attempted to re-focus attention on the underlying structural factors which determine life-chances in the UK. This analysis distinguishes between shorter-run, cyclical factors and longer-run, structural factors. Thus, our analysis illustrates in graphic detail a child's likelihood of living in a household dependent on welfare payments; their chances of attending a school at which they can expect to gain minimal qualifications; their chances of being trapped in long-term unemployment; their chances of achieving financial security; and their chances of dying early from disease. What we have shown is that some localities – notably in the old industrial regions – are characterised by multiple and enduring forms of deprivation.

This map of poverty and inequality raises important political questions. In the late 1980s apparent growth in inequality was seen as a necessary – and even desirable – consequence of rapid economic growth in the 'new enterprise culture'. It was the growth in consumption and services – made possible by spiralling asset inflation, especially in housing – which underpinned employment in the South. Those in the North who worried about the consequences of the country's shrinking manufacturing base were famously dismissed as 'moaning minnies'. From the perspective of the mid-1990s, however, it is apparent that entrenched poverty, concentrated in the old industrial regions in large measure, reflects the continued decline of the UK as a manufacturing economy. Entrenched unemployment, which is the consequence of this trend, and the parallel explosion in low-paid service jobs are fuelling poverty and are contributing to the UK's increasing public sector deficit as the social security bill has mushroomed. A vicious circle of decline was established in the 1980s. Now some politicians and economists accept mass unemployment as necessary for 'non-inflationary growth', but in so doing so they are, in practice, accepting that endemic poverty will be an enduring feature of British society.

Ironically, at the very point that the political system is turning its back on the poor, we have shown that social scientists have better information about poverty and its spatial distribution than ever before. What we conclude from the analysis in this paper is that the concentration of poverty in the old industrial regions reflects the deindustrialisation of the British economy. Thus, tackling poverty is not simply an issue of redistribution but must encompass a concern with wider economic issues and, specifically, a concern with rebuilding shattered regional economies.

ACKNOWLEDGEMENTS

We would like to thank James Cornford, Helen Stevens, Chris Philo and two anonymous readers for comments on an earlier draft of this chapter.

NOTES

1. J K Galbraith, *The Culture of Contentment* (Sinclair Stevenson, 1992).
2. Commisson on Social Justice, *Social Justice: strategies for national renewal* (Vantage/Institute for Public Policy Research, 1994).
3. W Hutton, 'Dispossessed one third at root of Britain's crisis', in *The Guardian*, 18 January 1993.
4. European Commission, *Competitiveness and Cohesion: trends in the regions (Fifth Period Report on the Social and Economic Situation and Development of the Regions in the Community)* (Office for Official Publications of the European Communities, 1994).
5. Due to problems of data compatibility, we have excluded the Scottish old industrial regions from our analysis.
6. Although the tables in this chapter refer to standard regions, the extent of poverty in each of the Objective 2 regions can be assessed from the figures. Figure 6.1 annotates county boundaries which are also superimposed on each of the subsequent figures which map the 'five great evils'. The Objective 2 regions are largely aggregations of counties, and their areal extents can be ascertained from the figures.

7. The concept of the 'five great evils' was also recently resurrected by the Commission on Social Justice to provide a picture of poverty at the national level: see Commission on Social Justice (see note 2).

8. For a description of the method used to produce these cartograms, see D Dorling, 'Visualising the geography of the population with the 1991 census', *Population Trends*, Vol 76 (Summer, 1994), pp29-39.

9. This approach has the disadvantage of obscuring some intra-regional differences, although these can be clearly seen in the figures. In particular, the relatively poor position of London is obscured at the standard region level, but can be clearly seen in the cartograms (see also Chapter 4). There is, of course, no optimal areal scale at which socio-economic data can be analysed.

10. For a theoretical treatment of the notion of 'life-chances', see R Dahrendorf, *Life Chances: approaches to social and political theory* (Weidenfeld and Nicholson, 1979).

11. For this study figures were collected for every secondary school in England and Wales which was not a 'special school' and which provided the Department of Education and the Welsh Office with examination results in 1993. These results were allocated to wards via the postcode of the school, and by allocating results to wards without schools by distributing pupils to their nearest wards in line with the numbers of 13-year-olds counted in those wards at the time of the 1991 census.

12. 'Positive equity' is the current market value of a home less the mortgage still owed on that home (when the former is greater than the latter), and can be estimated from building society records. It is used here as a proxy for overall levels of housing conditions.

13. The average level of positive equity has been calculated for all borrowers who purchased their home between 1988 and 1991, and whose home is worth more than their mortgage. Market values at the end of 1993 were used to estimate current levels of positive equity. We can assume that where middle-aged, more affluent people have moved and accumulated equity on housing transactions or through inherited wealth or by other means, levels of positive equity tend to be highest and housing conditions tend to be best.

14. Of course, 'poor' households in 'rich' regions can face particularly severe housing problems. For instance, rents tend to be higher where houses are more expensive. Moreover, 'poor' households in these areas will be compelled to take on large levels of debt in order to buy houses, while the provision of social housing in such areas will also be more constrained than elsewhere.

15. Among other things, mortality records indicate both the causes of death thought most likely and the postcode of the usual residence of the deceased, along with their age and sex. It is possible, in combination with census records, to estimate how many people could be expected to die in a particular ward under the age of 65 given the age and sex profile of the population in that ward, and then to compare that figure with the number of people who die nationally at each age for each sex.

7 High-tech places: poverty in the midst of growth

Doreen Massey and John Allen

INTRODUCTION: THE HIGH-TECH WORKPLACE AND FORMS OF ECONOMIC GROWTH

Imagine a high-tech workplace in Cambridge, maybe on the 'science park'. A modern, probably architect-designed building set among green lawns and ample parking space. The place is full of windows, and the entrance hall – complete with smiling receptionist (it is part of her job) – has easy chairs and large potted plants. Such buildings have become icons of economic growth in our times. They embody knowledge-based industry, high technology, a pleasant working environment. They represent – or so some would say – a foretaste of the future. This, of course, is already an assertion which can be questioned. Not everywhere will be like this. This is one of the privileged parts, and privileged places, within the British economy. Not that far away, in Oxfordshire and Berkshire for instance, you will find other 'rich places' too.

However, what we want to argue in this chapter is that, even here, in the midst of privilege and prosperity, there is inequality. An inequality which in this case, as was suggested could occur in Chapter 1, finds affluence and poverty side by side in the same place. This is not so much a tale of two cities, though, as it is one of different worlds of work which overlap and accompany each other. It is a world of scientist-engineers on the one side, and a world of nannies, cleaners and security guards on the other. Moreover – and this is a really important point – this is not an inequality which results from differences in the level of economic growth: that is, from there being more economic success in one place or part of the economy than in another. It is rather an inequality structured at the very heart of this kind of growth itself.

Growth can take many different forms, and each different form of growth has different social and economic implications. As has been discussed, in previous chapters, the kind of economic growth which took place in the 1980s across the UK was marked by widening income differentials, with some groups monopolising the well-paid jobs, other groups effectively being constrained to meet their needs through low-paid service work, and others again being excluded from the whole process – unable to get work of any sort. This kind of growth thus had particular implications for who benefited relative to (or even at the expense of) whom, for which sectors of the economy grew and which were held back, and for which places and regions experienced most of the benefits of growth. It is not sufficient, therefore, simply to call for more economic growth as if, in itself, it is necessarily a good thing. It is also vital to think about the *form* of growth being asked for. Take a close look at our iconic, high-tech workplace. In fact, its functioning, as we have indicated, is sustained by a wide range of groups of people and by a wide range of social relations. Embedded within these relations, structured into the very mechanisms of economic growth operating here, is – as we shall see – deep social inequality.

The account that follows is based upon two related pieces of research. One set out to explore some of the local labour market dynamics which result from a concentration of highly paid scientist-engineers in 'rich places' such as Cambridge. Of particular interest here was the impact of men's working lives in high-tech upon the organisation of domestic life at home. The other piece of research sought to understand the reasons behind the growth of a variety of low-waged service jobs in precisely such 'rich places' as Cambridge. The 'two sides of growth', as it were, represented a particular focus of our study and one characteristic of Cambridge in the 1980s. It is in this sense that our general concern is with a particular form of high-tech growth laid down in the 1980s.[1]

IN THE WORKPLACE: SCIENTIST-ENGINEERS

The heart of these high-tech workplaces is scientific and technical research-based production. Among the key workers on whom this process depends are scientist-engineers working, in one way or another, on research – into new products, new processes, new ways of designing software, and so on.[2]

As the day begins for them, these scientist-engineers – who are mainly young, mainly white (over 90 per cent) and mainly male (over 90 per cent) – arrive individually and at different times. This is a world away from the massed ranks of factory workers, arriving to clock in at the same hour. For the scientist-engineers, working hours are unfixed. Some turn up as early as 7.30 am or 8.00 am, others roll in at 10.00 am or even 10.30 am. Part of the 'wealth' of these jobs, and of the people who fill them, is the relatively high degree of control which each employee has over when and how they work. The scientist-engineers are also well-paid – maybe not on the level of the 'whizz-kiddery' of the City, but enough to enable ample home-ownership in Cambridge or in one of the surrounding villages, one or more new cars and a large collection of consumer-durables. At the very least, their existence is 'comfortable'. These are also jobs which are part of a career-structure. These young men expect to move on. Turnover of staff at the workplace is indeed high, not because this is casual labour (although some are working on consultancy contracts) but as a means of gaining promotion and a more substantial increase in salary. In their individual lives, in imitation of the industry in which they work, these people are successful. Even in the recent downturn in the early-1990s, when times have been comparatively (for them, that is) hard, they at least know that they have highly-valued, tradeable skills.

There are other sides of this picture, however, even for the scientist-engineers. For these are high-pressure jobs. Personal choice over time of arrival should not be taken to imply a low workload. Most of these young men will work a long week. Even when the basic contractual hours agreed with the company are (say) 37, almost everyone will consistently work far more. It is common to work late at night, to work at the weekends, to work Bank Holidays, to fail to take annual leave. Work also spills over into the home, penetrating the domestic environment. Almost all of these men have a modem at home, and a study. Some of them will have been working before they arrive at the high-tech workplace, and many will later put in an odd hour at home overnight. When they are at home washing-up, or apparently playing with the children, their minds may be elsewhere – at work – juggling with the latest knotty problem. Sometimes too they must go to conferences, or be on call for customers, or fly off to California. Their jobs demand that these men be both temporally and spatially 'flexible'.

It is interesting to ponder just why the working hours in this part of the economy have to be so long. There seem to be three reasons. First, these companies – and the way in which they compete among themselves – quite simply demand it. In this part of the economy, time is certainly money. Companies compete with each other by promising to come up with a solution to a customer's problem, or to design a new 'widget', before their competitors can. In the tender for the job, the working hours required will be compressed to a minimum. Delivery-date will be part of the competition. All of this inevitably means that the work is squashed into too few working days. This is exacerbated by the inherently unpredictable nature of research, in that things can go wrong or solutions may be harder to find than had initially been thought. Or again, since the time taken in drawing up the tender documents does not bring in money, it tends to get squeezed out of the 'normal' working day. Or yet again, part of the competition may hinge upon guaranteeing the customer 24-hours-a-day and 7-days-a-week cover: if anything goes wrong, the scientist-engineer will be there immediately to put it right. The very success of the companies in this part of the economy, the very fact of their economic growth, is dependent upon long and unpredictable hours being worked by these people within them. The other two reasons why the working hours are so long are the competitive career-structure of the employees and their involvement with their work. They can get very engrossed in its problem-solving nature, can find it very hard to tear themselves away. In one way or another, paid employment and its demands form the centrepiece of their lives. It dominates everything else. We shall see later what are the implications of this for those whose lives are in some manner shared with the lives of these successful young men.

IN THE WORKPLACE: CLEANERS AND SECURITY GUARDS

You do not even have to leave the science park or its high-tech buildings, however, to uncover the traces of what can be termed the 'new working poor'. Walk around the research laboratories at 6.00 or 7.00 in the morning, and you will discover a different type of workforce from that of the preoccupied scientist-engineers. The women arriving have come to clean the buildings, and the men about to leave are the security guards nearing the end of their 12-hour shift. An unseen workforce, often only visible in the half-light, these cleaners and security guards represent the low-paid, low-status end of high-technology growth, even in its most prestigious parts, sectors, localities. Both cleaners and security guards are likely to be earning around £3 per hour, but this figure hides as many differences in their respective working experiences as it reveals of what they hold in common.

Most cleaners work part-time, usually in the small hours of the morning or in the late evening. Two-hour shifts are normal, and a week's work will invariably total less than the 16 hours required to bring them within the national insurance threshold. Many will have earnings too low to pay income tax. The majority of cleaners will be excluded from the benefits and entitlements that the scientist-engineers take for granted. Not all will be poor: some will be working to supplement their family income (through non-taxable earnings), but others urgently need the work merely 'to keep them going'. Security guards work full-time, although the term conveys little of the experience of having to work rotating shift systems which lead to 60- or even 72-hour working weeks. The industry does not have to be organised in this way – in the US, for instance, the pattern of work is similar to that of manufacturing – yet, because that is the norm in the UK, guards have little choice but to put in the hours if they want to achieve anything approaching a basic wage. Ironically, they probably put in as many hours as the scientist-engineers, yet the difference lies in the 'poverty' of security work. Whereas the scientist-engineers – as noted earlier – tend to be obsessed with their work, unable to find the hours to satisfy their interests, guards are faced with the task of how to fill empty time. The product of security is that 'nothing happens', and the skill is in finding ways of passing time, whether it be through cards, conversation, reading magazines, or listening to the radio.

Despite the different worlds of work experienced by cleaners, guards and scientist-engineers, the former two (and sometimes all three) share a *contract labour* status. Few firms on the science park will employ their own cleaners or security guards, and most will subcontract this kind of work. The effect of this is to 'impoverish' employment in two ways. First, through the wage reductions that almost invariably accompany the movement of a contract from one private contractor to the next. As the cost of labour in both industries represents a major factor in the winning and losing of contracts, the pressure is always there to reduce the wages of the workforce, either directly or indirectly through the removal of various supplementary benefits (sick pay, holiday pay and the like). A second way in which employment may be 'impoverished' through subcontracting is that job security is limited to the length of the contract. When a contract changes hands, whether or not a cleaner or a guard still has a job is largely down to the discretion of the incoming management or the will of the client, the high-tech company. In cleaning, it is custom and practice to pass a workforce from one private contractor to the next, on the understanding that the company losing the contract will be unable to place them. That said, the possibility is always there that it is your job that will have to go. Likewise in contract security, when a firm loses a contract, most long-standing guards will be moved to other sites and the rest placed in a central pool to cover absentees. The client, however, still has the power of veto over who is and who is not taken on under a new contract. If your face does not fit, then 'you are out'.

The vulnerability of contract employment may also be shared by the scientists in the same building, but the difference rests with the ability to sell their much-wanted skills in the high-tech labour market. A contract status may be freely entered into by a young researcher, whereas for the cleaner and the guard it is likely to be something that is imposed. It is not simply the 'lack' of skills that marks one kind of contract work off from another, though, it is also the lack of visibility attached to cleaning and security work. In the case of cleaning, it is the cleaners themselves rather than the work performed which tends to be unseen. Even when cleaners *are* employed during the 'working day', they tend to occupy different spaces within the building, take their breaks at different times, and slip out of the building noticed only by the security guard. The small room in which they store the machinery and cleaning materials, read newspapers and magazines, as well as keep their personal effects, may be adjacent to a room full of problem-solvers and computers, but the latter – unlike the cleaners – will very likely be oblivious to what is next to them. Similarly, although much security work takes place at night, in the daytime it is often only the outline of the guard which is visible as the high-tech staff pass in and out. Staff quite often 'look right through you' as you stand by the entrances and exits of the building. To say that a workforce is hidden, then, is not to say that it cannot be seen. Part of the 'impoverishment' of work (as opposed to employment) in contract cleaning and security is that your presence is only noted if something is wrong – a blocked toilet, a stained carpet, the theft of a wallet, or the outbreak of a fire. These are not the 'poor places' mentioned in Chapter 1, therefore, but rather dominated spaces in which cleaners and security guards live their working lives alongside the 'more important' hours and highly visible comings and goings of the scientist-engineers. They are close to one another in terms of physical proximity, yet they are far apart in terms of social presence.[3]

Poverty at the heart of growth is hence not just about low wages; it is also about the loss of fringe benefits, the precariousness of employment and the 'impoverishment' of work. These low-status contract services represent one element of the 'underside' of growth in 'high tech' Cambridgeshire, an element which, certainly in the case of security, is absolutely crucial to the ability of the scientist-engineers to work the long hours that they do.

BEYOND THE WORKPLACE: PARTNERS, NANNIES AND MORE CLEANERS

But there are also other social relations required, and at the same time other social groups, to maintain these high-tech icons of economic prosperity. The hours called for in the scientific-engineering jobs, along with the related demands for temporal and spatial 'flexibility', mean that the people who hold such jobs would find it very difficult to take on any great duty in caring for others outside of the workplace. It is quite clear that a single parent, for instance, however otherwise well-qualified, could not do these jobs. Indeed, the way that these jobs are organised means that, ideally, the people who fill them need to have someone else to look after *them*.

And they do. A good number of the scientist-engineers (between 60 and 70 per cent in a recent survey) live with female partners. It is clear that the lives of these women are quite deeply affected by the demands of this particular aspect of economic growth. In effect, the flexibility claimed of the employees by their companies – the expectation that these men should be highly flexible in the organisation of their domestic environments – turns itself into a *constraint* upon the lives of female partners. This happens in a variety of ways. Most obviously, it is the partners who shoulder by far the greater burden of the whole range of domestic labour, including, where there are children, the task of child-rearing. This burden goes beyond the 'normal' inequality of the sexual division of labour in the late-twentieth century first-world home. The women themselves comment on the specific impact of the organisation of their men's working lives. Its unpredictability is almost as much of a problem as the sheer number of hours worked. The men themselves comment on not seeing their children growing up.

This organisation of domestic life affects in turn the ability of the women to have their own working lives outside of the home. The women have either decided to give up on having careers of their own, or are held back in the careers that they do decide to follow. Their spatial range of job choice, and of possible travel-to-work arrangements, may be restricted by the decision to adapt to the needs of the man's job ('*someone* has to pick up the children', and they have to be reliable, not flexible). They also avoid jobs which themselves demand long or even full-time hours, or which entail unpredictability, or which might occasionally involve them in travel beyond the local area, or which might involve conferences or social networking. Thus it is that the social requirements of economic growth in one part of the economy (in this case high-tech) impose constraints on the labour-market potential of other people. Potentially, indeed, they are holding back growth in other parts of the economy.

Sometimes an alternative, or additional, solution is found to the problem of how these high-tech workers are to be looked after. This is to pay for it: to buy in domestic services, to eat out, to employ a nanny. Although the levels of this kind of behaviour are not extraordinarily high, there is no doubt that such commercialisation of domestic labour is above the national average in a place such as Cambridge. This implies that other groups are being added to the range of those necessary to service high-tech industry: people whose hourly wages are low enough to be employable out of the incomes of others whose salaries are high enough, and who do not have the time to do all the work of self-servicing.[4] This also means that another form of economic inequality is structured into this kind of growth. At its worst, this would point to the development of local labour markets in part polarised between high-earners (in this case largely male) on the one hand and those (mainly female) who service them on the other. As with the cleaners and security guards at the workplace, the inequality is not just in terms of wage levels. The home-cleaners, child-minders and nannies often have little of the security of employment of the key workers, and they also do not have pension schemes or sick pay. Yet they too may find themselves working unpredictable hours. In the case of nannies, for example, the requirements for 'adaptability' and 'flexibility', for putting paid work first, are passed on to them from the high-tech workplace. When the scientist-engineers need to work late, and the partner is unavailable, nanny is telephoned and asked to stay on. The requirements for time-flexibility in high technology reach well beyond the portals of the high-status places of work.

Staying on late may also mean missing the last bus home to the council estates on the edge of the city where many of these service workers live. For nannies, as much as for the cleaners and security guards, their secondary position in the labour market is mirrored in their housing opportunities. The physical and social distances between the owner-occupied houses of the scientist-engineers in the outlying villages and the impoverished council estates, on which many at the bottom end of the service labour markets live, is simply another expression of a particular kind of unequal growth. Such neighbourhoods, blighted by both local and national restrictions on public housing expenditure, compound poverty and inequality at the workplace with poverty and inequality beyond it.[5]

CONCLUSION

Look more closely at the high-tech icons of economic prosperity, then, and you will see worlds of work other than those of the highly paid and the highly skilled. In many ways, the working – and indeed the non-working – lives of cleaners, guards and nannies are part of the hidden geography of poverty referred to in Chapter 1. This is not an accidental geography, however, but rather one that is integral to the kind of growth that a high-tech future represents.[6]

NOTES

1. This chapter is based on work by the authors in two ESRC-funded projects, R000-23-3004 and R000-23-3008. On both projects work was carried out with Nick Henry, now of the Department of Geography, University of Birmingham. For an outline of the 'South-East Programme'

and its conceptualisation of growth, see J Allen, *The Nature of a Growth Region: the peculiarity of the South-East* (Faculty of Social Sciences, The Open University, Occasional Paper Series No. 1, 1992).

2. For further details on high-tech places, see D Massey, P Quintas and D Wield, *High-Tech Fantasies: science parks in society, science and space* (Routledge, 1992).

3. See J Allen and M Pryke, 'The production of service space', *Environment and Planning D: society and space*, Vol 12 (1994), pp453-75.

4. For further reading on the commercialisation of domestic labour, see N Gregson and M Lowe, *Servicing the Middle Class: class, gender and waged domestic labour in contemporary Britain* (Routledge, 1994).

5. See also P Crang and R Martin, 'Mrs Thatcher's vision of the "New Britain" and the other sides of the Cambridge phenomenon', *Environment and Planning D: society and space*, Vol 9 (1991), pp100-30.

6. For a discussion of the relation of high-technology working hours to policies of a shorter working day/week, see D Massey, 'Masculinity, dualisms and high-technology', forthcoming in *Transactions of the Institute of British Geographers*.

8 Missing the boat: poverty, debt and unemployment in the South-East

John Mohan

INTRODUCTION: THE END OF THATCHERITE ILLUSION?

Politicians are often given to quoting variants on President Kennedy's aphorism that poverty (in the USA) would be eliminated because 'a rising tide would lift all boats'. The USA's experience suggests that in fact an increasing number of people have not caught the boat, and that many have sunk almost without trace. Here I suggest that, even in the most prosperous regions of the UK, large numbers of people also have missed the boat, and that current trends suggest rising numbers of people to have fallen overboard. This means that, while the government has relied on a 'trickle-down' theory in which the benefits of economic growth are supposed to cascade downwards so that ultimately everybody benefits, the evidence suggests that in practice 'trickle-down' economics are failing to work (or at least are failing to work in all places). Specifically, the notion of the South-East region (henceforth, the SE) as being uniformly prosperous is erroneous: there may have been some truth in that in the late-1980s (although still not for all social groups) but it is certainly not true now, as there are growing problems of social polarisation and poverty. In addition, the rapid economic growth during the 1980s brought with it its own problems – of excessive living costs and house prices particularly. National economic policies introduced to cope with this, such as the increases in interest rates in the late-1980s, have had a particularly adverse effect on the SE as many individuals have been unable to repay their mortgages.

It follows that economic recovery will be patchy and difficult due to the accumulated debts pressing on many residents of the region, limiting consumption expenditures.

I shall develop these arguments through analyses of data on employment trends and on unemployment, statistics on poverty and on low incomes, and also indicators of homelessness and indebtedness, concentrating on the SE, including London and East Anglia. The chapter has two principal aims: to chart the impacts on the SE as a whole resulting from the recent recession, and to consider the extent of inequalities within the SE as and where appropriate. In addition, comparisons are drawn on occasion with the position of other places and regions within the UK, so as to put the SE's situation in a wider context. First, however, some wider comments on the significance of these geographical areas in relation to the national political economy may be in order.

Whereas the boom in these locations was often regarded as resulting from the entrepreneurial activities and enterprise culture of their residents, in practice a number of public expenditure programmes have underwritten the prosperity of the SE. Consequently it is disingenuous − even vacuous − to claim that the South grew on the basis of its own efforts.[1] Indeed, some commentators argue that the Thatcher administrations underwrote the growth of incomes in the South at the expense of the withdrawal of, or restriction of growth in, public support for the North.[2] This is particularly evident if one contrasts the dramatic cuts in support for nationalised industries in the North (and their eventual privatisation) with the impacts of defence-related expenditures on economic growth in the SE.[3] The 1988 Budget was, of course, the most graphic manifestation of this, since 60 per cent of its benefits went to the SE, which contained 30 per cent of the national population.

More generally the SE was held up by the government as a model for other regions to follow. A deregulatory economic strategy was pursued, alongside promoting the internationalisation of the economy, with London at its heart as a major financial centre. This led to dramatic growth in the service sector and to the decline of traditional manufacturing. The accompanying rhetorics of Conservative ideology − self-reliance, property ownership, entrepreneurship, independence, flexibility − have been absorbed by the southern electorate to a greater degree than elsewhere, and hence the more rapid progress of (for instance) council house sales in the region. Yet the difficulties now being experienced in the housing market pose particular problems for this vision of Conservatism, as statistics on house repossessions and negative equity make clear. In addition, the type of growth experienced in the region has been associated with widening income polarisation, to an extent not evident elsewhere in the country.

EMPLOYMENT AND UNEMPLOYMENT

We should recall that only in the mid-1980s, less than seven years ago, the press was full of reports about the overheating in the SE and about the difficulties that employers were having with recruitment. With house prices booming, the problem seemed to be where to find the additional workers: as the comedian Phil Cool put it at the time, the M25 represented Margaret Thatcher's Berlin Wall, because those living outside it had almost no prospect of earning enough to enable them to move within it. Unemployment rates of less than 3 per cent were not uncommon, with many areas recording rates under 2 per cent.

The position in the mid-1990s is, however, substantially different. The region's economy is losing jobs in absolute terms more rapidly than anywhere else: between June 1990 and May 1993 the SE lost 579,000 jobs, which is more than the total for the rest of the UK put together. The SE began the recession with 23.3 per cent of national unemployment (June 1990), but has since accounted for 43.7 per cent of the growth in unemployment (more than twice of its proportionate share).[4] Unemployment rates in a number of localities in the SE now exceed the national average, in many cases for the first time (and remember that the national average itself is relatively high).

In April 1994, there were 16 'travel-to-work areas' in the SE where unemployment rates exceeded the national average of 9.7 per cent of the workforce. These were in part coastal areas such as Brighton (12.4 per cent), Clacton (14.9 per cent), Harwich (14.4 per cent), Sittingbourne/Sheerness (13.9 per cent), Thanet (15.9 per cent) and Hastings (12.8 per cent).[5] Of course, since these rates refer to April and are not seasonally adjusted, they ignore the possibility that in the coastal locations some individuals will find work for the duration of the tourist season, although such work is often associated with low pay and poor terms and conditions of service. There are hence issues of uneven development *within* the

SE's economy, distinguishing between these peripheral resorts and many other localities in the SE.

In inner London, the position is much worse. Estimates for March 1994 show that, while the UK unemployment rate was then 9.9 per cent, the rates for individual London boroughs were as high as 23.8 per cent (Hackney) and 23.7 per cent (Tower Hamlets); and in four other boroughs unemployment was over 20 per cent, with six boroughs recording rates between 15 and 20 per cent.[6] It is true that at the level of electoral wards London and the SE do not have the extremely high levels of unemployment recorded in some industrial cities such as Liverpool or Newcastle. This can be shown by using the ward statistics for the 1991 Census, which give figures for those without work as a percentage of the economically active population. Of the 100 wards with the highest rates on this indicator, only 13 are in London. By contrast, 24 of these wards are in Liverpool or in its neighbouring authorities of Knowsley or Sefton. Nevertheless, four wards in both Hackney and Tower Hamlets, two in Southwark and one each in Newham, Lewisham, and Lambeth each experience unemployment rates of at least 24.9 per cent (see also observations in Chapter 4 about patterns of deprivation in London).[7] The 1991 Census indicated that some 250,000 children in London were living in households where there was no adult in paid employment,[8] meanwhile, and since unemployment in London has risen substantially since 1991 this figure is surely an underestimate. If these unemployment figures for London suggest that there has been some convergence between regions, and hence an ending of the 'North-South divide', it is appropriate to note that this reflects the SE's unemployment rate approaching that experienced in the rest of the country, rather than the rest of the country catching up with the SE (see also Chapter 2).

LOW INCOMES, POVERTY AND INDEBTEDNESS

INCOMES AND INCOME POLARISATION

The available statistics on income levels do not allow much to be said about the experiences of particular places within regions, and so we have to rely on the Census and other data as surrogates for information about incomes. Of course, the SE still has the highest per capita incomes in the UK, and the highest proportions of people able to access the private middle-class welfare state (private healthcare, private education, occupational pensions and so on). Nevertheless, some parts of the SE have perhaps surprisingly high proportions of people on low incomes. Data from the Low Pay Unit (LPU) shows the proportion of full-time employees whose incomes fall below various thresholds for low pay. Here I use the Council of Europe's Decency Threshold of £215.50 per week, which is based on 68 per cent of average gross weekly earnings of all full-time employees on adult rates in the UK. For the SE as a whole, LPU figures show that 21.7 per cent of full-time employees earned less than this amount (compared to 31.1 per cent for Britain as a whole). However, in four counties (Essex, Kent, East Sussex and the Isle of Wight) the proportion was at or above the national average, while for the East Anglia region the proportion was 34.9 per cent, reflecting the continued importance of (low-paid) agricultural employment there. The figure for London as a whole was 14.8 per cent, but in 15 boroughs over 20 per cent of full-time employees earned less than this figure and in Tower Hamlets (29 per cent) and Bromley (28.4 per cent) the proportion approached the national average, while the next highest proportion was in Redbridge (25.8 per cent).[9]

The SE is also a region characterised by large, and widening, income disparities. The ratio of the incomes of the top 10 per cent of workers to those of the bottom 50 per cent has increased, from 4.85 in 1980-81 (indicating that people in the top 10 per cent of the income distribution earned, on average, 4.85 times as much as did people in the bottom 50 per cent) to 6.71 in 1991-92. Even in 1980-81 this ratio was 9 per cent above the average for England as a whole; by 1991-92 it was 14.7 per cent greater than the average for England. For all other regions in England, the ratio in 1991-92 lay between 4.78 (Northern region) and 5.36 (North West).[10] As Peck and Shutt point out, this is a comment on the particular type of growth experienced in the SE: because of the priority attached to financial services, in which there was extremely rapid growth as a result of deregulation of financial markets, there emerged an extremely polarised overall income distribution.[11] In addition, because of the nature of the new jobs created in the SE, and the lack of investment in training, many unskilled workers joined the ranks of the long-term unemployed: simultaneously, skill shortages thereby co-existed with large-scale unemployment within certain parts of the SE.

FREE SCHOOL MEALS

Data on eligibility for and take-up of free school meals provides
another insight into low incomes and the extent of dependence on
benefit. Local education authorities (LEAs) have a duty to provide
free school meals if a child's parents are on income support, and so
relevant figures are available for LEAs. For London boroughs in
1993 on average 28.2 per cent of secondary school pupils were
eligible for free school meals. However, the figures ranged from
7.75 per cent in Kingston to 64.9 per cent in Tower Hamlets, and in
15 contiguous inner London boroughs over 30 per cent of the
school population were eligible.[12]

Comparable data on free school meals are available for the period
1989-92,[13] allowing comparisons between inner London (the former
ILEA area), outer London (the remaining boroughs included in the
former Greater London Council) and the rest of the SE. The focus
is on primary school children since lower proportions of secondary
pupils actually take school meals, and the figures refer to actual
take-up of free school meals rather than to eligibility, the figures for
which would be higher. Firstly, for inner London there were 47,548
pupils on free school meals in 1989, but this figure had risen to
61,016 by 1992, an increase of 13,468 (28 per cent). As a result,
33.4 per cent of pupils in this area were on free meals by 1992.
These high proportions were to be expected given the high levels
of social deprivation in inner London. Secondly, the figures for
outer London show some dramatic increases, although this is partly
due to the low starting base from which percentage changes have
been calculated. The number of primary pupils taking free school
meals rose from 34,023 to 54,762, an increase of 20,739 (60.9 per
cent). Particularly rapid increases were experienced in some boroughs
which had previously experienced relatively low levels of free
school meal take-up in 1989, presumably reflecting the very low
levels of unemployment prevailing at that time. For example, in
Bromley, Croydon and Havering there were increases in take-up of
75 per cent; in Richmond and Sutton increases of over 80 per cent;
in Redbridge the numbers doubled; and Merton saw a 269 per cent
increase (from 537 to 1,982). While the average figures for outer
London indicate that 14.4 per cent of primary pupils were on free
meals, in four boroughs (Brent, Haringey, Newham and Waltham
Forest) the figures exceeded 20 per cent.

As for the SE excluding London, an additional 38,042 children took free school meals in 1992 compared with 1989, and the proportion so doing rose dramatically from 6.45 per cent to 10.8 per cent. However, this figure was still well below the figure for England (excluding London) of 16.5 per cent, although only 2 per cent below the average for non-metropolitan English counties of 12.8 per cent. In total, by comparison with 1989, an additional 72,249 pupils in primary schools in London and the SE were taking free school meals. The growth in take-up outside London again provides convincing evidence of the impact of the recession on household incomes. The total number of primary pupils on free school meals in London and the SE in 1992 was 205,349, or 14.8 per cent of the primary school population.

Data for 1993 includes numbers taking free meals in nursery schools, and thus is not strictly comparable with the earlier figures, but the percentages taking free meals show increases over previous years. In the constituent boroughs of inner London the average percentage of pupils in primary and nursery schools taking free meals was 35.7 per cent (nearly twice the national average of 18.3 per cent), and was over 40 per cent in Hackney (42 per cent) and Tower Hamlets (47 per cent). For outer London boroughs the average percentage on free school meals was 16.8 per cent (slightly below the national average), but in four boroughs (Brent, Haringey, Newham and Waltham Forest) the figure exceeded 24 per cent. Finally, in the outer SE the proportion of children on free school meals approached the national average in East Sussex (18 per cent) and in Bedfordshire (17 per cent). Overall in 1993 some 245,000 primary and nursery pupils in London and the SE received free school meals.

INCOME SUPPORT

The different regions used by the Department of Social Security (DSS) for collection of data mean that comparability with other statistical sources, and calculation of the proportion of people on income support over time, are both impossible.[14] What can be said, though, is that the total number of income support recipients in Great Britain increased from 4.16 million in 1989 to 5.51 million in 1993, an increase of 32.4 per cent (and the increase in England was 36.3 per cent). The totals for the London South and London North DSS regions were 1.15 million in 1989 and 1.81 million in 1993, an increase of 57 per cent; the percentage increases in the London

North and South regions were 57 and 58 per cent respectively, and an additional 666,000 claimants were therefore added to the rolls in the SE. When the numbers for the dependants and partners of claimants are added in, there are 3.18 million people in the London North and London South regions living in households dependent partly or wholly on income support payments.[15] In addition, in the SE there are 458,000 people who receive housing benefit without receiving income support (these are people whose incomes are above income support levels without being sufficiently high to enable them to pay their rents in full). It might be argued that to use 1989 as the start-date for this time series gives an unbalanced impression of the difficulties facing the SE, since large percentage changes emerge through being calculated on a low base. Yet the addition of two-thirds of a million income support claimants in one region in four years amply demonstrates the impact that both the recession and the growth of part-time employment has had on the SE.

HOUSEHOLD INDEBTEDNESS

A major element in this is housing-related debt, and some figures on this are given in the next section. Data provided by Citizens Advice Bureaux (CABx) are useful in showing the effects of economic changes on households and individuals. CABx are a free service and are open to all without discrimination, and so would be expected to provide a reasonable indicator of the numbers of households and individuals requiring advice on a range of problems. Although there are some 700 CABx in the UK, they are not distributed evenly; they depend on funding from various sources, for instance from local authorities, and therefore are subject to the funding decisions and the financial positions (to say nothing of the ideological predispositions) of local authorities. There are also complications caused by changes in the areal units for which the National Association of CABx aggregates its statistics, and by changes in the numbers of bureaux (closure of a bureau obviously restricts the capacity of the service to deal with inquiries), which prevent analysis of changes over time. But some indication can still be obtained of the extent to which individuals have felt it necessary to seek advice on specific matters, and hence on the extent to which problems in various categories have indeed arisen in the SE (and elsewhere).[16]

Firstly, the numbers of inquiries to bureaux indicate the impacts of various forms of economic stress on individuals lives. In the CABx's SE region (basically Kent and Sussex) the numbers of enquiries related to consumer and debt problems per bureau rose from 1,390 in 1988-89 to 2,117 in 1992-93, and since 1983-84 enquiries per bureau in this category had risen by 135 per cent. In the opinion of CABx officials, this is most likely to be related to debt problems rather than to consumer problems.[17] Secondly, CABx statistics indicate the different significance in different places of problems faced by individuals. Thus, across the various CABx regions consumer and debt problems actually account for a lower proportion of bureau caseload in the SE than they do nationally, although in the Chiltern and Eastern regions (both over 24 per cent) debt is also slightly over-represented compared to the national average. By contrast, housing and property issues – which nationally account for 9.6 per cent of caseload – account for over 12 per cent of CABx enquiries in its London divisions and 11 per cent in its SE region (broadly, Kent and Sussex), whereas in the North of England the figure is typically around 8.5 per cent. Social security issues are also over-represented in London, and the three London divisions find that social security accounts for between 25 and 31 per cent of bureau enquiries compared to 24 per cent nationally.[18] In general debt and employment issues now account for much higher proportions of CABx workload than they did, say, ten years previously.[19]

RELATIVE DEPRIVATION: INDICATORS FROM THE 1991 CENSUS

Historically, indicators of deprivation have been constructed using Census data and because of the lack of data for individuals from the Census – due to confidentiality restrictions – it has not proved possible to estimate with any degree of accuracy the numbers and proportions of individuals suffering from various forms of deprivation. However, the 1991 Census includes a 2 per cent Sample of Anonymised Records (SARs) for individuals, from which it is possible to calculate the numbers of individuals lacking access to certain types of amenities and also lacking access to paid employment. These statistics are drawn on here.[20]

The SARs allow us to calculate not just the proportion of individuals or households in an area who lack certain amenities –

such as access to a car, or who live in accommodation lacking certain basic facilities – but also to calculate the proportions of the population lacking more than one of a range of amenities. Taking eight criteria which are relevant to an assessment of deprivation, Fieldhouse calculated the proportion of individuals in each of 278 areas lacking two or more basic amenities.[21] On these figures some 8.6 per cent of the UK population were regarded as experiencing multiple deprivation, but this proportion is geographically highly variable. The statistics calculated in this way show that deprivation is overwhelmingly concentrated in large urban authorities (see also Chapter 4). Thus, of the 20 authorities scoring highest on two or more indicators, 12 are London boroughs; of the top 10, eight are London authorities. Tower Hamlets (35.6 per cent) leads the way, followed at some distance by Hackney (26 per cent), Newham (22.2 per cent), Islington (20.7 per cent) and Camden (20.1 per cent). Although the dominant feature of these statistics is the prominence of London authorities, some areas elsewhere in the SE score surprisingly highly. Thus, Brighton (11.2 per cent) scores more highly than South Tyneside (11.1 per cent); Luton (11 per cent) is ranked above Sunderland (10.9 per cent); and Portsmouth and Reading (both 10.7 per cent) both score more highly than Sheffield (10.6 per cent) and Gateshead (10.2 per cent). However, at the other end of the scale some established geographical differences reassert themselves. For example, Havering and Bromley (both 5.3 per cent) and Harrow (5.2 per cent) are ranked 213, 216 and 217 out of the 278 areas, while Bexley (4.6 per cent) is the lowest-placed London borough on this indicator, being ranked 249. Of the lowest-scoring 20 areas based on the SARs and this criterion of multiple deprivation, 11 are from the SE of England with the rest generally being prosperous rural localities (and all of these have 4.3 per cent or less of their population experiencing multiple deprivation).

THE HOUSING MARKET: HOMELESSNESS AND MORTGAGE INDEBTEDNESS

HOMELESSNESS

Given the symbolic importance attached by the Conservatives to owner-occupation, the growth in homelessness during the 1980s and 1990s is a particularly damning indictment of the economic situation, and of the failures of the government's housing policies. The numbers accepted for permanent rehousing by local authorities, under the homelessness provisions of the various Housing Acts, has doubled in London from 16,400 in 1979 to 32,950 in 1993 (though peaking in 1992 at 37,840).[22] In seven London boroughs, the homelessness rate in 1991 was the equivalent of over 2 per cent of all households in the borough, rising to 2.9 per cent in Haringey and Islington.[23] London accounts for around a quarter of all households accepted for rehousing under the Housing Acts. Figures for the SE (excluding London) show that in 1992 and 1993 some 38,500 households were accepted as homeless.[24]

These official figures almost certainly underestimate the problems of homelessness, partly because homeless single people and childless couples are not usually provided with accommodation under the Housing Acts. In 1992 it was estimated that there were 39,500 single homeless people in London,[25] and the visible growth of people sleeping on the streets symbolises the difficulty that many individuals have in gaining access to anything other than hostel or short-life accommodation. The periodic moral panics about begging indicate the extent to which victim-blaming is part of official ideology, and the attempts to reduce the visibility of this issue (for example, the 'rough sleepers' initiatives or the closure of public spaces such as Lincoln's Inn Fields) indicate the government's sensitivity to an issue that exposes the negative consequences arising from both a lack of investment in housing and the punitive changes in benefit regulations. The problem has been most visible in central London, where there are at least some support services for the homeless; the experience of being homeless elsewhere in the region, especially in the outer Metropolitan area, is likely to be a much harsher one.

Some 43,000 households in London are living in inadequate temporary accommodation. There are some 20,000 children in short-term accommodation, which adversely affects their health and education as well as their family relationships. The cost of such temporary accommodation, fast approaching £500 million in London, will soon equate to an additional £90 for every council tax bill.[26] In addition, some 42,600 children in London (3.15 per cent of the city's children) live in households including two or more families: in other words, they are living among the 'hidden homeless'.[27] For those living in permanent accommodation the position is not always much better. For example, the Association of London Authorities estimated that approximately 245,000 children in London occupy overcrowded housing (at a density of over one person per room), of which 64,000 were at a density of 1.5 persons per room (severely overcrowded). In addition, 100,000 children in London live in non-self-contained accommodation, while 150,000 children in London live in homes without central heating.[28]

OWNER OCCUPATION: REPOSSESSIONS AND NEGATIVE EQUITY

Owner-occupation has been promoted vigorously by the Conservatives, notably through the 'right-to-buy' legislation, but also through the continuation of tax relief on mortgage interest payments. In the SE, the economic boom fuelled by both tax cuts and the deregulation of financial services led to spiralling house prices, a phenomenon given a further twist by the decision to end dual tax relief in the 1988 Budget. The uneven regional impact of this form of subsidy is not widely publicised. Even in the 1992-93 financial year, the cost of mortgage tax relief was estimated at £5.2 billion, of which £2.13 billion was available to households in London and the SE. The total peaked at £7.7 billion in 1990-91, of which over £3 billion was for households in London and the SE. These figures should be set against the size of public expenditure programmes on new housing, for example, or on policies designed to promote more balanced regional development. In so doing it quickly becomes apparent how much the SE is actually a subsidised region in relation to housing.[30]

The promotion of owner-occupation produced high – and ultimately unsustainable – house prices. However, the policies adopted nationally to contain borrowing and to prevent import penetration through imports of consumer goods, particularly the successive increases in interest rates from 1988 onwards, made it extremely difficult for many households to sustain high levels of repayments. As a result many households fell into arrears, saw their properties repossessed, or at best suffered from high levels of negative equity.

NEGATIVE EQUITY

A survey by the Council of Mortgage Lenders in April 1993 suggested that nationally some 300,000 households perceived them-

selves as being in a situation of severe negative equity, indicating
that they thought that their home was worth a lot less than their
mortgage. Of these, 155,000 (52 per cent) were located in the SE,
and 41,400 (14 per cent) were located in Greater London. Bank of
England figures suggest that the number of people suffering from
negative equity peaked at 1.8 million in the first quarter of 1993,
though, and then dropped to 1.2 million by the third quarter. If the
distribution by region of those actually suffering from negative
equity is indeed the same as those who perceived themselves as
suffering from severe negative equity, this would suggest that some
624,000 households in the SE, and a further 168,000 households in
Greater London, are in this position.[31] National estimates suggest
that negative equity totalled some £7.3 billion in 1993, and if this
figure was distributed proportionately to the number of households
experiencing severe negative equity, then households in the SE
(outside London) are in debt to the tune of some £3.8 billion while
within London this form of indebtedness would be approximately
£1 billion. This suggests an average debt of £6,000 for each
household suffering from negative equity, although in some sections
of the market (for instance in flats in some parts of London)
property prices have collapsed because first-time buyers are now
able to purchase houses rather than flats, leaving some flat-owners
effectively trapped.

HOUSE REPOSSESSIONS

Many households have found the repayments on their mortgages
beyond their means, and a consequence has been a rapid rise in
mortgage repossessions, although these have reduced since 1991
due to a combination of falling interest rates and more sympathetic
management on the part of building societies. Nevertheless, during
1991 there were still 62,900 repossession orders made in the SE:
35,784 in the SE outside Greater London, which alone accounted
for 27,154. In 1992 and 1993 a further 55,000 and 45,000 repossession orders were made in the SE and London, and figures for
the first quarter of 1994 indicate a continued fall to around 30,000
in the annual total.[32] Repossession can lead directly to homelessness, and it may be significant that in the non-metropolitan areas of
England mortgage arrears are the primary cause of up to 13 per
cent of cases of homelessness (the average for England as a whole is
8 per cent). It is likely that the proportion of cases of homelessness

due to repossession is higher in the SE than in most non-metropolitan districts, due to the generally higher rate of default and repossession in this region. In the period from January 1992 to end-March 1994, and using these percentages, it can be estimated that around 10,000 households in the SE and Greater London were made homeless because of mortgage arrears.[33] It is perhaps the ultimate irony that this has occurred because people were vigorously encouraged to become owner-occupiers in the first place, but those made homeless in this way were probably among the last to climb aboard the bandwagon (attracting high repayments relative to their incomes) and were then the first to fall off as repayments became unsustainable. For these unfortunate households, buying into the Conservative dream has meant the loss of that key icon of Conservatism – one's own home.

It is arguable that high levels of owner-occupation such as those common in the SE – up to 89 per cent in the Castle Point District of Essex, and over 80 per cent in some 30 other districts – are unsustainable in the context of current changes in the labour market which indicate a much greater reliance on part-time work. The financial commitment required to pay off a mortgage on the scale of those being offered in the late-1980s requires a degree of occupational stability which is becoming less and less common.[34] Furthermore, the difficulties that many households are experiencing in selling properties (because of negative equity) inhibits labour mobility, and may therefore be a drag on economic recovery as workers find themselves unable to relocate to areas where new sources of employment are available. Therefore, future housing policies surely need to offer a greater range of choice than was the case during the 1980s, when for many people owner-occupation seemed the only desirable option.

Moreover, at least some of the current problems experienced in the housing market are a direct result of the privatisation of council housing stock, the refusal to permit local authorities to reinvest the proceeds of disposals, and the decline in construction of housing for rent. Between 1979 and 1992, 402,000 council properties were sold in the SE and Greater London. This was a much higher proportion than elsewhere (in the SE outside of London 38 per cent of the council stock was sold) and it reduced the ability of councils to respond to housing needs.[35] Over the same period, 182,000 starts were made on new housing for rent (by local authorities and, increasingly, by housing associations). However, housing starts in London dropped below 3,000 between 1985 and 1990, and for the

region as a whole they dropped below 10,000 between 1987 and
1990. In both cases, new starts have been running at approximately
half of their 1979 levels.[36] The lack of availability of rented accommodation could potentially weaken London's competitive economic
position, given that its high levels of employment in services and
government includes large numbers of relatively low-paid staff who
work long and often unsocial hours. Proximity to their workplace is
essential to these staff, and the minimal new construction for rent in
central London thus severely limits the housing options available to
them. Indeed, due to the financial regime imposed on housing
associations, many developments that these organisations can pursue
of necessity involve cheap sites on the fringe of London, not sites in
the centre where they are most needed.[37]

CONCLUDING COMMENTS

The concentration of unemployment, poverty and deprivation in
inner London is hardly new (see also Chapter 4), but the problem
needs constant restatement because of the sheer numbers affected,
since the numbers unemployed in London are greater than in any
other region of the UK. This chapter has attempted to show not
only that genuine and concentrated problems of poverty exist
within the SE, but that there is also evidence of growing hardship
which on some indicators, even in some SE localities *outside* of
London, now exceeds that in parts of the UK usually thought of as
disadvantaged in comparison to the SE. As well as stressing the
concentrated poverty and disadvantage within London, the chapter
has hence sought to highlight the impacts of recent economic
change on the rest of the SE, and to point towards the challenges
which will face the region in the future. Economic difficulties are
now even affecting the affluent heartlands of the SE, and they are
therefore hitting many people who initially bought into the
Thatcherite dream. Changes in the organisation of work (notably
greater flexibility in the labour market alongside increased casuali-
sation and use of fixed-term contracts) now impact upon middle-
class occupations which formerly offered stable jobs for life, and
which – in conjunction with owner-occupation – had once seemed
to promise guaranteed prosperity.[38] Small wonder that, as Will
Hutton puts it, there is 'angst in Acacia Avenue' as economic
insecurity spreads to the suburbs and even to the shires.[39]

The SE and its adjacent areas do remain the most prosperous part of the UK, even so, but it is worth remembering the extent to which prosperity here has been subsidised by various government policies – mainly through taxation and government expenditure programmes – and that it is this subsidy which has enabled the region to sustain high levels of consumption. However, recession has weakened the economy of the region, and has exposed the extent to which the apparently favourable economic circumstances of the late-1980s were temporary and indeed fragile. There are growing problems of unemployment, low incomes and poverty. The rapid growth in, for example, free school meals take-up and benefit payments indicate the difficulties that some households are facing, and the rise in inquiries to CABx demonstrates the growing problems of indebtedness. If house repossessions are perhaps the most dramatic indicator of this, the longer-term consequences of negative equity may be more serious still because this inhibits labour mobility, and may mean that future expenditure for many households will be directed into repayment of excess debts rather than into savings and investment. The outcome could comprise a serious drag on the regional economy. Problems of unemployment have also hit the region with a vengeance, and the fact that regional unemployment rates have demonstrated some measure of convergence indicates not so much the economic success of the peripheral regions but the rapid rise in unemployment within the SE.

The wider political consequences of this situation remain to be played out. Three sets of comments seem appropriate. The first is that the difficulties now being experienced in the SE must be interpreted as a failure of Thatcherism. The Thatcherite project relied on deregulation and on letting market forces operate freely, but it was subsequently unable to deal with either the costs of market failures or the externalities of rapid economic growth. As a result, large numbers of individuals now bear the costs of that failed deregulatory experiment. Secondly, the 1994 local election results seem to indicate that the support of localities once regarded as Conservative heartlands can no longer be taken for granted by the government. Thirdly and possibly more worrying, though, are the effects that the polarisation within the region – especially between the dispossessed of inner London and those in secure, full-time employment – may have in the long term. The potential social conflict to which this might lead is already being foreshadowed, especially within London, by increases in racial attacks, by a greater incidence of drug-related crime, and by growing public fear of crime (although this is not confined to the SE: see also Chapter 1). It would, of course, be oversimplistic to read off such incidents from economic changes. However, these developments do suggest that the nation is becoming *less* at ease with itself rather than more (to adopt the Prime Minister's phraseology). The fact that at least some Conservatives recognise the need for commitment to full employment is ample proof of the effect of economic decline on the Conservative electoral heartlands.

NOTES

1. R Martin, 'Deindustrialisation and state intervention: Keynesianism, Thatcherism and the regions', in J Mohan (ed), *The Political Geography of Contemporary Britain* (Macmillan, 1989), pp87–112.

2. A Gamble, *The Free Economy and the Strong State: the politics of Thatcherism* (Macmillan, 1994); B Jessop *et al*, *Thatcherism: a tale of two nations* (Polity, 1989).

3. R Hudson, 'Rewriting history and reshaping geography: the nationalised industries and the political economy of Thatcherism', in Mohan, *The Political Geography*, see note 1, pp113–29; J Mohan, 'Public expenditure, public employment and the regions', in R Martin and P Townroe (eds), *Regional Development in the 1990s: the British Isles in transition* (Jessica Kingsley, 1992), pp222–7.

4. J Peck and J Shutt, 'What kind of recovery in the South East?' (CLES European Research Network, Rethinking Urban Policy Bulletin 1, 1993).

5. *Employment Gazette*, June 1994. 'Travel-to-work areas' are the basic building blocks of the statistics used by the Department of Eployment, and there are around 280 of them, corresponding to local labour market areas.

6. I am grateful to Dave Taylor, Local Economic Policy Unit, South Bank University, for providing these statistics.

7. The source here is the 1991 Census.

8. Association of London Authorities (ALA), press release 93/182 ('One in five London children will spend Christmas in poverty').

9. The source of these statistics is the Low Pay Unit. The data refer to April 1993 and rates are at 1993 prices.

10. The source here is Alan Milburn MP (in turn House of Commons library and House of Commons, *Hansard*, 12 January 1994 and 27 February 1994).

11. Peck and Shutt, 'What kind of recovery?' (see note 4).

12. ALA, Press release 94/5 ('One London child in three poor enough to

receive free meals'). These figures admittedly refer only to state schools, and because of the numbers of children educated privately this will represent an overestimate of the proportion of children living in poverty.

13. Statistics provided by the Department for Education.

14. Although the regions used for statistical purposes by the DSS cut across the boundaries of the UK's Standard Regions in several respects, broadly speaking the South-East and East Anglian standard regions correspond to the London North and London South regions used by the DSS.

15. *Hansard*, Written Answers, 21 April 1993, vol 223, cols 137-8; 18 October 1993, col 165; 2 November 1993, col 193.

16. National figures provided by NACAB *Annual Reports*, various dates, available from NACAB, 115 Pentonville Road, London N1 9LB.

17. Figures for trends per bureau in the South-East provided by David Martin, Area Development Officer, NACAB South East Area. Note that one part of the rise in enquiries may be the impact of the poll tax in terms of causing a rise in legal claims for debt, which might predispose households to seek bureaux advice.

18. These figures refer to the 1992-93 year and are drawn from the NACAB's *Annual Report*. The difficulty with analysing change over time is the reorganisation of the regional structure of the service from 22 to 19 regions in 1991-92, and also various reallocations of bureaux from one region to another, which mean that comparable statistics are not readily available from this source.

19. NACAB *Annual Reports*, various dates.

20. I am grateful to Ed Fieldhouse of Manchester University's Census Micro-data Unit for permission to quote the following statistics. See E Fieldhouse and R Tye, 'Deprived places or deprived people? explaining the ecological fallacy in studies of deprivation using the Sample of Anonymised Records (SARs)', forthcoming in *Environment and Planning A*, Vol 27 (1995).

21. The eight indicators were: not owning a car; not in paid employment; living in rented accommodation; lacking central heating; lacking a bath; lacking an inside WC; living in accommodation which is not self-contained; living at a density of more than one person per room; and being unemployed. The SARs for individuals are a 2 per cent sample of the Census, and where the population of a local government district is small it necessitates linking adjacent districts together for purposes of confidentiality. This means that there are 278 areas for which data are available, whereas there are some 459 local government districts in England, Wales and Scotland. Note that in Chapter 1 some scepticism is expressed about the use of statistical indicators which imply certain places in the South (such as Brighton) to be more deprived than certain places in the North (such as Tyneside). See also the analysis of different indices of deprivation as applied to urban areas given in Chapter 4.

22. Department of the Environment (DoE), *Households found Accommodation*

under the Provisions of the 1985 Housing Act, quarterly statistics. Note that because households which are deemed to have made themselves intentionally homeless were excluded from entitlement to rehousing in 1991, these statistics (which are a consistent series to reflect that legislative change) underestimate the extent of homelessness.

23. London Research Centre, *London Housing Statistics 1991*, Table 4.2. The boroughs included were Camden, Hackney, Hammersmith and Fulham, Haringey, Islington, Lambeth and Southwark.

24. DoE, *Households* (see note 22).

25. Communities and Houses in Central London (CHiCL), *Losing Heart: the impact of government policy on housing association development in central London* (CHiCL, 1992), p10.

26. SHAC/London Housing Unit, *Your Place or Mine? A report on homelessness* (SHAC, 1993), pp3-4; and on the costs of temporary accommodation, see CHiCL, *Losing Heart* (see note 25).

27. D Dorling, 'Children and housing in Britain' (unpublished mimeo, Department of Geography, University of Newcastle upon Tyne, 1993).

28. ALA, press release 93/182 (see note 8).

29. *Hansard*, Written Answers, 17 June 1992, vol 209, cols 537-8.

30. For example, expenditure on various forms of regional and urban policy assistance by the UK Government is currently some £400 million and falling; it is dwarfed in comparison with the hidden subsidies through mortgage relief, or through other public expenditure programmes such as defence procurement, which overwhelmingly benefit the SE: see R Martin, 'Remapping British regional policy: the end of the North-South divide?', *Regional Studies*, Vol 27 (1993), pp797-806; Mohan, 'Public expenditure' (see note 3).

31. *Housing Finance*, February 1994, Table 7 and p18.

32. The source of these repossession statistics is the Lord Chancellor's Department. Note that repossession orders do not equate with the number of properties actually repossessed because, while orders may be made, this does not mean that the property was eventually repossessed.

33. Calculated from DoE, *Households* (see note 22).

34. I am grateful to Peter Williams, Council of Mortgage Lenders, for this observation.

35. *Regional Trends*, 1994, Table 6.11.

36. DoE, *Housing and Construction Statistics*, 1979-89 and 1982-92.

37. CHiCL, *Losing Heart* (see note 25).

38. It is interesting to compare the assessment given here with that contained in a text which reflects upon the key (and then successful) role of the SE as *the* middle-class region of the UK, as the crucial location where people have been 'getting their feet on the ladder' of middle-class wealth and well-being (even if they subsequently move elsewhere): see M Savage *et al, Property, Bureaucracy and Culture: middle-class formation in contemporary*

Britain (Routledge, 1992) esp Chapter 8.

39. W Hutton, writing in *The Guardian*, 2 August 1994.

9 Geographical perspectives on poverty, health and health policy in different parts of the UK
Sarah Curtis

INTRODUCTION

This chapter considers how health and poverty are related in different areas of Britain, and also the relevance of these relationships for health policy. Space does not allow a comprehensive treatment of these topics here, so examples have been selected as illustrations. The discussion starts with a consideration of some of the evidence concerning the geography of health differences, and then discusses these in the context of some recent health policy developments.

HEALTH DIFFERENCES AND POVERTY

There is a good deal of evidence that, on average, health is worse for those living in poverty than for wealthier groups in Britain, and this has several implications in terms of health care policies. Firstly, the existence of these health inequalities demonstrates the continuing need for measures to improve health outcomes for the poorest members of society, especially measures which are directed at health promotion and illness prevention. The 'new public health movement' has also emphasised the fact that these measures will require a co-ordinated response from a number of sectors of the British political economy, since health services alone cannot act effectively on all of the processes leading to health differences.[1] A further implication is that, on average, poor people need to consume relatively more curative health care than do more privileged groups because of their higher levels of illness, and that it may therefore be necessary to target additional health care resources towards them.

Health differences have been demonstrated between social groups defined in terms of various dimensions of social position, and they can also be seen clearly in studies which compare populations of different geographical areas. This evidence is the subject of a very extensive research literature which cannot be reported in detail here. Some of the most widely publicised reviews of the findings include the report of a working group chaired by Sir Douglas Black published in 1980 (widely referred to as the 'Black Report') and in Whitehead's update to this review in 1987, demonstrating continuing evidence for health inequalities during the 1980s. These reports were later published together.[2]

Since we have more comprehensive statistical data on death than on health during life, much of the evidence in these studies concerns differences in mortality. Various dimensions of socio-economic position show an association with mortality, and the less privileged groups generally show higher overall mortality levels. These associations must be viewed as patterns which apply across groups of people, and not necessarily to all individuals within a group (or in a locality). Analysis of the longitudinal study by Goldblatt and others[3] has produced data such as that shown in Table 9.1, which presents 'standardised mortality ratios' for males aged 15-64 at death.[4] Data from this survey have been used to show that there are differences in death rates between occupational social class groups in the population, with those in unskilled manual work having poorer health than those in professional jobs. (Unemployed people also show higher levels of mortality than those in employment.) Mortality is also associated with other indicators of socio-economic position and wealth, such as housing status, level of education and car ownership. Those in local authority rented housing have worse mortality rates than owner-occupiers. Those with no educational qualifications have worse mortality rates than those with higher education. Those living in households without cars typically have higher mortality than those with access to a car. Multivariate statistical analysis also shows that these factors have independent associations with health, so that the health differences noted here probably reflect complex links between disadvantage and ill-health, rather than simple direct causal relationships.[5] Direct information on income in relation to health is not systematically available in Britain, but as poverty is linked to disadvantages in terms of employment, housing and education, the associations summarised above and in Table 9.1 all point to the health disadvantages of those living in poverty.

TABLE 9.1: **Mortality differences in relation to various indicators of socio-economic position, using 'standardised mortality ratios' (SMRs) for males aged 15-64 in the period 1971-81**
(Endnote 4 explains how SMRs are calculated)

Indicator of social position	SMR
social class	
I	67
II	77
IIINM	105
IIIM	96
IV	125
V	189
housing tenure	
owner-occupied	85
privately rented	108
local authority rented	117
car ownership	
2 or more cars	77
1 car	90
none	122
educational qualifications	
degree	51
higher qualification	75
A-level	87
none	104

Source: Derived from P Goldblatt, *Longitudinal Study: mortality and social organisation, 1971-1981, England and Wales, Series LS8* (OPCS, HMSO, 1990).

Most studies of inequalities in health have used standardised mortality indicators which control for variation in the age structure of the groups concerned. Studies within age groups show that the most striking and persistent differences in death rates concern premature adult mortality between 45 years and retirement age.[6] However, socio-economic differentials in mortality are also evident for children as well as for older people. Table 9.2 shows information on infant mortality and mortality among children, which also demonstrate social class differences.[7] In addition to information on mortality, there are some data relating to differences in levels of health and illness in the population. Morbidity information is much more limited in scope than data on death rates.[8] Nevertheless, sources such as the *National Survey of Morbidity in General Practice*[9] and morbidity registers for diseases such cancer[10] can be used to demonstrate variations in morbidity. Research using the survey of morbidity in general practice has shown, for instance, that patients in professional and managerial classes consult their doctor less frequently for conditions which doctors rate as 'serious' than do those in manual semi- or unskilled jobs.

TABLE 9.2: **Male infant and child mortality rates according to social class of parents for years 1979-81 and 1982-83**

Class	Infant mortality per 100,000 live births	Deaths per 100,000 children aged 1-15
I	867	24.24
II	964	24.08
IIN	1,008	26.30
IIM	1,153	32.45
IV	1,510	38.33
V	1,814	56.76

Source: OPCS, *Occupational Mortality: childhood supplement, 1979-1980, 1982-1983, England and Wales*, Series DS8 (OPCS, HMS), 1988).

Self-reported illness has also been recorded since 1972 in the *General Household Survey* (GHS), a national sample of British households. Social class differences in long-standing illness, with less-privileged social classes being more likely to report illness, have been a consistent feature of the annual results from this question of the GHS (see Table 9.3).[11] Information on self-reported illness differs from information on medically diagnosed illness, since it depends significantly on the individual's perception of their own state of health. However, when responses are considered in the aggregate, there is an association between self-reported illness and medically diagnosed illness and health service use, and self-reported illness is still considered to be useful data for health planning purposes. A more comprehensive source of information on health and morbidity which is independent of health service use is the *Health and Lifestyle Survey* which collects information from national samples of the population and demonstrates social group differences in variables such as body mass index, lung function and psycho-social health, as well as asking questions on the respondent's perception of their own health.[12] Figure 9.3 (see further on) shows examples of social group differences in health reported in this survey. Males in the 40-59 age group in manual occupations were more likely to report illness than those in non-manual occupations.

TABLE 9.3: **Prevalence of reported 'limiting' long-standing illness, 1991, showing percentage of people reporting illness by sex and social class**

Social class	Men	Women
professional	12	12
employer/manager	13	14
intermediate/junior non-man	15	17
skilled manual	19	18
semi-skilled manual	20	24
unskilled manual	21	26

Source: OPCS, *General Household Survey, 1991* (OPCS, HMSO, 1993).

Socio-economic position is not the only characteristic which is associated with health differences. Variations in morbidity and mortality are associated with other aspects of social position such as gender[13] and with ethnicity.[14] Most importantly for the discussion here, though, there are also important geographical differences.

GEOGRAPHICAL DIMENSIONS OF HEALTH DIFFERENCE

Of particular interest in this discussion is evidence that mortality differences are associated with the type of area in which people live. These geographical differences can be observed in comparisons of different regions of the country, and are broadly summarised in terms of a North-South divide with Scotland, Wales and North-West England showing worse average mortality than South-East England (see also Chapter 2).[15] In addition, there seems to be an association with levels of urbanisation, since inner-city areas show higher mortality and morbidity levels on average than suburban and rural areas (see also Chapters 4 and 5). At the more local scale, small areas show differences in mortality which are strongly associated with the socio-economic profiles of their resident populations. Areas with higher levels of socio-economic deprivation typically show higher levels of mortality. For example, analysis of the Cancer Registry Statistics in South-East England has also shown that people living in deprived neighbourhoods who suffer from cancer of the lung, of the breast or of the prostrate have poorer five-year survival rates than do those from affluent neighbourhoods who suffer from the same diseases.[16]

Similarly, there are geographical differences in morbidity statistics of the type mentioned above. In 1991 the Population Census included information on self-reported long-term illness for the first time, so that there is now a new source of information collected right across the country which offers considerable scope for analysis of socio-geographical variations in this aspect of population health. Figure 9.1, for example, shows the pattern of long-term illness reported in the Census for District Health Authorities in London (standardised for demographic variation). It illustrates how areas with higher proportions of unskilled manual workers tend to be areas with larger proportions of people reporting illness. There are also regional variations in health reported in the *Health and Lifestyle Survey*.[17] These regional differences in mortality and morbidity can be only partly explained by the geographical distribution of socio-economic groups, however, and it seems likely that the geography of health and illness results from the combined effects of a range of socio-economic and environmental factors. Furthermore, the general patterns described above do not apply equally for all causes of illness and death. Different diseases each have their own distinctive epidemiological characteristics, and the relevant risk factors vary from one disease to another.[18]

Especially interesting for the discussion here is the fact that the relationship between health and social variables seems to be manifested differently in different geographic settings. Figure 9.2 shows regional mortality differences cited by Jacobsen *et al*,[19] demonstrating how male social class differentials in mortality differ according to region of residence, there being more pronounced differences in Scotland and the North of England than in the South-West and East Anglia. In addition, the mortality rate for a particular social class varies from one region to another: compare, for example, the mortality rate for professionals in Scotland with the lower rate for

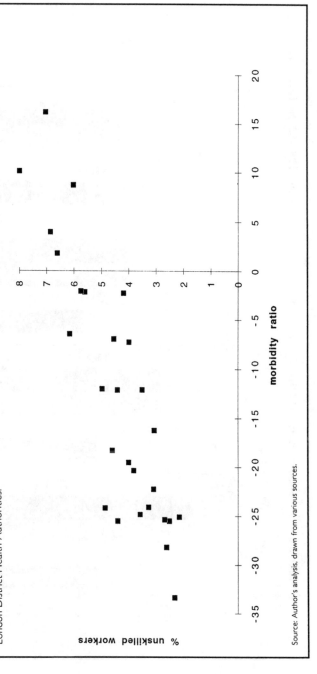

Figure 9.1: **Standardised rates of reported long-term illness from 1991 Census and proportion of unskilled workers: data for London District Health Authorities**

Data is presented in terms of 'morbidity ratios', standardised for demographic variation, with a ratio of 0 equating to the average rate for all London District Health Authorities.

Source: Author's analysis, drawn from various sources.

Figure 9.2: **'Standardised mortality ratios' (SMRs) for men aged 20-64, 1979-80 and 1982-83, by region and social class**

Endnote 4 explains how SMRs are calculated.

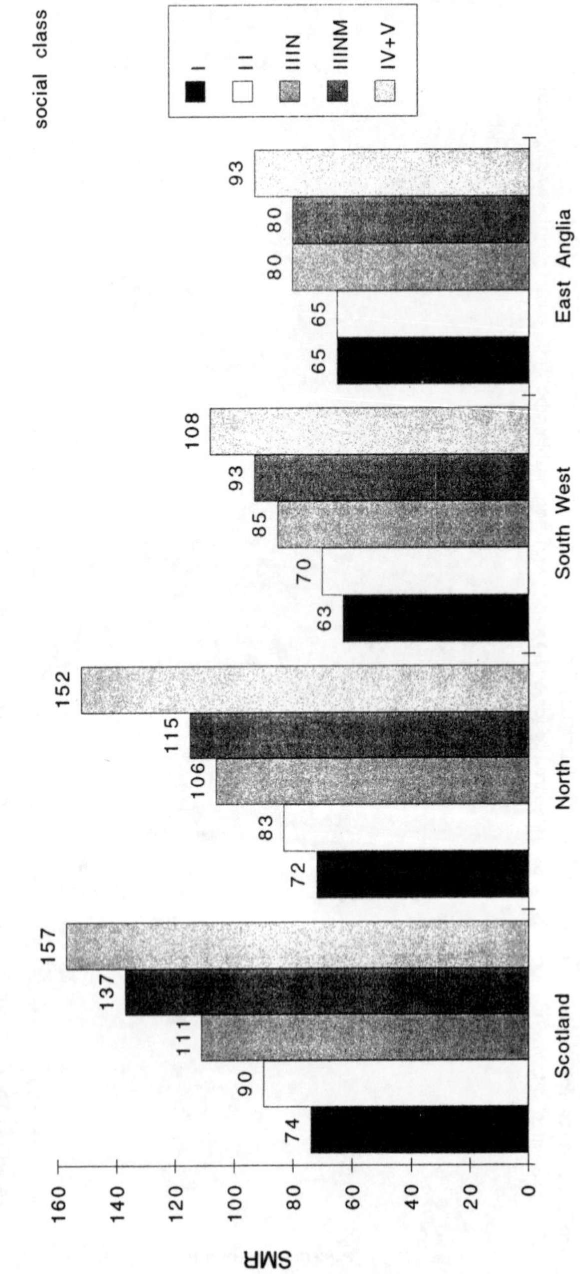

Source: B Jacobsen, A Smith and M Whitehead, *The Nation's Health: a strategy for the 1990s (Second Edition)* (King Edward's Hospital Fund for London, 1988).

the same group in East Anglia. Fox and Goldblatt have also found differences in the social class gradients in mortality between 'families' of areas classified using Census data on demographic and socio-economic characteristics,[20] while social class differentials in morbidity appear to vary according to the area of residence of respondents to the *Health and Lifestyle Survey*. Not only is there a regional effect on social gradients in health, but there is seemingly also an effect associated with the type of area, as illustrated in Figure 9.3. Manual workers have worse health than non-manual workers in each type of area, but the situation for each social group varies between high status residential areas, rural resort towns, cities and traditional manufacturing/industrial areas. Figure 9.3 shows that non-manual workers living in cities have a greater propensity to report illness than manual workers in rural or resort areas.

Eames and colleagues have demonstrated differences in the small area association between mortality and deprivation between different regional health authorities,[21] and Phillimore has shown that the geographical association between mortality and area deprivation indicators is different in urban areas as compared to rural areas. Furthermore, his study of two apparently similar urban areas in the North-East of England showed that the strength of the local geo-graphical association between area social conditions and health was quite different. He thus suggests that conditions specific to parti-cular areas can indeed have significant effects on social health inequalities.[22] Analysis using multi-level modelling techniques, which provide a more powerful statistical test of individual and area effects in health differences, suggest that while much of the geographical variation in health is due to the *composition* of the population (especially varying spatial concentrations of people living in poverty), there are also effects due to *context* (where type of area seems to influence the association between individual deprivation and health status).[23]

These examples from the literature on health inequalities demon-strate that disadvantaged (and poor) groups in British society have consistently worse health on a number of different indicators. Also, they reveal that differences in the health experience between rich and poor people depend to some extent upon the particular area where they live. The next section considers why this finding is important for health policy.

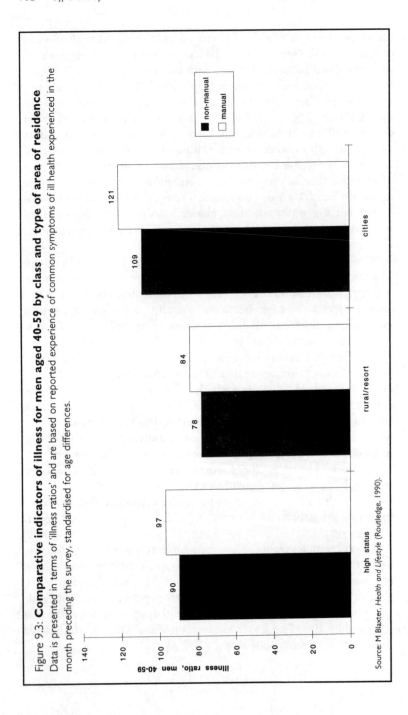

Figure 9.3: **Comparative indicators of illness for men aged 40-59 by class and type of area of residence**
Data is presented in terms of 'illness ratios' and are based on reported experience of common symptoms of ill health experienced in the month preceding the survey, standardised for age differences.

Source: M Blaxter, *Health and Lifestyle* (Routledge, 1990).

HEALTH INEQUALITIES AND HEALTH POLICY

The socio-geographic dimensions of health difference have several implications for health policy. Firstly, some (although not all) of the differences in health are likely to be associated with variations in the outcome of the health service, and this may reflect differences in the level of health provision or variation in the effectiveness of healthcare per unit of resource. Authors such as Charlton have attempted to assess the geographical variation in 'avoidable mortality' which is that proportion of deaths which are considered to be preventable by adequate provision of good quality healthcare.[24] Although their methodology has been questioned,[25] it has attracted a good deal of attention because, if the health service *is* achieving worse outcomes in some areas than in others, this must be a cause for concern for a National Health Service (NHS) which was founded on principles of equity in access to health care in relation to need. It is also clear that, since there are social and geographical differences in health, there will be corresponding differences in need for health care at the regional and local level. These differences in need will relate to both the amount of health resources required and also to the ways in which it is appropriate to deliver healthcare. Thus, health resource allocation must be informed by geographical indicators of mortality, morbidity and socio-economic conditions.

However, there may be problems in trying to apply standard indicators of population health need in a systematic way across the whole UK. The discussion above has shown that the relationship between social factors and health varies geographically, so that the health need implications suggested by any one 'deprivation' indicator may have to be interpreted differently from place to place. Furthermore, because the health status of the population varies in the ways described above, targets for health improvement should take account of local conditions. It may hence not be appropriate or feasible to try to realise national targets for health and healthcare improvement at the local level in areas where the health status of the population is very different from the national average.

These issues will now be considered in the course of discussing two examples of recent developments in national health and health service policy. There have, of course, been many recent policy developments in the healthcare sector in Britain, and one of the major challenges for the NHS in recent years has simply been the difficulty of keeping pace with the rapid organisational changes being forced upon it. The following discussion focuses particularly on two selected policy issues which are central here: the question of resource allocation is considered first, and then attention turns to the introduction of an 'internal market' for state healthcare as coupled with the expansion of independent healthcare.

CHANGES IN RESOURCE ALLOCATION

The system of resource allocation in the NHS has important implications for the availability of funds for provision of NHS care to poor populations in different parts of the country. Since the report of the Resource Working Allocation Party in 1975,[26] there has been an attempt by the Department of Health to make its allocation of resources to the Regional Health Authorities (RHAs) responsive to regional differences in population need for health care. Between 1975 and 1989 the formula used for regional resource allocation in England included statistics on regional mortality rates in an attempt to shift resources towards areas where population health was worse. To some extent this objective was achieved, since regional budgets did grow more rapidly in regions outside of the South-East. However, as the changes were implemented during a period of overall restraint on expenditure, the redistribution of resources resulted in relatively severe resource limitations in regions deemed to be spending above target. Throughout this period the RHAs in the South and East of England (where average mortality rates were relatively favourable and relative resource reductions were most strongly felt) argued that the formula was an inadequate reflection of the healthcare needs of their population, since it did not take account of the effects leading from high levels of poverty and deprivation in London's inner city.[27] To the extent that these complaints were justified, it may be argued that poor people in the South-East lost out in terms of health care resourcing compared with disadvantaged populations in the North-West.[28]

In 1989 the regional funding formula was revised and the contribution of mortality information was reduced.[29] Critics of the new scheme argue that, once again, information on social deprivation has been left out of the equation and that the new formula does not make sufficient allowance for geographical differences in health. Moreover, some commentators have suggested that the changes in the system of regional resource allocation have now enabled government to enhance resources for regions in the South and East of the country, where the largest proportions of Conservative voters (and of wealthier people) are concentrated.[30] A further failing of the new resource allocation formula is the fact that it still only partially compensates RHAs for the additional costs resulting from sparsity in rural areas.[31] This may mean that deprived rural populations are relatively disadvantaged in health terms compared with those in urban areas (see also Chapter 5). The results of the most recent review of the regional resource allocation formula for the NHS[32] proposes inclusion of information on both self-reported illness and social conditions, which would go some way towards meeting the criticisms of the existing method.

Although RHA budgets are determined without reference to the distribution of poor populations, there have been changes in the remuneration of general practitioners which aim to improve local funding of family doctor services for disadvantaged populations. The case for these changes was set out in the Government's policy document 'working for patients', which brought in a number of changes in general practitioners' contracts. In particular, additional 'deprivation' payments could be made to practices which draw patients from electoral wards identified as 'deprived' according to an indicator developed by Professor Jarman and colleagues.[33] This indicator is not simply a measure of social deprivation: it combines information on a number of population characteristics which doctors have recognised to be likely to increase their workloads. The Census indicators for small areas which go to make up the Jarman indicator are shown in Table 9.4. Wards scoring above a particular threshold value on this indicator are defined as 'deprived' for the purposes of calculating deprived area payments, and the thinking behind this measure is certainly well intentioned as a way to enable doctors to cope more effectively with the needs of disadvantaged populations.

A number of criticisms have been directed at the scheme as it has been implemented, though, and these are clearly set out by Senior.[34] Firstly, patients suffering socio-economic deprivation will only be likely to benefit if their doctor is drawing a large number of patients from 'deprived' wards, and disadvantaged patients living in otherwise affluent areas will not attract any additional resources. Secondly, electoral wards with quite high levels of social deprivation but which fall just below the threshold will not qualify, which seems an arbitrary distinction to make with little correspondence to population needs. Thirdly, and as noted above, the associations between small area indicators of deprivation and health differences have been

TABLE 9.4: **The components of the 'underprivileged areas score' proposed by Jarman**
Data from the Census is used to classify areas according to a score based on the characteristics as listed below of the resident population in an area.

elderly population living alone
children under 5 years
single parent households
unskilled/manual workers
unemployed people
overcrowding
recent movers
people from New Commonwealth/Pakistan

Source: B Jarman, 'Identification of underprivileged areas', *British Medical Journal*, Vol 286 (1983), pp1705-6.

shown to vary across the country, which means that the indicator may not reflect differences in need for the family doctor equally well in all districts. Fourthly, it has often been argued that the Jarman indicator emphasises inner-city deprivation of the type experienced particularly in London, but that it does not accurately reflect rural deprivation. Finally, the information used has been based on the 1981 Population Census, and as a consequence is now becoming significantly outdated. Therefore, the resource allocation process for general practices with respect to poor and disadvantaged populations is probably not operating in a very even-handed way across the country, principally because of a failure to take seriously the local geography of health and heath care needs.

This example, considering aspects of resource allocation, shows how area of residence will influence health care resourcing in the state sector. Methods for targeting health resources towards poor populations are here seen to be rather 'blunt instruments' which are not very responsive to the complexity of the geography of health inequalities. This is not to claim that it is inappropriate to target additional health service resources towards areas with relatively large populations living in poverty, but the evidence does suggest that the mechanisms currently in use to do this are not as well designed as they might be. Furthermore, there is no system to 'ring fence' these additional funds in some way, so as to reserve their use for poor populations in an area. Also, during a period of general restraint on health spending these additional funds are likely to be used to retain existing service levels, not to *improve* services for local poor people.

ENCOURAGING MARKET COMPETITION IN HEALTHCARE

The previous section was concerned with the ways in which central government allocates resources for health, and this section now illustrates the ways in which certain mechanisms operating at the level of the District Health Authority (DHA) can influence how these resources are spent in local areas. Although it is impossible to do justice to the topic in this short piece, it does seem appropriate to mention here the impact of the health policies which have recently led to the introduction of market forces into the NHS.

One of the major changes to the NHS introduced in 1991 was the separation of the 'purchasing' function of the NHS (which uses public money to commission healthcare for the population) from the 'provision' function (the delivery of healthcare). The NHS reforms have also made it possible for providers such as hospitals and community health services to opt out from the managerial control of the local DHA, and in so doing to become semi-autonomous 'healthcare trusts'. Providers within the NHS are now in competition with the independent sector to supply state-funded healthcare in the new 'internal market'. By introducing purchasing powers for certain 'fund-holding' general practices, the NHS reforms have also created conditions for competition between purchasers.

Supporters of the 'internal market' argue that the pressures of market competition will force providers to be more responsive to patient needs, and to offer more patient choice and better value for money in the state sector. This will supposedly benefit users by making healthcare more acceptable and effective, and by making public resources go further in terms of levels of provision. On the other hand, there is concern among critics of the 'internal market' that financial considerations may weigh more heavily with purchasers and providers than criteria of patient care. Geographers have pointed out that market forces tend to produce very uneven patterns of service provision from one place to the next, and the British independent health sector is a good example of where this kind of geographical unevenness has been produced. Private hospital development has been particularly concentrated in the South-East, notably in the outer London area, while in other parts of the country it remains more sparse.[35] This suggests that market forces lead to a distribution of healthcare which has more to do with profitability than with healthcare need in the population.

Clearly the success or failure of the internal market in the NHS will depend heavily on how effectively it is 'managed' by those with local responsibility for commissioning health services. The actions of local purchasers can have profound effects on the healthcare provision for disadvantaged populations in a local area. DHAs have a responsibility to assess the needs of their resident populations for healthcare, and to specify contracts accordingly. Fund-holding general practitioners have to do the same for their practice patients. Methods for local needs assessment are still being developed, however, and the priorities and ideologies of local healthcare managers are likely to vary considerably in terms of how and to what extent they consider the needs of people living in poverty. In some areas of the country their decision-making is hampered by a lack of good information about populations needing healthcare. For example, population data from the Census are thought to be particularly inaccurate in some inner-city areas, and the needs of groups such as the homeless and travellers (who form important categories of the poor population in some areas) are particularly difficult to assess. A further (and spatial) aspect of the arrangements for 'purchaser competition' is the fact that the development of fund-holding general practices, which are intended to 'compete' with DHAs in the commissioning of healthcare, is geographically uneven. For instance, in the North-East Thames RHA only 10.5 per cent of doctors are fund-holders, compared with 20.4 per cent in the South-West Thames RHA and over 30 per cent in the Mersey RHA.[36] Patients in areas with more general practitioner fund-holders will have the advantage of a wider effective choice of 'purchaser' than is available to patients in areas with few fund-holders.

For patients with private health cover, the expansion of the independent sector in Britain has provided an alternative source of care to which they resort if they find the care delivered by the NHS unacceptable. Statistics collected in the *General Household Survey* have shown that 1 per cent of people from the less-privileged unskilled manual social classes have independent health insurance, compared with 27 per cent of people from the more privileged professional classes.[37] This is not a surprising finding, and largely reflects the greater ability of wealthier people to afford health insurance premiums. In some cases, private health insurance is provided as a part of the remuneration package for employees (overall, about one-third of people with private insurance cover have the subscription fully paid by their employer). It means, of course, that poor people are much less likely than wealthy people to have the option of using privately funded alternatives to NHS care. Thus, a two-tier system of access to healthcare has begun to develop in some parts of Britain, to the disadvantage of the least well-off. This effect is particularly evident in areas where the independent sector is most highly developed, notably in South-East England.

A further mechanism for the introduction of market forces into state healthcare has been the insistence upon competitive tendering for ancillary work such as hospital cleaning and laundry. This has brought some reduction in the costs of these parts of the NHS, but often at the cost of worsening pay and working conditions for the employees concerned. People working in ancillary health services are low paid, and competitive tendering has therefore been to the detriment of significant numbers of relatively poor people.[38] This is one example of how the role of the NHS as an employer, as well as a provider of healthcare, is important for the less wealthy population of Britain. Such a role is often particularly significant in inner-city areas where the NHS has long been a major local employer of low-paid service sector workers.

In a number of ways, therefore, the introduction of an 'internal market' for healthcare may have important effects for the poor population of Britain. This market is variable in its operation from place to place, so that the impact of the 'internal market' for both rich and poor patients is likely to depend partly on the area in which they are living. In general, market forces do not tend to be strongly influenced by considerations of equity, and, unless they are effectively managed, they seem intrinsically likely to act to the disadvantage of the poorest members of society.

'THE HEALTH OF THE NATION': GOVERNMENT POLICY FOR HEALTH IN BRITAIN

The policy statements set out in the recent *The Health of the Nation* document[39] represent a step forward in health policy in some respects, since they focus clearly on the outcomes of public services in terms of the health of the population. The policy sets targets for the improvement of health, focusing on certain health 'priorities' (heart disease, cancer, sexually transmitted diseases, mental illness, accidents), and it is therefore also directing attention towards conditions which are typically most common among the disadvantaged and poor groups in society. It also emphasises the importance of collaboration between health services and other 'partners' such as social services, environmental health, education, industry and the community in attempting to achieve health improvements for the British population. *The Health of the Nation* may therefore have the potential to promote action to improve the health of poor populations.

Yet the emphasis in the document is *not* towards the reduction of health inequalities. The most striking and indeed most criticised aspect of the first version of this document, when it was circulated for consultation, was its lack of attention to health inequality: a lack which effectively led the policy as a whole to ignore the health situation of disadvantaged and poor populations in Britain.[40] Although the revised document did make more reference to the importance of taking into account health differences between social groups, most of the relevant discussion appeared in the form of an appendix. Furthermore, the targets for health improvement set here relate to the population as a whole, and do not specify health improvements for particular social groups or areas. By pursuing these targets, improvements to average health might eventually be achieved *without* really tackling health differences and the health disadvantages of the poor.[41] Measures to promote better health in the poor population will need to be directed partly at changing individual health behaviour, but also at modifying structural factors in society which influence social differences in health. The 'educative' model of health promotion, which is based on the idea that people will change their health behaviour if they receive information on healthy lifestyles, is manifestly less effective for populations living in poverty. Health education needs to be more sensitive to the fact that healthy diets are more difficult to afford on a limited income, for instance, and that the immediate relief from the pressures of poverty offered by drinking and smoking may seem more important than the possible future gains from abstinence. Recognition should also be given to the likelihood that many of the factors which are significant for the health of poor people are very difficult for them to act on individually. Shortages of good quality affordable housing, lack of a minimum wage policy, environmental pollution, the social stress of living in poverty in run-down areas, food pricing policies, tobacco and alcohol advertising strategies: all of these are examples of such structural factors. New public health strategies and 'empowerment' models of health promotion[42] are more sensitive to these problems. They show us that many of the dimensions of inequality considered in this volume are relevant to health, and that policies for health gain need to go beyond provision of health services if they are to be really effective.

This chapter has demonstrated the significance of health inequalities which disadvantage poor people in different parts of the UK. I have argued that central government policies, relating to resource allocation, the development of 'internal markets' and targets for health outcomes, are quite unresponsive to the particular needs of poor people in specific areas of the country. However, at the local level, DHAs and health professionals may nevertheless decide to make greater equality in health one of their aims. In order to intervene effectively, they are likely to take into consideration the geography of health which so clearly shows how social and environmental deprivation interact with health in different ways in different places.

NOTES

1. Anon, 'Editorial: back to the future – the reinvention of public health', *Lancet* (1988), pp157-9; J Ashton (ed), *Healthy Cities* (Open University Press, 1992); C Martin and D McQueen (eds), *Readings for a New Public Health* (Edinburgh University Press, 1989).
2. P Townsend, N Davidson and M Whitehead, *Inequalities in Health* (Penguin, 1988).
3. P Goldblatt, *Longitudinal Study: mortality and social organisation 1971-1981, Series LS8* (OPCS, HMSO, 1990).
4. The 'standardised mortality ratio' (SMR) is a measure which compares the numbers of deaths actually observed in a particular population, over a given time, with the number which would be expected if the death rates in each age and sex group of the population were the same as for those of a reference population. In this case the reference population is the national population (of England and Wales). The ratio is therefore 'standardised' in the sense that it enables population comparisons which control for the differences in demographic structure between social groups or between geographical areas. This is necessary because death rates are naturally higher in older populations than in younger ones, so it is not very useful to compare mortality data that has not been standardised. The method of standardisation is technically described as 'indirect'. The

ratio expresses 'observed' deaths as a percentage of 'expected' deaths, thus: SMR = (observed deaths/expected deaths) x 100. An SMR of 110 indicates relatively high mortality, with observed deaths 10 per cent above those in the reference population (allowing for age and sex differences), while an SMR of 90 indicates relatively low mortality, with observed deaths 10 per cent below the 'expected' number. An SMR of 100 obviously indicates death rates identical to those in the reference population.

5. The reference here to 'independent' effects means that, while the different factors affecting health (social class, education, housing, etc.) are themselves inter-related, in statistical terms they also seem to have some *separate* links with health. The implication is that the cumulative health risks associated with these factors considered all together will *not* be the same as the risk associated with any one factor alone.

6. R Illsley, J Le Grand and C Mullings, *Regional Inequalities in Mortality* (Suntory Toyota International Centre for Economics and Related Disciplines, London School of Economics, Discussion Paper WSP/57, 1991).

7. OPCS, *Occupational Mortality: childhood supplement, 1979-1980, 1982-1983, England and Wales, Series DS8* (OPCS, HMSO, 1988).

8. K Jones and G Moon, *Health, Disease and Society* (Routledge and Kegan Paul, 1987) especially pp73-83.

9. P McCormick and M Rosenbaum, *Morbidity Statistics from General Practice, 1981-82, Series MB5 No. 2* (OPCS, HMSO, 1990).

10. OPCS, *Cancer Statistics Registration, 1987, Series MB1, No. 20* (OPCS, HMSO, 1993).

11. OPCS, *General Household Survey, 1991* (OPCS, HMSO, 1993).

12. M Blaxter, *Health and Lifestyle* (Routledge, 1990).

13. A Miles, *Women, Medicine and Health* (Open University Press, 1991); J Popay, M Bartley and C Owen, 'Gender inequalities in health: social position, affective disorders and minor physical morbidity', *Social Science and Medicine*, Vol 36 (1993), pp21-32.

14. R Balarajan and L Bulusu, 'Mortality among immigrants in England and Wales, 1979-83', in M Britton (ed), *Mortality and Geography: a review in the mid-1980s, England and Wales, Series DS9* (OPCS, HMSO, 1990), pp103-21; M Marmot, A Adelstein and L Bulusu, *Immigrant Mortality in England and Wales, 1970-78: causes of death by country of birth (Studies on Medical and Population Subjects No. 47* (OPCS, HMSO, 1984).

15. M Britton, 'Geographic variation in morality since 1920 for selected causes', in Britton, *Mortality and Geography* (see note 14), pp28-48.

16. V Carstairs and R Morris, *Deprivation and Health in Scotland* (Aberdeen University Press, 1991); P Townsend, P Phillimore and A Beattie, *Health and Deprivation: Inequality and the North* (Croom Helm, 1988); C Schrijvers, J Mackenbach, T Lutz, M Quinn and T Coleman, 'Deprivation and Cancer Survival', in Thames Cancer Registry, *Cancer in South East*

England, 1991 (Thames Cancer Registry, 1994), pp54-5.
17. Blaxter, *Health and Lifestyle* (see note 12), p12.
18. Britton, 'Geographic variation' (see note 15), p17; M Gardner, P Winter and D Barker, *Atlas of Mortality from Selected Diseases in England and Wales, 1968-1978* (Wiley, 1984).
19. B Jacobsen, A Smith and M Whitehead, *The Nation's Health: a strategy for the 1990s, Second Edition* (King Edward's Hospital Fund for London, 1988), p113.
20. A Fox and P Goldblatt, *The Longitudinal Study: socio-demographic mortality differentials, Series L5.1* (OPCS, HMSO, 1982).
21. S Curtis, M Eames *et al,* 'Geography of coronary heart disease in England: the implications for local health planning', *Health Education Journal,* Vol 52/2 (1993), pp72-8.
22. P Phillimore, 'Mortality variations within two poor areas in North East England', *The Statistician,* Vol 39 (1990), pp373-83. See also P Phillimore and R Reading, 'A rural advantage? urban-rural health differences in Northern England', *Journal of Public Health Medicine,* August 1992, pp.290-9.
23. M Gould and K Jones, 'Analysing perceived limiting long-term illness using UK Census microdata' (paper given at Sixth International Medical Geography Symposium, Vancouver, British Columbia, Canada, July, 1991); S Shouls, P Congdon, S Curtis and M Green, 'Modelling inequality in reported long-term illness: combining individual and area characteristics' (Queen Mary and Westfield College, Department of Geography, Research Paper, forthcoming).
24. J Carlton *et al,* 'Geographical variations in mortality from conditions amenable to medical intervention', *The Lancet* (1983), pp691-6.
25. R Carr-Hill *et al,* 'Variations in avoidable mortality and variations in health care resources', *The Lancet* (1987), pp789-92.
26. DHSS, *Sharing Resources for Health in England: report of the Resource Allocation Working Party* (DHSS, HMSO, 1976).
27. N Mays, 'Measuring morbidity for resource allocation', *British Medical Journal,* Vol 295 (1987), pp176-767.
28. Jones and Moon, *Health, Disease and Society* (see note 8), pp24-5.
29. G Royston *et al,* 'Modelling the use of the health services by populations of small areas to inform the allocation of central resources to larger regions', *Socio-Economic Planning Sciences,* Vol 26 (1992), pp169-80.
30. J Mohan, *A National Health Service? The restructuring of health care in Britain since 1979* (Macmillan, forthcoming).
31. I Watt and T Sheldon, 'Rurality and resource allocation in the UK', *Health Policy,* Vol 26 (1993), pp19-27; I Watt, A Franks and T Sheldon, 'Health and health care of rural populations in the UK: is it better or worse?', *Journal of Epidemiology and Community Health,* Vol 48 (1994), pp16-21.

32. R Carr-Hill, T Sheldon, P Martin, S Peacock and G Hardman, 'Allocating resources to health authorities: development of method for small area analysis of use of inpatient services', *British Medical Journal*, Vol 309 (1994), pp1046-9; P Smith, T Sheldon, R Carr-Hill, S Martin, S Peacock and G Hardman, 'Allocating resources to health authorities: results and policy implications of small area analysis of inpatient services', *British Medical Journal*, Vol 309 (1994), pp1050-4.

33. T Delamonthe, 'Deprived areas payments', *British Medical Journal*, Vol 300 (1990), pp1609-10; B Jarman, 'Identification of underprivileged areas', *British Medical Journal*, Vol 286 (1983), pp1705-6.

34. M Senior, 'Deprivation payments to GPs: not what the doctor ordered', *Environment and Planning C: Government and Policy*, Vol 19 (1991), pp79-94.

35. J Mohan and K Woods, 'Restructuring health care? the social geography of public and private health care under the British Conservative Government', *International Journal of Health Services*, Vol 15 (1985), pp197-217; J Mohan, 'Commercialisation and centralisation: towards a new geography of health care', in J Mohan (ed), *The Political Geography of Contemporary Britain* (Macmillan, 1989), pp224-37.

36. Department of Health, *Health and Personal Statistics for England, 1993* (DoH, HMSO, 1993), Tables 6.16 and 6.17, pp99-100.

37. OPCS, *General Household Survey, 1987* (OPCS, HMSO, 1989).

38. J Mohan, 'Spatial aspects of health care employment in Britain 2: current policy initiatives', *Environment and Planning A*, Vol 20 (1988), pp203-17; N Small, *Politics and Planning in the National Health Service* (Open University Press, 1989), pp99-100.

39. Department of Health, *The Health of the Nation: a strategy for health in England* (Cm.1986, HMSO, 1992).

40. Radical Statistics Health Group, 'Missing: a strategy for the health of the nation', in British Medical Journal, *The Health of the Nation: the BMJ view* (BMJ, 1991), pp9-18.

41. C Bryce, S Curtis and J Mohan, 'Coronary heart disease: trends in spatial inequalities and implications for healthcare planning in England', *Social Science and Medicine*, Vol 38 (1994), pp677-90.

42. T Ashton, 'The healthy cities project: a challenge for health education', *Health Education Quarterly*, Vol 18(1) (1991), pp39-48; A Root, 'Oxford blues', *Health Services Journal*, 19 January 1995, pp32-3.

10 'Poor places' and beyond: summary findings and policy implications

Chris Philo, James McCormick and CPAG [1]

POVERTY AND A GEOGRAPHICAL PERSPECTIVE

There *is* poverty in the UK. Organisations such as CPAG have long recognised this, of course, but it is important that this view is held more widely. The time has come for all of us to wake up to the fact that poverty exists, and to consider the kinds of responses that might be appropriate – from the level of national government down to that of the individual citizen. As Fran Bennett recently stated, poverty needs to be returned to the agendas of politics and policy, and a 'new burst of energy' is required to generate fresh thinking, enthusiasm and (even) optimism in the struggle against poverty. [2]

Debates about whether 'absolute' poverty exists in the UK must not be allowed to obscure the reality of many people enduring hard, constrained and unforgiving lives from having so few financial and other resources at their disposal. This acknowledges, as this volume has shown, the enormous inequalities between the 'haves' and the 'have-nots' in this country. The 'relative' view of poverty is more helpful here. In line with the broader position taken by CPAG, then, this volume has tracked the existence of poverty as the manifest *exclusion, marginalisation* and *discrimination* endured by many people unable to partake in the 'normal' lifestyles, activities and possessions generally expected by the UK's population. [3]

There are parallels between taking a geographical perspective on poverty and accepting the 'relative' view, in that both adopt a *comparative* approach. Throughout this volume various comparisons and contrasts are drawn between the circumstances, indicators and experiences of different parts of the UK (North-South, city-countryside, old- and new-industrial regions). Talking about spatial inequalities and geographical unevenness in the distributions of wealth and poverty is to compare places in terms of their relative wealth or poverty, and it ties in closely with the claims and arguments about 'relative poverty' which are familiar to CPAG. It is hoped that the spotlight here on the geography of poverty, will offer a new slant on – and maybe sharpen – what anti-poverty activists are already saying about imbalances in well-being between individuals and social groups.

INVESTIGATING 'POOR PLACES': FINDINGS AND THEMES

The volume has demonstrated that there are 'poor places' in the UK and these places can be identified at a range of spatial scales (national, regional and local), but it acknowledges that the precise criteria used to measure the presence of poverty will lead to differences in the places identified (and in how the boundaries of these places are delimited). It may be that at the micro-scale of, say, the individual street or high-tech workplace it is better to speak of spaces whose 'impoverishment' is fleeting and subject to change depending on who is in the space concerned, on whether it is visible or invisible, regulated or left alone, upgraded or degraded (see Chapter 7). Often in these settings there may be a dramatic and shocking, if fluctuating, juxtaposition of poverty and wealth side-by-side. At the larger spatial scales of neighbourhoods, settlements, cities and regions it makes sense to speak of definite 'poor places' whose poverty is all too fixed and enduring, which exist in a kind of nested hierarchy (think of, say, the problems of a Tyneside outer-city estate nested within the problems of Tyneside as a whole and more generally within those of the North).[4] Such a hierarchy perhaps assists us in visualising how the apparently remote workings of the macro-economy have effects which are transmitted down the hierarchy, thus linking the 'national' to the 'local', and allowing a situation in which some places or regions 'win' at the expense of others.

Many 'poor places' are in one way or another hidden from the powerful people who are responsible for making decisions that affect them, and to people such as ourselves, and others, who may claim to know what they are like 'on the ground'. This is partly because getting to know the places concerned can be genuinely difficult for outsiders, but it is also surely because many of the decision-makers and experts do not really *want* to know them. Direct experience of these places may be virtually non-existent for the majority of decision-makers and experts – particularly those in Westminster and Whitehall – and understanding may be restricted to stereotypes conveyed in the media. It is therefore because poverty has a geography that it remains hidden from, or misrepresented to, much of comfortable UK society. The 'poor places' and often the people in them are cast as places of irresponsibility where people bring their fate on themselves by failing to be sufficiently entre-preneurial. It is because of this ignorance and distortion that government-led policy responses are commonly so inappropriate and do not help people in these 'poor places'. It is therefore vital to reveal the geography of poverty so as to challenge deficiencies in current policy. It is essential to underline that poverty has not been eradicated, to indicate that it is still very much there beyond (and even sometimes in: see Chapter 8) the well-to-do avenues of the UK's 'rich places'. This is why the many and various 'poor places' in the UK must be spotlighted, and why (to paraphrase Doreen Massey) the 'geography matters'.[5]

More specifically, the volume reveals a regional geography of poverty, showing how at the spatial scale of the regions broad distinctions can be drawn between those which are doing well and those which are not. The most obvious distinction is 'the North-South divide', which undoubtedly persists despite claims about its death, but it is also possible to identify a distinction termed here 'the Celtic divide'.[6] The latter is admittedly a contentious divide, one much complicated by cultural and other differences *within* the Celtic lands of Northern Ireland, Scotland and Wales, but paying attention to the regional geography of poverty does call for sensitivity to this – almost an 'East-West' – fracture which runs alongside, cross-cutting, the better-known 'North-South' one. Chapters 2 and 3 complement each other in this respect.[7]

Superimposed upon this regional pattern are other sets of differences between urban and rural UK, and between old-industrial and new-industrial UK. There may be other differences which could be considered here, but they are certainly ones which must be prominent in a volume such as this. This means that Chapters 4 and 5, and then Chapter 6 and 7, are also pairs which should be read in combination. There are many claims to be made about the changing structural circumstances within the areas covered by these four chapters, particularly when considering the connections between them that lead (say) attractive countryside places containing high-tech science parks to be much less blighted with poverty than are (say) despoiled urban/industrial places containing shut-down mines, steelworks and shipyards. There are also claims to be made about the imagery surrounding these areas – the decaying inner-city, the 'rural idyll', the smokestacked skyline, the high-tech science park – and about how these images are not incidental to the present and likely future well-being of the places being (mis)represented. Chapters 4 to 7 can only do so much in laying out such political-economic and social-cultural dimensions but, taken as a foursome, these contributions do spell out something of how 'real' and 'imagined' geographies intersect to create different concentrations of either wealth-creation or poverty-entrenchment.

Layered upon these regional and sub-regional patterns there are more local patterns to consider and in particular (as noted in Chapter 4 and echoed elsewhere) the peculiar fate of the hugely deprived inner- and outer-city housing estates. They arise as almost the emblem of poverty in the North and in the Celtic lands, and as the feared 'blots' which are the run-down 'no-go areas' in the still-wealthy heartlands of southern and eastern England. Chapter 8 performs a crucial function in showing how even within the prosperous South-East, this iconic region of Thatcherite success, there are now clear intra-regional inequalities and tracts of poverty. To some extent this reflects the problems experienced by certain of London's inner and outer boroughs, but there is also the possibility of, if not deep poverty, then undoubtedly serious financial pressures and worries building up behind closed doors in the 'stockbroker belt'. These complex geographies of poverty are linked to other phenomena such as housing, education and welfare support, but it is only in Chapter 9 that the volume turns away from a simple 'geographical' framework for analysis to consider a specific pheno-menon – in this case health and healthcare provision – and how there are variations in healthcare (and, indeed, health itself) through-out the country.[8] The view proposed in this volume is that anti-poverty policies will always be 'impoverished' if they fail to grasp these many geographies: if they fail to see that policies have to work in a range of different, nested and inter-connected human environments.

Common themes begin to emerge from all of the chapters about how the national restructuring of the economy impacts more harshly upon certain places and regions than it does upon others. The move from an older industrial base (sometimes now characterised as 'Fordist') to a newer one ('post-Fordist'), however fragmented and incomplete this transition may be, has involved a siphoning of capital investment (and thus jobs, services, higher-quality retailers, financial dealings) from certain places and regions towards other places and regions.[9] Sometimes the new places and regions have been overseas, reflecting the international context of restructuring, but they have also been elsewhere in the UK, maybe nearby but often quite distant. The shifts from the North to the South, from the old-industrial to the new-industrial regions, and from the inner cities to suburbs and green-field sites, may be messier than such simple descriptions can convey: but shifts have still occurred along something like these lines. In the wake of this relocation of economic activity there have been profound social effects, notably because the people left behind in the abandoned places and regions – people who for a host of reasons cannot simply 'get on their bikes' and follow capital – are likely to suffer unemployment, under-employment, poor services and a downgraded commercial and financial environment (see in particular Chapters 1, 4 and 6).

To some extent something similar has happened in the agricultural sector of the economy as well, given a restructuring which has left many marginal rural areas[10] with a barely (if at all) viable agricultural base, and with others dominated by capital-intensive farming which brings wealth to a few but does little for the thousands of local people who can take no part in it. Even in the latter areas many farmers are now in trouble because they have become over-capitalised as a result of the open-ended promises made under the Common Agricultural Policy (CAP) which are now being pulled back. The spectre of poverty is never far away for many farmers and other people struggling to survive in a countryside which has now become less a 'rural idyll'– if it ever was for some people – and more a prison (see also Chapter 5). The presence of what might be termed 'genteel poverty' in rural areas needs to be exposed, then, as does the presence of what might be termed 'middle-class poverty' in suburbia (as in Chapter 8).

There are a number of other common themes which are covered in the chapters of the volume, many of which echo the remarks made in Chapter 1 about the processes which fuse together in dragging particular 'poor places' ever deeper into the snares of

poverty. The mutually reinforcing 'evils' of unemployment, under-
employment, declining services, withdrawing commercial-financial
activity, running-down of education, welfare and health provisions,
increasing incidences of crime, drug-abuse, delinquency and the
suchlike are mentioned again and again. There has not been the
space here to analyse these 'evils' in the detail that each one really
demands, nor to investigate more fully the mixing together of these
'evils' in specific places.

ASSISTING 'POOR PLACES': POLICY RESPONSES

As Bennett asserts, there is indeed the need for 'a new burst of
energy' in the formulation and execution of anti-poverty policies,
whoever is responsible – or is prepared to take responsibility – for
such policies. A volume such as this one, with the chief objective of
highlighting the geography of poverty in the UK, does not lead
necessarily to policy recommendations. This being said, if a key
feature of 'relative poverty' in the UK is the geographical unevenness
of wealth and poverty from place to place and from region to
region, then it is important that attention should be given to
policies which could rectify this unevenness – and which in so
doing would serve as vital tools for a broader attack on poverty in
all of its aspects. Indeed, it is important that this final chapter should
be forward-looking and assert there is nothing *inevitable* about what
some writers are (rightly) calling 'the crisis of our times'.

An obvious matter for debate (aired particularly in Chapter 4)
concerns the extent to which anti-poverty policies should be *area-
based* or not. Given that the volume has investigated the geographies
of poverty, and has highlighted 'poor places', it might seem logical to
argue for area-based solutions. Indeed, having isolated the vulnerable
places the proposal would be for anti-poverty policies directed at
and implemented within them. To some extent this logic is compelling
and should frame policy responses, but it must never be forgotten
that the roots of poverty are *not* straightforwardly to be found within
the places and regions affected (somehow neatly sealed within their
geographical boundaries). Rather, the causes of poverty 'in place'
derive from many different sources and locations beyond that place,
and this must be taken on board in policy formulation and execution.
Policies with no eye to the national picture – with no sense of

planning at a national scale through the mechanisms of national government – will always be flawed. Further, the complexity of the poverty map, with in some places the very poor living alongside the very rich, makes it impossible to devise sound local measures. Neither would it be satisfactory to replace universal rights with localised discretion. It takes remarkably little for discretion to become discrimination. Moreover, poor people must be able to rely on consistent provision to meet their basic needs. In very general terms, then, area targeting from the bottom up (at the local community level) must meet with macro-economic and other broadbrush strategies from the top-down (at the national governmental level).

COMMUNITY INITIATIVES

There are other reasons why we need certain anti-poverty policies which are, if not simply area-based, then certainly place-sensitive. Most contributions to the volume have discussed poverty in specific areas, as felt and voiced by local people and communities, and have at least gestured to the kinds of responses that such people and communities make about the problems in their area. Moreover, a salient finding of recent research by the Commission on Social Justice[11] is that, for all of the difficulties faced by many people in places throughout the UK, not all of them are passively 'accepting their lot'. There are numerous signs of locally-based resistance and progress, and these efforts must be taken as a cue for what *can* be achieved in the teeth of social and geographical divides between 'comfortable UK' and 'hardship UK'. Common strands here include a range of community development initiatives (credit unions, food co-operatives, child care networks), and it is significant how women have been active in these initiatives. These women have commonly had to fight not just the authorities but also their neighbours and even relatives, and have had to counter the apathy and scepticism as well as the hostility of young men confused by a loss of role and purpose in the face of mass unemployment (as Bea Campbell has explained when trying to account for the slippage of such young men into criminality, delinquency and violence[12]).

Such locally-based responses should be encouraged in whatever ways possible, partly as an element in a wider politics of neighbourhood empowerment which can perhaps be facilitated through official channels. It may be that current national-level policies offer an opening for local initiatives to secure funding, and there is evidence that under the rubric of the 'City Challenge' scheme (see below) a number of 'grass-roots' projects – such as a women's training centre in Lewisham, funded through the Deptford City Challenge[13] – are indeed emerging which arguably comprise local responses to what is needed. Local people need to feel that they have some control over their destinies, that these are not being dictated in form and content from above (even by the most well-meaning of anti-poverty activists). This is crucial to the success or otherwise of local responses and particularly so when cultural issues such as Celtic resentment of the 'English' dimension of social policies are considered, as in Chapter 3.

These claims about policies requiring a place-sensitivity relate to questions about the need for utilising more formal local political-administrative structures in the struggle against poverty. Indeed, it is all very well to talk about empowering local responses to poverty, but there are difficult issues to be addressed about how to engineer a combination of political and administrative units which are large enough to deliver anti-poverty policies with some chance of success, but which remain close enough to the concerns and efforts of local communities to allow real accountability. It must be wondered if in a Britain of the 'quango state', as created over the last few years by the Tories, such attentiveness and accountability is really possible. There may be potential in the regional focus of some quangos, or in the regional management structures of others, to outline the space for anti-poverty (and related) policies which will end up being well-matched to the specific needs of specific 'poor places'. Present and projected reforms in the management of the Benefits Agency and its service delivery might offer the possibility for piloting initiatives in certain places and regions, for instance.[14]

However, while there may be strong arguments for ensuring benefit delivery is place sensitive (eg, in providing interpreting services in areas where people from a particular ethnic minority are concentrated), there could be serious dangers in setting benefit levels and criteria for eligibility to reflect local circumstances. There must be doubt about whether the fundamentally undemocratic nature of government by quango can ever deliver what is required in a fashion that can be effectively challenged and reworked from below, and so – although this is to engage with ongoing controversies about the proper political-administrative-geographical shape of government in the UK – the suggestion must be that only decentralisation, as coupled to a reinvigoration of local government, can provide the framework necessary to support or to launch place-sensitive anti-poverty policies. Further, as mentioned above, the complexity of the poverty map, with the very poor living alongside the very rich, could make it impossible to devise sound local measurements. Neither would it be satisfactory to replace universal rights with localised discretion. It takes remarkably little for discretion to become discrimination, as we have said. Moreover, people in poverty more than others must be able to rely on consistent provision to meet their basic needs.

VOLUNTARY AND CHARITABLE INITIATIVES

Voluntary organisations – including many charities and churches – also have a vital role to play in the policy mix, a role that anti-poverty activists are gradually coming to accept as valid (even given continuing fears about the presence of a voluntary sector legitimating the withdrawal of state involvement). As Campbell explains, '[i]n the Nineties, many estates in Britain are being galvanised not by political parties but by traditional charities which are modernising their social base ... by breaking away from their role as rescuers of the perishers'.[15] Thus, on one estate in Belfast it is only Save the Children who provide any local services, in the form of a desperately-needed Family and Children Centre, while in Miles Platting and Ancoats (Manchester) nothing was happening until people from the local churches got together to establish a Development Trust, which is now achieving extraordinary things given its size. As with the local initiatives mentioned above, a general willingness to encourage, champion and if possible materially assist such efforts on the part of voluntary organisations must be developed.

This obviously dovetails with claims about local instances of battling against poverty, and it is clear that the voluntary sector has often been adept at creating or facilitating such local projects, but there is also something to be said about the importance of voluntary and charitable organisations with a national coverage who are prepared to adopt an anti-policy stance (and often a stance more committed to positive action than are the tiers of either national or local government). The contribution of CPAG is relevant here, and there is little doubt that the commitment of such an organisation to networking, to helping in the co-ordination of anti-poverty ideas and actions from a variety of sources, should be included in the overall portfolio of anti-poverty policies. Moreover, an extremely significant function that organisations such as CPAG can perform (in conjunction with others such as academics) lies in helping to foster a new national-level 'discourse' opposing poverty, one that sensitises all of us to the continued existence of poverty in the UK, and one which lays out in an unsentimental fashion the moral and political imperatives that must be widely accepted if this poverty is to be eradicated.

GOVERNMENT INITIATIVES

It might be objected that the sorts of initiatives described so far are not enough on their own, that they are *coping strategies* which are at best ameliorative instead of being preventative. An awareness of the macro-economic trends which cause poverty, including some knowledge of the necessarily uneven working of the macro-economy which leads to wealth in some places and regions but poverty in others, is essential in Westminster and Whitehall. Without a sensibility that regards inequality as objectionable, there can be no will on the part of national government to intervene – either in the economy or in the benefits system – so as to generate conditions in which some *levelling* of the surface of wealth and poverty surface can be attained (a levelling where 'poor places' get richer, preferably without 'rich places' having to be made substantially poorer).

There is a variety of unfashionable but surely still tenable arguments to be made for reversing the trend to dismantle 'deprived area' programmes, and in this connection there are numerous geographical studies which chart the rolling back of the map of regional aid (the withdrawing of incentives packages and advance factory building schemes) and then make claims about the need for their reinstatement.[16] At the same time, care must be taken in assessing the positive and negative dimensions to the kinds of policy responses which have been favoured by the Tories in recent years. Their approach of seeking to develop public-private partnerships in the regeneration of crumbling local economies, partnerships where the common model is for initial public funding gradually to be replaced by self-funding, can certainly boast some successes in bringing investment, employment, housing and an improved commercial environment to certain places and regions. But many poor people in such places and regions – perhaps living on estates not all that distant from the new developments initiated by, for instance, the Urban Development Corporations (UDCs) – will probably ask themselves what benefits they have experienced as a result of these developments, and it may be that the achievements of the UDCs, 'enterprise zones' and the suchlike have actually served to sharpen social-geographical divides between wealth and poverty rather than to alleviate them.[17] Questions must be posed about whether or not something like the 'City Challenge' programme will achieve more in the way of genuinely assisting 'poor places' – the early signs are perhaps encouraging (see above) – but anti-poverty activists must remain wary of the extent to which such partnership initiatives remain democratic enough, sufficiently able to incorporate inputs from local people, to produce measures, activities and events suitable for reducing local poverty. The role of national government in supporting these initiatives is one that should remain, then, but it may be that more traditional strategies for macro-economic management in the interest of protecting the UK's 'poor places' should be re-implemented.

Although we have argued for 'bottom-up' anti-poverty initiatives which are place sensitive and specific it is also the case that 'top-down' universal anti-poverty strategies will be of particular advantage to poor people in poor places. A significant part of the national government's anti-poverty agenda should involve a restructuring of the whole benefits system. The broad argument of many anti-poverty activists (for example, the Commission on Social Justice) is that the benefits system has to change because it is based on an outdated notion of the single family breadwinner, and because it is *inflexible* in the face of a more flexible labour market. More particularly, it is apparent that the system as it currently operates discourages people from trying to do something to improve their circumstances, it often being simply not worth their while to chase work should there be any available locally. This 'trap' of the benefits system is supposedly the same across the UK,[18] but it is clear that its impact is spatially unequal because in those 'poor places' where work is available it tends to be poorly-paid – often thanks to being unskilled, part-time and regarded as 'women's work' – and hence the system is less likely to encourage people into work than is the case in more fortunate places where better-paid work is available. A simple set of reforms would hence institute less steep benefits tapers (slower withdrawal of benefits after earning more) and a higher earnings disregard across the board, along with greater National Insurance protection, and – although not obviously a 'geographical' policy – the likely consequence would nonetheless be to improve the situation for poor people in 'poor places'.

Further possibilities arise here, including the consideration of some form of universal 'basic income' (now called by some a 'citizen's income'),[19] - an amount paid to each citizen as of right. However, as well as the practical difficulties of raising the funds necessary to set the level high enough to make a difference, it could be criticised for undermining a commitment to intervene in the macro-economy which would ensure the creating, redistributing and crediting of work (some of which is currently unpaid) so as to allow every UK citizen to *earn* a decent income. Additional policies which should be considered – appropriately enough given the specific brief of CPAG – revolve around a radical expansion of both childcare and pre-school child education facilities, along with new 'family-friendly' employment policies on parental leave (return to work guarantees for women and statutory leave opportunities for men). It may be that few other reforms could have such a powerful influence in terms of both freeing up time for poor (notably single) parents to gain employment, and in enhancing the future abilities of people to be creative and successful in pulling themselves *and their places* away from the snares of poverty.

NOTES

1. This chapter was drafted by Chris Philo, drawing upon materials from James McCormick and several people associated with CPAG – Peter Golding, Carey Oppenheim, Robin Simpson, Robert Walker and Sally Witcher.

2. F Bennett, 'Introduction' (Paper given at conference on *From the Margin to the Mainstream, Pathways out of Poverty in the 1990s*, held at the Directory of Social Change, London, 25 April 1994).

3. F Bennett, 'Introduction' (see note 2). Sally Witcher suggests underlining how exclusion and marginalisation are not simply about access to money, they are also about the various ways in which certain people in certain circumstances are more-or-less deliberately discriminated against.

4. One of the readers also makes the good point that we should not forget here about the *people* 'nested' in these places.

5. D Massey, 'Introduction: geography matters', in D Massey and J Allen (eds), *Geography Matters: a reader* (Cambridge University Press, 1984), pp1-11.

6. As explained in Chapter 3, 'Celtic UK' includes Northern Ireland, Scotland and Wales, but not Cornwall.

7. It must be admitted that the logic of how these two chapters have been

composed does mean that the problems of the English Midlands, notably the clear difficulties experienced by many people in the West Midlands, end up being somewhat overlooked here (although see Chapter 6).

8. The intention had initially been to include a chapter on the connections between housing and the geography of poverty, but unfortunately this chapter had to be abandoned.

9. For an accessible introduction to the argument about a transition from a Fordist form of industrial organisation to a post-Fordist one (otherwise identified as a 'regime of flexible accumulation'), see D Harvey, *The Condition of Postmodernity: an enquiry into the origins of social change* (Basil Blackwell, 1989), Part II. See too the critical use of ideas about the spatial manifestations of Fordism and post-Fordism, as linked into a substantive study of changes in the 'older' UK industries with particular reference to North-East England, found in D Sadler, *The Global Region: production, state policies and uneven development* (Pergamon, 1991). Works such as these can usefully be read in tandem with a text that continues to be extremely useful in explaining recent sectoral and spatial shifts in Britain's industrial base, D Massey, *Spatial Divisions of Labour: social structures and the geography of production* (Macmillan, 1984).

10. 'Marginal' in the sense of containing lands and topographies which are difficult to farm, and which are usually given over to sheep raising. As it happens such areas tend to be spatially peripheral as well, tending to be sited in northerly and westerly parts of mainland Britain.

11. James McCormick's work with the Commission on Social Justice has provided these examples.

12. Campbell, *Goliath: Britain's dangerous places* (Methuen, 1993). She argues powerfully in this respect about a new 'social landscape' where it has become impossible for many people to make a 'legal living', and where the normal situation involves 'men on the loose' in 'raging posses', often younger men who have chosen to exit from what few points of social contact organised around notions of 'equality' and 'grace' (notably the school) remain open to them. Chris Philo acknowledges here a recent presentation by Campbell that he was fortunate enough to attend: B Campbell, 'Analysis of, and solutions to, poverty in the UK' (Paper given at conference on *From the Margin to the Mainstream, Pathways out of Poverty in the 1990s*, held at the Directory of Social Change, London, 25 April 1994).

13. Chris Philo acknowledges here Yvonne Hepburn's contribution to a workshop on 'enterprise and economic development in partnership with communities' run at conference on *From the Margin to the Mainstream, Pathways out of Poverty in the 1990s*, held at the Directory of Social Change, London, 25 April 1994.

14. One of the readers asks 'should benefit policy be made explicitly spatial, reflecting and responding to the characteristics of the locality? Could this

be a way of responding to the problem of how to cope with variations in housing costs?'.

15. Campbell, *Goliath* (see note 12).

16. See, for instance, C M Law, 'Regional development policies and economic change', in M Pacione (ed.), *Progress in Industrial Geography* (Croom Helm, 1985), pp219-48; H D Watts, 'Industry', in T Bayliss-Smith and S Owens (eds), *Britain's Changing Environment from the Air* (Cambridge University Press, 1990), pp133-59.

17. There are numerous reviews and critiques of UDCs, for instance, and two useful papers are M Goodwin, 'The city as commodity: the contested spaces of urban development', in G Kearns and C Philo (eds), *Selling Places: the city as cultural capital, past and present* (Pergamon, 1993), pp145-62; D Sadler, 'Place-marketing, competitive places and the construction of hegemony in Britain in the 1980s', in Kearns and Philo, *Selling Places* (see above), pp175-92.

18. This being said, Peter Golding suggests that there *is* some regional 'inconsistency' in the benefit system relating to the management of the 'social fund', the allocation of housing benefits and local government response to debt. One of the readers also wonders if the 'revolution of managerial responsibility in the Benefits Agency opens the door to greater territorial injustice', particularly if this involves (as it may do) the breaking up of the Agency into quasi-autonomous regional units.

19. CPAG does not really endorse a 'citizen's income', but Carey Oppenheim argues that the views of the organisation are not so far away in their preference for something 'more like a contingency-based citizen's income: ie. non-means tested/non-contributory benefits based on entitlement in particular circumstances such as unemployment, sickness, etc'.

Now's the time to join CPAG!

We can help you ... with the facts on poverty and social security.

You can help us ... in the fight against poverty.

CPAG membership gives you access to all the latest — on welfare rights, income inequalities, perspectives on policy, and lots more!

And CPAG members give us the support we need to ensure that poverty is at the heart of the agenda, whatever political party is in power.

Send off the form and join CPAG now.

☐ I would like to join CPAG as a Rights Member £40
(Rights Members receive the *National Welfare Benefits Handbook* and *Rights Guide*, the *Welfare Rights Bulletin* and CPAG's *Poverty Magazine*)
or
☐ I would like to join CPAG as a Comprehensive Member £53
(Comprehensive Members receive CPAG's social policy publications **as well as** all the publications received by Rights Members)
☐ I enclose a cheque/PO (made out to CPAG) for £ _____

Name _____

Organisation (if applicable) _____

Address _____

_____ Postcode _____

Send with payment to CPAG, 1-5 Bath Street, London EC1V 9PY

Education divides: poverty and schooling in the 1990s

CHILD POVERTY ACTION GROUP

Teresa Smith and Michael Noble

Have the education reforms of the 1980s and 1990s benefited the chances and welfare of all children? *Education Divides* is the first book to bring together the views of parents and all the relevant research findings to show the real impact of recent changes on the education of children from low-income families.

Opting out and open enrolment, 'formula funding' for schools, pre-school provision, the school meals service and the hidden costs of schooling – such as clothing and 'voluntary contributions' – are all examined.

Education Divides presents a stark picture of growing inequalities in funding, educational standards and quality. Today, children from poor families are less likely than their better-off peers to do well in examinations or to stay on in education – and the gap is widening. Increasingly, barriers to learning are going up for many children – children for whom 'choice' and 'diversity' can turn out to be no choice at all.

The authors propose measures to create real choices and real quality of educational opportunity for **all** children.

160 pages   0 946744 76 9   February 1995   £7.95

Please send .... copy/ies of *Education Divides* @ £7.95 each (incl p&p).

I enclose a cheque/PO for .... payable to CPAG Ltd

Name ....

Address...

....

.... Postcode ....

Return payment with order to
CPAG Ltd, 1-5 Bath Street, London EC1V 9PY

Family Fortunes: pressures on parents and children in the 1990s

CHILD POVERTY ACTION GROUP

Sue Middleton, Karl Ashworth and Robert Walker

Family Fortunes is the first book to examine the economic and social pressures on parents and children today. Uniquely, children speak for themselves about how they cope with pressures to spend, including peer pressure to conform in their choice of clothes and other possessions. Parents explain the strategies they deploy to deal with their children's demands: from saying 'no' to giving in gracefully. Parents and children describe how outside pressures from the media, the advertising industry and school lead to incessant battles because of financial difficulties.

There is also the first formulation of a poverty line for children using a minimum budget standard drawn up and agreed by mothers from all walks of life. Based on the views of mothers and children, *Family Fortunes* is an original contribution to debates on poverty and relative deprivation, the meaning of participation in society and the realities of social exclusion.

| 176 pages | 0 946744 68 8 | December 1994 | £7.95 |

Send a cheque/PO for £7.95 (incl p&p) to
CPAG Ltd, 1-5 Bath Street, London EC1V 9PY

Putting the Treasury First: the truth about child support

Alison Garnham and Emma Knights

Putting the Treasury First is the first book to assess the impact of the Child Support Act on child maintenance arrangements.

The authors examine:
- the background to the passing of the Act
- the first year of the Child Support Agency in operation, based on CPAG's nationwide monitoring of implementation of the Act
- the experiences of parents directly affected by the scheme

There are comprehensive proposals for immediate changes to the scheme, as well as wider-ranging proposals for tackling child poverty and creating a genuine system of 'child support' in the long term.

Putting the Treasury First is an essential aid for anyone campaigning against the Act or wishing to find out more about the impact of the legislation.

May 1994	0 946744 64 5	£6.95

The Cost of a Child

Living standards for the 1990s

Nina Oldfield and Autumn C S Yu

CHILD POVERTY ACTION GROUP

This new study adds to the growing evidence that income support does not meet even the most minimal needs of children. The research was carried out by the Family Budget Unit at the University of York, and is the first systematic reassessment of the basic benefit scales since the Beveridge Report in 1948.

The study uses two 'budget standards', or specific baskets of goods and services which when priced represent two standards of living. There is a modest-but-adequate standard representing the cost of the average child, and a low cost budget reduced to necessities.

Behind the bare statistics lie important findings which make a crucial contribution to tackling current issues – including VAT on fuel, the position of lone parents, subsidised child care, child benefit and levels on income support.

88 pages   0 946744 56 4   October 1993   £6.95

Please send .... copy/ies of *The Cost of a Child*

@ £6.95 each (incl p&p). I enclose a cheque/PO for

£ .... payable to CPAG Ltd

Name ....

Address ....

....

.... Postcode ....

Return payment with order to
CPAG Ltd, 1-5 Bath Street, London EC1V 9PY

Europe:
for richer or poorer?

CHILD POVERTY ACTION GROUP

Robin Simpson and Robert Walker (eds)

Now that the Maastricht Treaty has been ratified, the time has come for Europe to face the consequences for social policy and the poor.

The authors examine not only the Social Chapter, but also moves to guarantee a minimum income and services for children throughout the EC. They analyse the different social policy traditions – including detailed comparisons of family benefits and childcare provisions – within each member state, the geography of poverty throughout the Community, and tendencies towards 'Fortress Europe'. Uniquely, this analysis extends to the evolution of social policy in Eastern Europe, and the global impact of EC commercial policy on poorer countries outside the Community.

In this challenging collection, the contributors (from the EC and beyond) consider whether this 'marriage' of member states will benefit primarily commerce, the workforce, or *all* residents of the European Community.

144 pages   0 946744 55 6   1993   £6.95

Please send .... copy/ies of *Europe: for richer or poorer?* @ £6.95 each (incl p&p).

I enclose a cheque/PO for £ .... payable to CPAG Ltd

Name ....

Address ....

....

.... Postcode ....

Return payment with order to
CPAG Ltd, 1-5 Bath Street, London EC1V 9PY

WINDOWS OF OPPORTUNITY: public policy and the poor

Saul Becker (ed)

CHILD POVERTY ACTION GROUP

'A book attempting to set out policy goals for the nineties ... encompassing not only social security but employment opportunities, taxation and ... quality public services' – *THE GUARDIAN*

'Calls on all the major political parties to review their policies in order to abolish poverty by the end of the century' – *DAILY TELEGRAPH*

'Help(s) to re-orientate and re-invigorate what has become a stale debate about poverty' – *SOCIAL WORK TODAY*

'Expertise, clarity and readability, up-to-dateness, careful argument... You will not find anything better' – *BENEFITS*

144 pages   1991   0 946744 35 1   £6.95

Please send .... copy/ies of Windows of Opportunity @ £6.95 each (incl p&p)

I enclose a cheque/PO for £ .... payable to CPAG Ltd

Name ....

Address ....

....

.... Postcode ....

Return payment with order to CPAG Ltd, 1-5 Bath Street, London EC1V 9PY

CONSUMING CREDIT
Debt and poverty in the UK
Janet Ford

CHILD POVERTY ACTION GROUP

Consuming Credit examines the links between increased poverty, the growth of the credit industry and the problems of debt.

Issues examined include:
- the exclusion of the poor from some forms of credit, and how they are channelled into higher cost repayment schemes
- the concentration of debt amongst the poor
- the social and personal consequences of debt
- the burden that falls on women
- protection for credit users
- remedies

| 128 pages | 1991 | 0 946744 32 7 | £5.95 |

Please send .... copy/ies of the *Consuming Credit* @ £5.95 each (incl p&p).

I enclose a cheque/PO for £ .... payable to CPAG Ltd

Name ....

Address ....

....

.... Postcode ....

Return payment with order to CPAG Ltd, 1-5 Bath Street, London EC1V 9PY

The Exclusive Society:
citizenship and the poor
Ruth Lister

Throughout its 25 year history CPAG has been dedicated to the promotion of the rights of the citizen. The last decade has seen the obligations of citizenship stressed at the expense of such rights.

The Exclusive Society argues that poverty excludes millions from the full rights of citizenship, undermining their ability to fulfill either their private or social obligations. Ruth Lister demonstrates that it is impossible to divorce the rights and responsibilities which are supposed to unite citizens from the inequalities of power and resources that divide them.

The eighties saw the hijack of citizenship in the promotion of consumerism and the enterprise ethos. **The Exclusive Society** proposes a charter of social citizenship which can bridge the gap between common and self interest.

96 pages   0 946744 26 2   1990   £4.95

Excluding the Poor
Peter Golding (ed)

This ground-breaking study was one of the first to point out the increasing exclusion of a large and growing minority of the population from full participation in our society. **Excluding the Poor** presents original and detailed evidence to show how poverty is obstructing people from joining in a range of activities which others take for granted in everyday life.

By examining such areas as the modern leisure industry, information and communications, political processes and financial institutions, the contributors map new features of poverty peculiar to our times.

96 pages   0 903963 97 3   1986   £4.95

ORDER FORM (cash with order please)

Please send me: _____ copy/copies of *The Exclusive Society* @ £4.95 each   £ _____

_____ copy/copies of *Excluding the Poor* @ £4.95 each   £ _____

Prices include postage and packing

I enclose a donation towards Child Poverty Action Group's work   £ _____

I enclose a cheque/PO, payable to CPAG Ltd, for the sum of — TOTAL: £ _____

Please send me details of CPAG membership: YES/NO

Name _____

Address _____

_____

_____ Postcode _____

Return this form with your remittance to CPAG Ltd (Pubs), 1-5 Bath Street, London EC1V 9PY